Unity 3D UI Essentials

Leverage the power of the new and improved UI system for Unity to enhance your games and apps

Simon Jackson

BIRMINGHAM - MUMBAI

Unity 3D UI Essentials

First published: January 2015

Production reference: 1270115

Published by Packt Publishing Ltd.
Livery Place
35 Livery Street
Birmingham B3 2PB, UK.

ISBN - 978-1-78355-361-7

www.packtpub.com

Credits

Author
Simon Jackson

Reviewers
Attilio Carotenuto
Adam Dawes
Javier García-Lajara Herrero
Dr. Sebastian T. Koenig
Simon Wheatley

Commissioning Editor
Akram Hussain

Acquisition Editor
James Jones

Content Development Editor
Sumeet Sawant

Technical Editor
Utkarsha S. Kadam

Copy Editors
Gladson Monteiro
Merilyn Pereira

Project Coordinator
Danuta Jones

Proofreaders
Simran Bhogal
Ameesha Green
Paul Hindle

Indexer
Priya Subramani

Graphics
Sheetal Aute

Production Coordinator
Nitesh Thakur

Cover Work
Nitesh Thakur

About the Author

Ever since my early years I have been a tinkerer, engineer, problem solver, and solution gatherer. In short, I love to break things apart, figure out how they work, and then put them back together, usually better than before.

I started way back when with my first computer, the Commodore Vic20. It was simple, used a tape deck, and forced you to write programs in basic or assembly; they were fun times. From there, I progressed through the ZX Spectrum +2 and the joyous days of modern graphics, but with the 30 minute load times from a trusty tape deck. Games were a passion of mine even then, which led to many requests for another gaming machine, but Santa brought me an Amstrad 1640, my first PC. From there, my tinkering and building exploded, and that machine ended up being a huge monstrosity with so many addons, tweaks, and fixes; I was Frankenstein, and this PC became my own personal monster crafted from so many parts. Good times.

This passion has led me down many paths, and I learned to help educate others on the tips and tricks I learned along the way; these skills have equipped me well for the future.

Today I would class myself as a game development generalist. I work with many different frameworks, each time digging down, ripping them apart, and then showing whoever would listen through my blog, videos, and speaking events how to build awesome frameworks and titles. This has been throughout many generations of C++, MDX, XNA (what a breath of fresh air that was), MonoGame, Unity 3D, The Sunburn Gaming Engine, HTML, and a bunch of other proprietary frameworks; I do them all. This gives a very balanced view of how to build and manage many different types of multiplatform titles.

I don't stop there, as I regularly contribute to the MonoGame project, adding new features and new samples before publishing it on NuGet. I also have several of my own open source projects and actively seek out any new and interesting ones to help with.

By day I am a lowly lead technical architect working in the healthcare software industry seeking to improve patients' health and care through better software (a challenge to be sure), but by night I truly soar! Building, tinkering, and educating whilst trying to push game titles of my own. One day they will pay the bills, but until then I still lead a double life.

More recently, I achieved the highly acclaimed reward of being a Microsoft MVP in the ID@Xbox program, for my evangelizing efforts in the game development space. This won't change much about me, but will give me additional tools to help game developers out there.

Lastly, you should check out my previous title, which has been one of Packt's best sellers since its release, especially if you want to learn more about Unity's 2D system. Check it out here: `http://bit.ly/MasteringUnity2DGameDevelopment`.

It truly has been a tormentous year but it looks to be getting better. Through it all, my wife Caroline has been my tiller, keeping me straight and true while I tend to my game development and writing efforts. Looking forward, I'll likely be crafting more of my own experiences with my kids pitching in; Caitlin, new to game development in school, being my sidekick, Jessica adding her colorful artistic talent to the mix, and the boys (Alexander and Nathan) no doubt trying to destroy my efforts through testing.

Additionally, a big thanks to my extended family (Mike and Marilyn) for helping out with the kids and keeping the writing area a kids-free zone for a few desperate hours. (It's amazing what a few hours respite can do.)

Also a big shout out to the PWSA (Prader-Willi Syndrome Association — `http://pwsa.co.uk`) for their help and support with Alexander, plus the Warrington Youth Club (`http://www.warringtonyouthclub.co.uk/`) for their exciting events to keep him entertained, especially in his more trying times. On that last thread, a very big thank you to Westland Drive respite (supported by Warrington council), who give us peace of mind and a night off from time to time; Alexander certainly loves his visits there.

Finally, thanks to the reviewers of this title (especially Simon W and Andrew D who joined me from my previous book); they kept me grounded and on target, although didn't help keeping the page count down. Thanks for your support guys!

About the Reviewers

Attilio Carotenuto is a senior game developer at Space Ape Games, based in London. There, he uses Unity to create awesome mobile and tablet strategy games such as *Samurai Siege*.

Attilio previously worked at King, developing *Farm Heroes Saga*, and EA Playfish, creating social games and tools based on the *The Sims* brand. Before that, he was a freelance game and web developer, using tools such as Unity, Cocos2D, Flash, and XNA.

He has previously worked with Packt Publishing on *Unity 3D Game Development* (a video tutorial) as a technical reviewer.

Recent projects, tutorials, and articles from Attilio can be found on his personal website, `www.attiliocarotenuto.com`.

Adam Dawes is a software developer and systems architect working at a cutting-edge online service development company.

He has long maintained a fondness for computer games. From the very first time Nightmare Park displayed its devious maze of pathways in green symbols back in 1980, he has been a player across a variety of genres and styles. Creating his own games has always been a hobby, and while he has no plans to become part of the professional games industry, Adam has a lot of fun developing his own titles nonetheless.

Over the last few years, Adam has also published three books of his own, the most recent of which, Windows 8 and Windows Phone 8 Game Development (published by Apress), explains everything you need to know to develop Windows 8 games in C# using the open source MonoGame platform.

More information is available from his website at `www.adamdawes.com`.

Javier García-Lajara Herrero was part of the booming video game industry in Spain, participating in the *Commandos* saga of Pyro Studios, where he developed as an artist, before continuing his career in different studies at Virtual Toys, Bitoon, and Unusual Studios.

He is now one of the professors at U-Tad University of Technology.

Always passionate about technical advances, he now researches and develops new proposals in games, virtual reality, and aerial photogrammetry of objects and environments with drones.

Dr. Sebastian T. Koenig received his PhD in human interface technology from the University of Canterbury, New Zealand, developing a framework for individualized virtual reality cognitive rehabilitation. He obtained his diploma in psychology from the University of Regensburg, Germany, in the areas of clinical neuropsychology and virtual reality rehabilitation.

Dr. Koenig is the founder and CEO of Katana Simulations, where he oversees the design, development, and evaluation of cognitive assessment and training simulations. His professional experience spans over ten years of clinical work in cognitive rehabilitation and over seven years of virtual reality research, development, and user testing. Dr. Koenig has extensive experience as a speaker at international conferences and as a reviewer of scientific publications in the areas of rehabilitation, cognitive psychology, neuropsychology, software engineering, game development, games user research, and virtual reality.

Dr. Koenig has developed numerous software applications for cognitive assessment and training. For his work on the Virtual Memory Task, he was awarded the prestigious Laval Virtual Award in 2011, for the Medicine and Health category. Other applications include the virtual reality executive function assessment in collaboration with the Kessler Foundation, NJ, USA, and the patent-pending Microsoft Kinect-based motor and cognitive training JewelMine/Mystic Isle at the USC Institute for Creative Technologies, CA, USA.

Dr. Koenig maintains the website `www.virtualgamelab.com` about his research and his software development projects. His website also contains a comprehensive list of tutorials for the game engine Unity.

Simon Wheatley first got into programming with the Sinclair ZX81 and then the Acorn BBC Micro. This hobby led onto a bachelor's degree in information technology, after which he embarked on an IT career working in the service, manufacturing, and higher education sectors.

Recently, he discovered Unity's new 2D tools and set about enthusiastically learning as much as possible about them while contributing plenty of errata to several recently published Unity books. Currently, he is developing an indie mobile game using Unity. When he isn't working, he can be found singing down at his local karaoke bar or out enjoying the fantastic British countryside!

www.PacktPub.com

Support files, eBooks, discount offers, and more

For support files and downloads related to your book, please visit www.PacktPub.com.

Did you know that Packt offers eBook versions of every book published, with PDF and ePub files available? You can upgrade to the eBook version at www.PacktPub.com and as a print book customer, you are entitled to a discount on the eBook copy. Get in touch with us at service@packtpub.com for more details.

At www.PacktPub.com, you can also read a collection of free technical articles, sign up for a range of free newsletters and receive exclusive discounts and offers on Packt books and eBooks.

https://www2.packtpub.com/books/subscription/packtlib

Do you need instant solutions to your IT questions? PacktLib is Packt's online digital book library. Here, you can search, access, and read Packt's entire library of books.

Why subscribe?

- Fully searchable across every book published by Packt
- Copy and paste, print, and bookmark content
- On demand and accessible via a web browser

Free access for Packt account holders

If you have an account with Packt at www.PacktPub.com, you can use this to access PacktLib today and view 9 entirely free books. Simply use your login credentials for immediate access.

Table of Contents

Preface

A new era has dawned, and Unity Technologies have taken a big, bold step. Not only have they delivered on some big promises for an all new and improved UI system for Unity projects, but they have also made the source for the new UI completely open source, giving everyday developers access to the inner workings of the new UI.

These are bold steps indeed. Many felt that the new UI wouldn't live up to the dream that was sold, as it had been years since they announced it was coming. Delays and rewrites made it look like it was never going to happen, leaving developers with either having to live with the existing legacy GUI or pay for some of the more advanced GUI systems on the asset store (such as NGUI).

Now, after a long and highly deliberated beta program, the new UI system is finally upon us. In some areas, it meets our expectations; in some, it falls a bit short (however, this is only the beginning). In other areas however, it has gone far beyond.

Throughout this title, we will peel back the layers of all this new technology to understand what each component does, how it fits together, and how to use it to build a fantastic new UI in our projects. Each chapter builds upon the last, to arm you (the reader) with all the knowledge required to assemble your UI within your projects. You will not just build on screen menus and options, but to embed UI elements within your 3D game world.

Not only have Unity released the new UI system, they have also given every developer access to the source that builds the UI, allowing you to better understand how things are built and enable you to extend the existing controls or even build your own. If you are feeling adventurous, you can even submit fixes or new features back to Unity for them to include within Unity itself.

Finally, we can now build what we want, how we want and best of all, it's completely *free* and available with the Free license for Unity. All hail and rejoice!

Now what are you waiting for? Pack up your towel, brew a freshly hot cup of tea, crack open this guide, and start exploring the all new universe of UI.

What this book covers

Chapter 1, Looking Back, Looking Forward, is a retrospective look at what Unity3D had to offer prior to 4.6 and an overview of what 4.6 and beyond brings to the table, including a high-level overview of all the new UI features.

Chapter 2, Building Layouts, covers the core elements of the new Unity UI system, the Canvas and Rect Transforms. These elements are the foundations of the new Unity UI system.

Chapter 3, Control, Control, You Must Learn Control, Unity UI introduces a heap-load of new UI controls to suit just about any UI need, from buttons and checkboxes to entire scrollable areas and layout masks. Here, we will delve deep into how to make the most of all the controls available.

Chapter 4, Anchors Away, provides a detailed walk-through of how to make the most of the new Unity UI anchor system and build responsive layouts/designs.

Chapter 5, Screen Space, World Space, and the Camera, Here we finally delve into one of the most highly anticipated parts of the new UI system: the ability to easily build perspective UI layouts and add UI elements as 3D objects within a scene.

Chapter 6, Working with the UI Source, looks at all the coding behind the UI framework and explores the new Event System and UnityEvent frameworks. The chapter finishes with a walk-through, the open source project for the UI system, allowing you to see just about every line of code Unity has written for the new UI.

Appendix, The 3D Scene Sample, talks about a flashy 3D demo scene, which was discussed in *Chapter 5, Screen Space, World Space, and the Camera,* to show off the UI. Because this wasn't the focus of the book, it was added as an optional appendix that you could follow if you wish. The instructions are also available online and as a downloadable package to enable developers of all levels to make use of it.

What you need for this book

- Unity3D V4.6+
- Visual Studio 2012 (Express, Pro, or higher); optional but recommended

Who this book is for

This book is for anyone with a solid understanding of Unity's core functionality and a decent grasp of C# scripting in Unity (although not required for just the core editor portions of the new Unity UI system). With this book, you'll be well placed to take advantage of the new UI feature set.

Conventions

In this book, you will find a number of styles of text that distinguish between different kinds of information. Here are some examples of these styles and an explanation of their meaning.

Code words in text, database table names, folder names, filenames, file extensions, pathnames, dummy URLs, user input, and Twitter handles are shown as follows: "For standards stake, you should add scripts into a folder called `Scripts` and scenes into a folder called `Scenes`."

A block of code is set as follows:

```
void OnGUI() {
  GUI.Label(new Rect(25, 15, 100, 30), "Label");
}
```

When we wish to draw your attention to a particular part of a code block, the relevant lines or items are set in bold:

```
public Texture2D myTexture;
void Start() {
  myTexture = new Texture2D(125, 15);
}
void OnGUI() {
  GUI.DrawTexture(new Rect(325, 15, 100, 15), myTexture,
    ScaleMode.ScaleToFit,true,0.5f);
}
```

New terms and **important words** are shown in bold. Words that you see on the screen, in menus or dialog boxes for example, appear in the text like this: "With the new **Unity UI** system, you can define several layout groups."

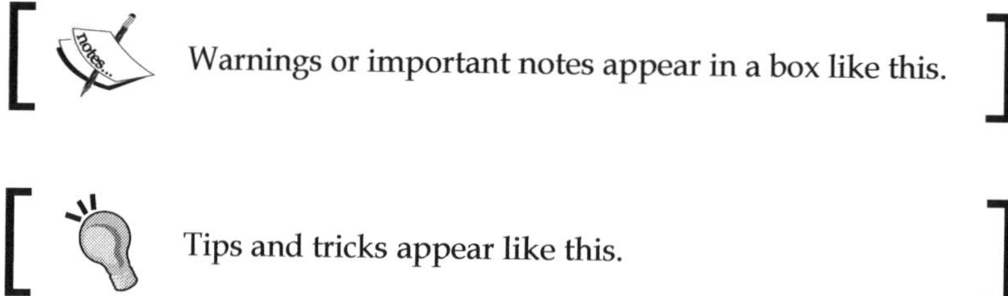

Warnings or important notes appear in a box like this.

Tips and tricks appear like this.

Reader feedback

Feedback from our readers is always welcome. Let us know what you think about this book—what you liked or may have disliked. Reader feedback is important for us to develop titles that you really get the most out of.

To send us general feedback, simply send an e-mail to `feedback@packtpub.com`, and mention the book title via the subject of your message.

If there is a topic that you have expertise in and you are interested in either writing or contributing to a book, see our author guide on `www.packtpub.com/authors`.

Customer support

Now that you are the proud owner of a Packt book, we have a number of things to help you to get the most from your purchase.

Downloading the example code

You can download the example code files from your account at `http://www.packtpub.com` for all the Packt Publishing books you have purchased. If you purchased this book elsewhere, you can visit `http://www.packtpub.com/support` and register to have the files e-mailed directly to you.

Additionally, the author has provided a support forum for the book. This forum provides direct support from the author on your queries and any forthcoming announcements regarding the title. You can find this forum at `http://bit.ly/Unity3DUIEssentialsForums`.

Downloading the color images of this book

We also provide you with a PDF file that has color images of the screenshots/diagrams used in this book. The color images will help you better understand the changes in the output. You can download this file from: `https://www.packtpub.com/sites/default/files/downloads/36170S.pdf`.

Errata

Although we have taken every care to ensure the accuracy of our content, mistakes do happen. If you find a mistake in one of our books—maybe a mistake in the text or the code—we would be grateful if you could report this to us. By doing so, you can save other readers from frustration and help us improve subsequent versions of this book. If you find any errata, please report them by visiting `http://www.packtpub.com/submit-errata`, selecting your book, clicking on the **Errata Submission Form** link, and entering the details of your errata. Once your errata are verified, your submission will be accepted and the errata will be uploaded to our website or added to any list of existing errata under the Errata section of that title.

To view the previously submitted errata, go to `https://www.packtpub.com/books/content/support` and enter the name of the book in the search field. The required information will appear under the **Errata** section.

Piracy

Piracy of copyright material on the Internet is an ongoing problem across all media. At Packt, we take the protection of our copyright and licenses very seriously. If you come across any illegal copies of our works, in any form, on the Internet, please provide us with the location address or website name immediately so that we can pursue a remedy.

Please contact us at `copyright@packtpub.com` with a link to the suspected pirated material.

We appreciate your help in protecting our authors, and our ability to bring you valuable content.

Questions

You can contact us at `questions@packtpub.com` if you are having a problem with any aspect of the book, and we will do our best to address it.

Additionally you can post questions directly to the author about the content of the title on the book's support forum at `http://bit.ly/Unity3DUIEssentialsForums`.

1
Looking Back, Looking Forward

The new Unity UI has long been sought by developers; it has been announced and re-announced over several years, and now it is finally here. The new UI system is truly awesome and (more importantly for a lot of developers on a shoestring budget) it's free.

As we start to look forward to the new UI system, it is very important to understand the legacy GUI system (which still exists for backwards compatibility) and all it has to offer, so you can fully understand just how powerful and useful the new system is. It's crucial to have this understanding, especially since most tutorials will still speak of the legacy GUI system (so you know what on earth they are talking about).

With an understanding of the legacy system, you will then peer over the diving board and walk through a 10,000-foot view of the new system, so you get a feel of what to expect from the rest of this book.

The following is the list of topics that will be covered in this chapter:

- A look back into what legacy Unity GUI is
- Tips, tricks, and an understanding of legacy GUI and what it has done for us
- A high level overview of the new UI features

Downloading the example code

You can download the example code files for all Packt books you have purchased from your account at http://www.packtpub.com. If you purchased this book elsewhere, you can visit http://www.packtpub.com/support and register to have the files e-mailed directly to you. Additionally, the author has provided a support forum for the book. This forum provides direct support from the author on your queries and any forthcoming announcements regarding the title. You can find this forum at http://bit.ly/Unity3DUIEssentialsForums.

State of play

You may not expect it, but the legacy Unity GUI has evolved over time, adding new features and improving performance. However, because it has kept evolving based on the its original implementation, it has been hampered with many constraints and the ever pressing need to remain backwards compatible (just look at Windows, which even today has to cater for programs written in BASIC (http://en.wikipedia.org/wiki/BASIC)). Not to say the old system is bad, it's just not as evolved as some of the newer features being added to the Unity 4.x and Unity 5.x series, which are based on newer and more enhanced designs, and more importantly, a new core.

The main drawback of the legacy GUI system is that it is only drawn in screen space (drawn on the screen instead of within it) on top of any 3D elements or drawing in your scenes. This is fine if you want menus or overlays in your title but if you want to integrate it further within your 3D scene, then it is a lot more difficult.

For more information about world space and screen space, see this Unity Answers article (http://answers.unity3d.com/questions/256817/about-world-space-and-local-space.html).

So before we can understand how good the new system is, we first need to get to grips with where we are coming from. (If you are already familiar with the legacy GUI system, feel free to skip over this section.)

A point of reference

Throughout this book, we will refer to the **legacy GUI** simply as **GUI**.

When we talk about the new system, it will be referred to as **UI** or **Unity UI**, just so you don't get mixed-up when reading.

When looking around the Web (or even in the Unity support forums), you may hear about or see references to **uGUI**, which was the development codename for the new **Unity UI** system.

GUI controls

The legacy GUI controls provide basic and stylized controls for use in your titles.

All legacy **GUI** controls are drawn during the GUI rendering phase from the built-in `OnGUI` method. In the sample that accompanies this title, there are examples of all the controls in the `Assets\BasicGUI.cs` script.

For GUI controls to function, a camera in the scene must have the GUILayer component attached to it. It is there by default on any **Camera** in a scene, so for most of the time you won't notice it. However, if you have removed it, then you will have to add it back for GUI to work.

The component is just the hook for the `OnGUI` delegate handler, to ensure it has called each frame.

Like the `Update` method in scripts, the `OnGUI` method can be called several times per frame if rendering is slowing things down. Keep this in mind when building your own legacy GUI scripts.

The controls that are available in the legacy GUI are:

- **Label**
- **Texture**
- **Button**
- **Text fields (single/multiline and password variant)**
- **Box**
- **Toolbars**
- **Sliders**
- **ScrollView**
- **Window**

So let's go through them in more detail:

All the following code is implemented in the sample project in the basic GUI script located in the `Assets\Scripts` folder of the downloadable code.

To experiment yourself, create a new project, scene, and script, placing the code for each control in the script and attach the script to the camera (by dragging it from the project view on to the **Main Camera** GameObject in the scene hierarchy). You can then either run the project or adorn the class in the script with the `[ExecuteInEditMode]` attribute to see it in the game view.

The Label control

Most GUI systems start with a **Label** control; this simply provides a stylized control to display read-only text on the screen, it is initiated by including the following `OnGUI` method in your script:

```
void OnGUI() {
  GUI.Label(new Rect(25, 15, 100, 30), "Label");
}
```

This results in the following on-screen display:

The **Label** control supports altering its font settings through the use of the `guiText` GameObject property (`guiText.font`) or `GUIStyles`. (See the following section on *GUIStyles* for more detail.)

To set `guiText.font` in your script, you would simply apply the following in your script, either in the `Awake/Start` functions or before drawing the next section of text you want drawn in another font:

```
public Font myFont = new Font("arial");
guiText.font = myFont;
```

You can also set the `myFont` property in **Inspector** using an imported font.

The **Label** control forms the basis for all controls to display text, and as such, all other controls inherit from it and have the same behaviors for styling the displayed text.

The **Label** control also supports using a Texture for its contents, but not both text and a texture at the same time. However, you can layer Labels and other controls on top of each other to achieve the same effect (controls are drawn implicitly in the order they are called), for example:

```
public Texture2D myTexture;
void Start() {
  myTexture = new Texture2D(125, 15);
}
void OnGUI() {
  //Draw a texture
  GUI.Label(new Rect(125, 15, 100, 30), myTexture);
  //Draw some text on top of the texture using a label
  GUI.Label(new Rect(125, 15, 100, 30), "Text overlay");
}
```

You can override the order in which controls are drawn by setting `GUI.depth = /*<depth number>*/;` in between calls; however, I would advise against this unless you have a desperate need.

The texture will then be drawn to fit the dimensions of the **Label** field, By default it scales on the shortest dimension appropriately. This too can be altered using `GUIStyle` to alter the fixed width and height or even its stretch characteristics.

`GUIStyles` and `GUISkins` are explained in the later *GUI styles and skins* section.

Texture drawing

Not specifically a control in itself, the GUI framework also gives you the ability to simply draw a Texture to the screen Granted there is little difference to using `DrawTexture` function instead of a Label with a texture or any other control. (Just another facet of the evolution of the legacy GUI). This is, in effect, the same as the previous `Label` control but instead of text it only draws a texture, for example:

```
public Texture2D myTexture;
void Start() {
```

```
    myTexture = new Texture2D(125, 15);
  }
  void OnGUI() {
    GUI.DrawTexture(new Rect(325, 15, 100, 15), myTexture);
  }
```

> Note that in all the examples providing a Texture, I have provided a basic template to initialize an empty texture. In reality, you would be assigning a proper texture to be drawn.

You can also provide scaling and alpha blending values when drawing the texture to make it better fit in the scene, including the ability to control the aspect ratio that the texture is drawn in.

> A warning though, when you scale the image, it affects the rendering properties for that image under the legacy GUI system.
>
> Scaling the image can also affect its drawn position. You may have to offset the position it is drawn at sometimes.

For example:

```
public Texture2D myTexture;
void Start() {
  myTexture = new Texture2D(125, 15);
}
void OnGUI() {
  GUI.DrawTexture(new Rect(325, 15, 100, 15), myTexture,
    ScaleMode.ScaleToFit,true,0.5f);
}
```

This will do its best to draw the source texture with in the drawn area with alpha blending (`true`) and an aspect ratio of `0.5`. Feel free to play with these settings to get your desired effect.

This is useful in certain scenarios in your game when you want a simple way to draw a full screen image on the screen on top of all the 3D/2D elements, such as pause or splash screen. However, like the **Label** control, it does not receive any input events (see the `Button` control for that).

There is also a variant of the `DrawTexture` function called `DrawTextureWithTexCoords`. This allows you to not only pick where you want the texture drawn on to the screen, but also from which part of the source texture you want to draw, for example:

```
public Texture2D myTexture;
void Start() {
  myTexture = new Texture2D(125, 15);
}
void OnGUI() {
  GUI.DrawTextureWithTexCoords (new Rect(325, 15, 100, 15),
    myTexture ,
  new Rect(10, 10, 50, 5));
}
```

This will pick a region from the source texture (`myTexture`) 50 pixels wide by 5 pixels high starting from position **10, 10** on the texture. It will then draw this to the `Rect` region specified.

> However, the `DrawTextureWithTexCoords` function cannot perform scaling, it can only perform alpha blending! It will simply draw to fit the selected texture region to the size specified in the initial Rect.
>
> `DrawTextureWithTexCoords` has also been used to draw individual sprites using the legacy GUI, which has a notion of what a sprite is.

The Button control

Unity also provides a **Button** control, which comes in two variants. The basic `Button` control which only supports a single click, whereas **RepeatButton** supports holding down the button.

They are both instantiated the same way by using an `if` statement to capture when the button is clicked, as shown in the following script:

```
void OnGUI() {
  if (GUI.Button(new Rect(25, 40, 120, 30), "Button"))
  {
    //The button has clicked, holding does nothing
  }
  if (GUI.RepeatButton(new Rect(170, 40, 170, 30),
    "RepeatButton"))
  {
    //The button has been clicked or is held down
  }
}
```

Each will result in a simple button on screen as follows:

The controls also support using a Texture for the button content as well by providing a texture value for the second parameter as follows:

```
public Texture2D myTexture;
void Start() {
  myTexture = new Texture2D(125, 15);
}
void OnGUI() {
  if (GUI.Button(new Rect(25, 40, 120, 30), myTexture))
  { }
}
```

Like the **Label**, the font of the text can be altered using `GUIStyle` or by setting the `guiText` property of the GameObject. It also supports using textures in the same way as the Label. The easiest way to look at this control is that it is a Label that can be clicked.

The Text control

Just as there is a need to display text, there is also a need for a user to be able to enter text, and the legacy GUI provides the following controls to do just that:

Control	Description
TextField	This is a basic text box, it supports a single line of text, no new lines (although, if the text contains end of line characters, it will draw the extra lines down).
TextArea	This is an extension of **TextField** that supports entering of multiple lines of text; new lines will be added when the user hits the enter key.
PasswordField	This is a variant of **TextField**; however, it won't display the value entered, it will replace each character with a replacement character. Note, the password itself is still stored in text form and if you are storing users' passwords, you should encrypt/decrypt the actual password when using it. Never store characters in plain text.

Using the **TextField** control is simple, as it returns the final state of the value that has been entered and you have to pass that same variable as a parameter for the current text to be displayed. To use the controls, you apply them in script as follows:

```
string textString1 = "Some text here";
string textString2 = "Some more text here";
string textString3 = "Even more text here";
void OnGUI() {
  textString = GUI.TextField(new Rect(25, 100, 100, 30),
    textString1);
  textString = GUI.TextArea(new Rect(150, 100, 200, 75),
    textString2);
  textString = GUI.PasswordField(new Rect(375, 100, 90, 30),
    textString3, '*');
}
```

A note about strings in Unity scripts

Strings are immutable. Every time you change their value they create a new string in memory by having the `textString` variable declared at the class level it is a lot more memory efficient.

If you declare the `textString` variable in the `OnGUI` method, it will generate garbage (wasted memory) in each frame. Worth keeping in mind.

When displayed, the textbox by default looks like this:

As with the **Label** and **Button** controls, the font of the text displayed can be altered using either a `GUIStyle` or `guiText` GameObject property.

Note that text will overflow within the field if it is too large for the display area, but it will not be drawn outside the `TextField` dimensions. The same goes for multiple lines.

The Box control

In the midst of all the controls is a generic purpose control that seemingly can be used for a variety of purposes. Generally, it's used for drawing a background/shaded area behind all other controls.

The `Box` control implements most of the features mentioned in the controls above controls (`Label`, `Texture`, and `Text`) in a single control with the same styling and layout options. It also supports text and images as the other controls do.

You can draw it with its own content as follows:

```
void OnGUI() {
GUI.Box (new Rect (350, 350, 100, 130), "Settings");
}
```

This gives you the following result:

Alternatively, you can use it to decorate the background of other controls, for example:

```
private string textString = "Some text here";
void OnGUI() {
  GUI.Box (new Rect (350, 350, 100, 130), "Settings");
  GUI.Label(new Rect(360, 370, 80, 30), "Label");
  textString = GUI.TextField(new Rect(360, 400, 80, 30),
    textString);
  if (GUI.Button (new Rect (360, 440, 80, 30), "Button")) {}
}
```

Note that using the Box control does not affect any controls you draw upon it. It is drawn as a completely separate control. This statement will be made clearer when you look at the **Layout** controls later in this chapter.

The example will draw the box background and the **Label**, **Text**, and **Button** controls on top of the box area and looks like this:

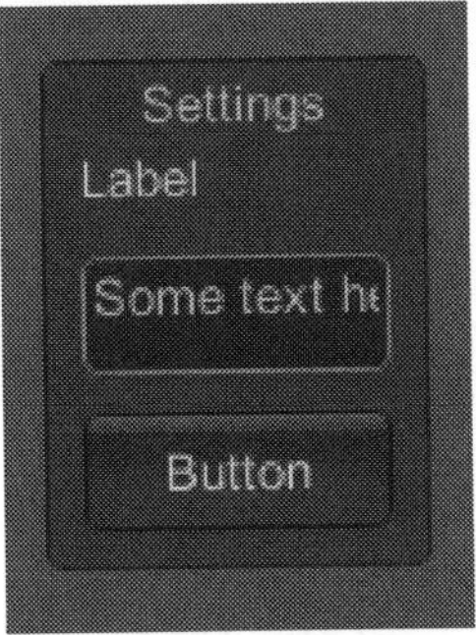

The box control can be useful to highlight groups of controls or providing a simple background (alternatively, you can use an image instead of just text and color).

As with the other controls, the **Box** control supports styling using `GUIStyle`.

The Toggle/checkbox control

If checking on / checking off is your thing, then the legacy GUI also has a `checkbox` control for you, useful for those times when you need to visualize the `on/off` state of an option.

Like the **TextField** control, you pass the variable that manages `Togglestate` as a parameter and it returns the new value (if it changes), so it is applied in code as follows:

```
bool blnToggleState = false;
void OnGUI() {
blnToggleState = GUI.Toggle(new Rect(25, 150, 250, 30),
blnToggleState, "Toggle");
}
```

This results in the following on-screen result:

As with the **Label** and **Button** controls, the font of the text displayed can be altered using either a `GUIStyle` or `guiText` GameObject property.

Toolbar panels

The basic GUI controls also come with some very basic automatic layout panels: the first handles an arrangement of buttons, however these buttons are grouped and only one can be selected at a time.

As with other controls, the style of the button can be altered using a `GUIStyles` definition, including fixing the width of the buttons and spacing.

There are two layout options available, these are:

- The Toolbar control
- The Selection grid control

The Toolbar control

The `Toolbar` control arranges buttons in a horizontal pattern (vertical is not supported).

Note that it is possible to fake a vertical toolbar by using a selection grid with just one item per row. See the *Selection grid* section later in this chapter for more details.

As with other controls, the **Toolbar** returns the index of the currently selected button in the toolbar. The buttons are also the same as the base button control so it also offers options to support either text or images for the button content.

The **RepeatButton** control however is not supported.

To implement the toolbar, you specify an array of the content you wish to display in each button and the integer value that controls the selected button, as follows:

```
private int toolbarInt;
private string[] toolbarStrings ;
Void Start() {
  toolbarInt = 0;
  toolbarStrings = { "Toolbar1", "Toolbar2", "Toolbar3" };
}
void OnGUI() {
  toolbarInt = GUI.Toolbar(new Rect(25, 200, 200, 30),
    toolbarInt, toolbarStrings);
}
```

The main difference between the preceding controls is that you have to pass the currently selected index value in to the control and it then returns the new value.

The Toolbar when drawn looks as follows:

As stated, you can also pass an array of textures as well and they will be displayed instead of the text content.

The SelectionGrid control

The **SelectionGrid** control is a customization of the previous standard **Toolbar** control, it is able to arrange the buttons in a grid layout and resize the buttons appropriately to fill the target area.

In code, `SelectionGrid` is used in a very similar format to the `Toolbar` code shown previously, for example:

```
private int selectionGridInt ;
private string[] selectionStrings;
Void Start() {
  selectionGridInt = 0;
  selectionStrings = { "Grid 1", "Grid 2", "Grid 3", "Grid 4" };
}
void OnGUI() {
  selectionGridInt = GUI.SelectionGrid(
  new Rect(250, 200, 200, 60), selectionGridInt, selectionStrings, 2);
}
```

The main difference between **SelectionGrid** and **Toolbar** in code is that with **SelectionGrid** you can specify the number of items in a single row and the control will automatically lay out the buttons accordingly (unless overridden using `GUIStyle`).

The preceding code will result in the following layout:

On their own, they provide a little more flexibility than just using buttons alone.

The Slider/Scrollbar controls

When you need to control a range in your games. GUI or add a handle to control moving properties between two values, like moving an object around in your scene, this is where the **Slider** and **Scrollbar** controls come in. They provide two similar *out-of-the-box* implementations that give a scrollable region and a handle to control the value behind the control.

Here, they are presented side by side:

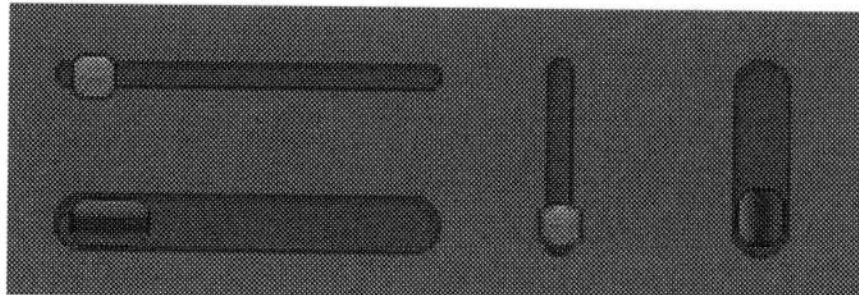

The **slimmer Slider** and **chunkier Scrollbar** controls can both work in either horizontal or vertical modes and have presets for the minimum and maximum values allowed.

Slider control code

In code, the Slider control code is represented as follows:

```
private float fltSliderValue = 0.5f;
void OnGUI() {
  fltSliderValue = GUI.HorizontalSlider(new Rect(25, 250, 100,30),
    fltSliderValue, 0.0f, 10.0f);
  fltSliderValue = GUI.VerticalSlider(new Rect(150, 250, 25, 50),
    fltSliderValue, 10.0f, 0.0f);
}
```

Scrollbar control code

In code, the Scrollbar control code is represented as follows:

```
private float fltScrollerValue = 0.5f;
void OnGUI() {
  fltScrollerValue = GUI.HorizontalScrollbar(new Rect(25, 285,
    100, 30), fltScrollerValue, 1.0f, 0.0f, 10.0f);
  fltScrollerValue = GUI.VerticalScrollbar(new Rect(200, 250, 25,
    50), fltScrollerValue, 1.0f, 10.0f, 0.0f);
}
```

Like **Toolbar** and **SelectionGrid**, you are required to pass in the current value and it will return the updated value. However, unlike all the other controls, you actually have two style points, so you can style the bar and the handle separately, giving you a little more freedom and control over the look and feel of the sliders.

Normally, you would only use the **Slider** control; The main reason the **Scrollbar** is available is that it forms the basis for the next control, the ScrollView control.

The ScrollView control

The last of the displayable controls is the **ScrollView** control, which gives you masking abilities over GUI elements with optional horizontal and vertical **Scrollbars**. Simply put, it allows you to define an area larger for controls behind a smaller window on the screen, for example:

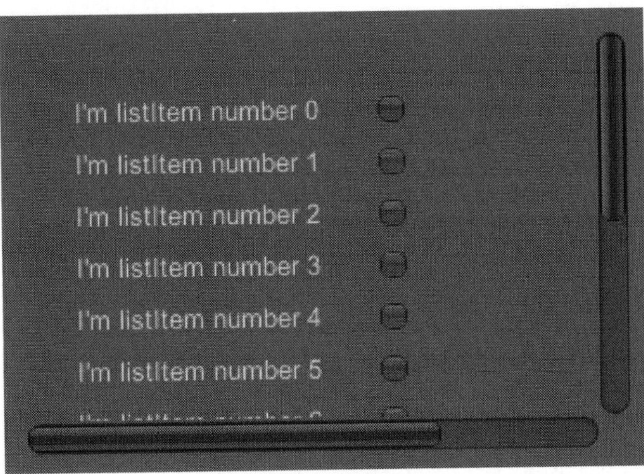

Example list implementation using a ScrollView control

Here we have a list that has many items that go beyond the drawable area of the **ScrollView** control. We then have the two scrollbars to move the content of the scroll viewer up/down and left/right to change the view. The background content is hidden behind a viewable mask that is the width and height of the **ScrollView** control's main window.

Styling the control is a little different as there is no base style for it; it relies on the currently set default `GUISkin` (see the following **GUIStyles** section). You can however set separate `GUIStyles` for each of the sliders but only over the whole slider, not its individual parts (bar and handle). If you don't specify styles for each slider, it will also revert to the base `GUIStyle`.

Implementing a **ScrollView** is fairly easy, for example:

1. Define the visible area along with a virtual background layer where the controls will be drawn using a `BeginScrollView` function.
2. Draw your controls in the virtual area. Any GUI drawing between the ScrollView calls is drawn within the scroll area.

Note that 0,0 in the **ScrollView** is from the top-left of the **ScrollView** area and not the top-left-hand corner of the screen.

3. Complete it by closing the control with the `EndScrollView` function. For example, the previous example view was created with the following code:

```
private Vector2 scrollPosition = Vector2.zero;
private bool blnToggleState = false;
void OnGUI()
{
  scrollPosition = GUI.BeginScrollView(
  new Rect(25, 325, 300, 200),
  scrollPosition,
  new Rect(0, 0, 400, 400));

  for (int i = 0; i < 20; i++)
  {
    //Add new line items to the background
    addScrollViewListItem(i, "I'm listItem number " + i);
  }
  GUI.EndScrollView();
}

//Simple function to draw each list item, a label and checkbox
void addScrollViewListItem(int i, string strItemName)
{
  GUI.Label(new Rect(25, 25 + (i * 25), 150, 25), strItemName);
  blnToggleState = GUI.Toggle(
  new Rect(175, 25 + (i * 25), 100, 25),
  blnToggleState, "");
}
```

In this code, we define a simple function (`addScrollViewListItem`) to draw a list item (consisting of a label and checkbox). We then begin the **ScrollView** control by passing the visible area (the first `Rect` parameter), the starting scroll position, and finally the virtual area behind the control (the second `Rect` parameter). Then we use that to draw 20 list items inside the virtual area of the **ScrollView** control using our helper function before finishing off and closing the control with the `EndScrollView` command.

[If you want to, you can also nest **ScrollView** controls within each other.]

The `ScrollView` control also has some actions to control its use like the `ScrollTo` command. This command will move the visible area to the coordinates of the virtual layer, bringing it into focus. (The coordinates for this are based on the top-left position of the virtual layer; 0,0 being top-left.)

To use the `ScrollTo` function on **ScrollView**, you must use it within the **Begin** and **End** `ScrollView` commands. For example, we can add a button in **ScrollView** to jump to the top-left of the virtual area, for example:

```
public Vector2 scrollPosition = Vector2.zero;
void OnGUI()
{
  scrollPosition = GUI.BeginScrollView(
  new Rect(10, 10, 100, 50),
  scrollPosition,
  new Rect(0, 0, 220, 10));

  if (GUI.Button(new Rect(120, 0, 100, 20), "Go to Top Left"))
    GUI.ScrollTo(new Rect(0, 0, 100, 20));

  GUI.EndScrollView();
}
```

You can also additionally turn on/off the sliders on either side of the control by specifying the `BeginScrollView` statement using the `alwayShowHorizontal` and `alwayShowVertical` properties; these are highlighted here in an updated `GUI.BeginScrollView` call:

```
Vector2 scrollPosition = Vector2.zero;
bool ShowVertical = false; // turn off vertical scrollbar
```

```
bool ShowHorizontal = false; // turn off horizontal scrollbar
void OnGUI() {
scrollPosition = GUI.BeginScrollView(
  new Rect(25, 325, 300, 200),
  scrollPosition,
  new Rect(0, 0, 400, 400),
  ShowHorizontal,
  ShowVertical);
  GUI.EndScrollView ();
}
```

Rich Text Formatting

Now having just plain text everywhere would not look that great and would likely force developers to create images for all the text on their screens (granted a fair few still do so for effect). However, Unity does provide a way to enable richer text display using a style akin to HTML wherever you specify text on a control (only for label and display purposes; getting it to work with input fields is not recommended).

In this HTML style of writing text, we have the following tags we can use to liven up the text displayed.

<b></b>

This gives text a **Bold** format, for example:

```
The <b>quick</b> brown <b>Fox</b> jumped over the <b>lazy Frog</b>
```

This would result in:

The **quick** brown **Fox** jumped over the **lazy Frog**

<i></i>

Using this tag will give text an **Italic** format, for example:

```
The <b><i>quick</i></b> brown <b>Fox</b><i>jumped</i> over the
<b>lazy Frog</b>
```

This would result in:

The ***quick*** brown **Fox** *jumped* over the **lazy Frog**

<size></size>

As you can probably guess, this tag will alter the **Size** of the text it surrounds.

For reference, the default size for the font is set by the font itself.

For example:

```
The <b><i>quick</i></b> <size=50>brown <b>Fox</b></size> <i>jumped</
i> over the <b>lazy Frog</b>
```

This would result in:

The ***quick*** **brown Fox** *jumped* over the **lazy Frog**

<color></color>

Lastly, you can specify different colors for text surrounded by the Color tag. The color itself is denoted using its 8-digit RGBA hex value, for example:

```
The <b><i>quick</i></b> <size=50><color=#a52a2aff>brown</color>
<b>Fox</b></size> <i>jumped</i> over the <b>lazy Frog</b>
```

Note that the color is defined using normal RGBA color space notation (`http://en.wikipedia.org/wiki/RGBA_color_space`) in hexadecimal form with two characters per color, for example, RRGGBBAA. Although the color property does also support the shorter RGB color space, which is the same notation but without the A (Alpha) component, for example,. RRGGBB

The preceding code would result in:

The quick brown **Fox** jumped over the **lazy Frog**

(If you are reading this in print, the previous word brown is in the color brown.)

You can also use a color name to reference it but the pallet is quite limited; for more details, see the Rich Text manual reference page at `http://docs.unity3d.com/Manual/StyledText.html`.

For text meshes, there are two additional tags:

- `<material></material>`
- `<quad></quad>`

These only apply when associated to an existing mesh. The material is one of the materials assigned to the mesh, which is accessed using the mesh index number (the array of materials applied to the mesh). When applied to a quad, you can also specify a size, position (*x*, *y*), width, and height to the text.

> The text mesh isn't well documented and is only here for reference; as we delve deeper into the new UI system, we will find much better ways of achieving this.

Common control features

The legacy GUI system does also have some features for controlling flow, control selection, and targeted behavior. When it was introduced in Unity V2, it was a huge step up from the previous component-based system.

Grouping controls

The legacy GUI allow you to group controls together on the screen, making all positions for the group relative to the group's position. This means that if you started a group at position X 50 and Y 50, then all child control positions within the group would start at 50,50 when they define their position as 0,0.

Like the **ScrollView** control, each group has a beginning and an end to define the scope of all the controls within the group, for example:

```
void OnGUI() {
  //Start a group at position 50, 50. 150 width and 60 height
  GUI.BeginGroup(new Rect (50,50,150,60));
  //Draw a label with a 10, 10 offset in the group
  GUI.Label(new Rect (10, 10, 100, 30), "Label in a Group");
  GUI.EndGroup();
}
```

Here the label is drawn within the group bounds, and as the group starts at X 50, the Labels screen position will be at `X 60 (50 + 10)`. Anything positioned or overflowing the group's bounds will not be drawn.

The group, like other controls, can also specify content within the group as text or a texture with appropriate `GUIStyles`.

> What is odd is that unlike the rest of the controls, if you specify text content in the function, the default color of text is white, whereas if you specify text in the content parameter for the `BeginGroup` function, the text in the group is black by default. It's also left justified instead of centered.
>
> Additionally, by default the group does *not* support Rich Text Formatting unlike the other controls, so you will need to apply `GUIStyle` to change that.

Naming controls

With each control that you implement through script, you can name them as you place them; this is essential if you want to control flow and access to each field from the keyboard or to derive logic based on the currently selected/focused control.

Now unlike most other Unity functionality, you cannot directly name controls, there is no Name field on the properties of the controls as they are just commands to the GUI system to draw things to the screen, kind of like a rendering pipeline.

So to name GUI controls in Unity, we simply need to tell the GUI system that the next control we are going to draw has a name, as follows:

```
string login = "Would you like to play a game?";
void OnGUI() {
  GUI.SetNextControlName("MyAwesomeField");
  login = GUI.TextField(new Rect(10, 10, 200, 20), login);
}
```

Getting in focus

With names defined on controls, you could then define which control you were focusing on. To focus on a specific control, you would simply need to call:

```
GUI.FocusControl("MyAwesomeField");
```

This would then change the user's input focus or selection to the specific GUI control with that name.

Once you have a control in focus, you then discover the name of the specific control in focus by calling:

```
string selectedControl = GUI.GetNameOfFocusedControl();
```

If the control in focus has a name, it will return the name you set for that control. If no control is in focus or the control in focus has no name, it will return an empty string.

The logon example

As an example of using the previous naming and focus capabilities, you can build a simple logon GUI for a user to enter with validation behavior and some usability features.

To demonstrate, we will create a user registration form where the user can enter a username and password to register with your game. The password however will have to be more than six characters long for security reasons (no weak passwords here).

To start, create a new script called `IntermediateGUI` in your project (the full sample can be found in the project available with this book in the code download) and replace its contents with the following:

```
using UnityEngine;
[ExecuteInEditMode]
public class IntermediateGUI : MonoBehaviour {

  public string username = "Enter username";
  public string password = "Enter password";
  private bool passwordInError = false;
  private string passwordErrorMessage =
    "<color=red>Password too short</color>";
}
```

This gives a basic class with some of the parameters you might expect in a logon or registration form.

To this we'll add a simple function to validate the password entered to ensure it meets our stringent security policy:

```
void CheckUserPasswordAndRegister()
{
  if (password.Length < 6)
  {
    //If the password is not long enough, mark it in error
    //and focus on the password field
    passwordInError = true;
    GUI.FocusControl("PasswordField");
  } else
  {
    passwordInError = false;
GUI.FocusControl("");
    //Register User
  }
}
```

With that in place, now we can add our GUI controls:

```
void OnGUI() {
  //A tidy group for our fields and a box to decorate it
  GUI.BeginGroup(new Rect(Screen.width / 2 - 75,
    Screen.height / 2 - 80, 150,160));
  GUI.Box(new Rect(0,0,150,160), "User registration form");
```

```
    GUI.SetNextControlName("UsernameField");
    username = GUI.TextField(new Rect(10, 40, 130, 20), username);
    GUI.SetNextControlName("PasswordField");
    password = GUI.PasswordField(new Rect(10, 70, 130, 20),
      password,'*');
    if (passwordInError)
    {
      GUI.Label (new Rect (10, 100, 200, 20),
        passwordErrorMessage);
    }
    if (Event.current.isKey &&
        Event.current.keyCode == KeyCode.Return &&
          GUI.GetNameOfFocusedControl() == "PasswordField")
    {
      CheckUserPasswordAndRegister();
    }
    if (GUI.Button(new Rect(80, 130, 65, 20), "Register"))
    {
      CheckUserPasswordAndRegister();
    }
    GUI.EndGroup();
  }
```

Note that the `Event` keyword here relates to the legacy GUI event system for handling user input. See the **Event** section later in this chapter for more information.

This is **NOT** to be confused with the `UnityEvent` system introduced with the new UI system.

These results are shown in the following GUI screen:

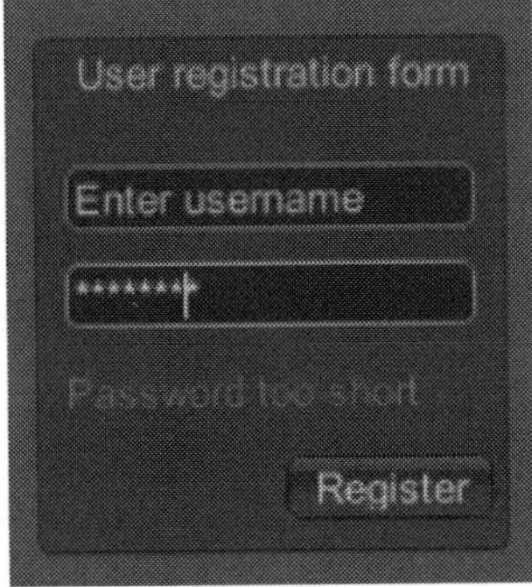

In this example, we draw a box, a text field, and a password field together with a simple button within a group, which is then centered on the screen.

We check whether the user hits the *Enter* key and whether they are on the password field (checked using the `GUI.GetNameOfFocusedControl()` function) and we try to register them. The same happens if the user clicks on the **Register** button.

If the user's password is longer than six characters, then they are registered; if not, then the `passwordInError` flag is set to `True`, which causes the additional label to be drawn, this then warns the user that their password could be broken easily by a 6-year-old.

Don't forget to add the `IntermediateGUI` script to an active GameObject in a scene or **Main Camera** to see the result!

Tooltips

Each of the GUI controls can also have a tooltip associated with it to display some additional text when it is either in focus or the mouse is hovering over the control.

Adding a tooltip is simple; you just need to replace the content of the control when it is being drawn using the `GUIContent` class. For example, we can update the **Register** button in the previous script as follows:

```
if (GUI.Button(new Rect(80, 130, 65, 20),
    new GUIContent("Register", "My Tooltip")))
{
  CheckUserPasswordAndRegister();
}
```

With the tooltip defined, we just then need to display the current tooltip somewhere on the screen, usually as a label, but it can be any control that can display text (input fields are not recommended however), so add the following after the button block but before `EndGroup()`:

```
GUI.Label (new Rect (10, 120, 65, 20), GUI.tooltip);
```

This simply gets the content of the current tooltip in focus and returns the tooltip text for that control.

`GUIContent` also has several other options for displaying text and texture variants, so it's worth checking out some more.

The Window control

The last weapon in the legacy GUI arsenal is the `Window` control. As the name suggests, this defines a separate drawable window for your controls.

[The window behavior is similar to **ScrollView**; however, it is just one layer. Any controls drawn outside the bounds of the window are simply not drawn.]

[But there is nothing to stop you using a **ScrollView** control inside a Window to achieve the same thing however.]

With this separate Window, we can control many things, including:

- The modal nature of the **Window**

[Modal means that this window is the only one you can control; non-modal means it is a side-by-side window]

- The drag state of **Window**; as in, the window can be dragged by holding on with a mouse or touch
- The draw order of each **Window**; this allows sorting of draw windows on top of each other
- The specific **Window** in focus, if there are multiple side-by-side windows or a modal window

This opens lots of possibilities with a GUI **Window**.

[The full **Window** example can be found in the **BasicGUI** script in the sample project, displaying all the same controls as before but within a single separate **Window** control.]

To create a **Window** control, you first need to define a new method callback for the Window using the following signature:

```
void DoMyWindow(int windowID)
{
}
```

This method is where you will add all your GUI code using the previous examples; each control is positioned is based off the top-left position of the window when it is displayed (same as the **Group** and **ScrollView** controls described earlier).

Additionally, you can specify any of the previous options for the window, for example:

```
void DoMyWindow(int windowID)
{
  GUI.Label(new Rect(25, 15, 100, 30), "Label");
  // Make the window Draggable
  GUI.DragWindow();
}
```

With your `Window` method in place, you just need to call the `GUI.Window` function to open it along with the property to track the **Window's** location:

```
private Rect rctWindow1;
void OnGUI()
{
  Rect rctWindow1;
  rctWindow1 = GUI.Window(0,
  rctWindow1,
  DoMyWindow,
  "Controls Window");
}
```

This calls **Window** control into view using:

- An ID for the window
- The `Rect` position for where **Window** will open
- The delegate method for the GUI contents of **Window**
- A name/title for the window

If you want a modal window, then you would need to instantiate the window with the `GUI.ModalWindow` function instead of the `Window` function:

```
rctWindow1 = GUI.ModalWindow(0, rctWindow1, DoMyWindow, "Modal
  Controls Window");
```

If we take all the controls together (that we have created so far in this chapter), it would create a **Window** view, as shown in the following screenshot:

For a complete end-to-end example, please see the code download package, which has all this defined.

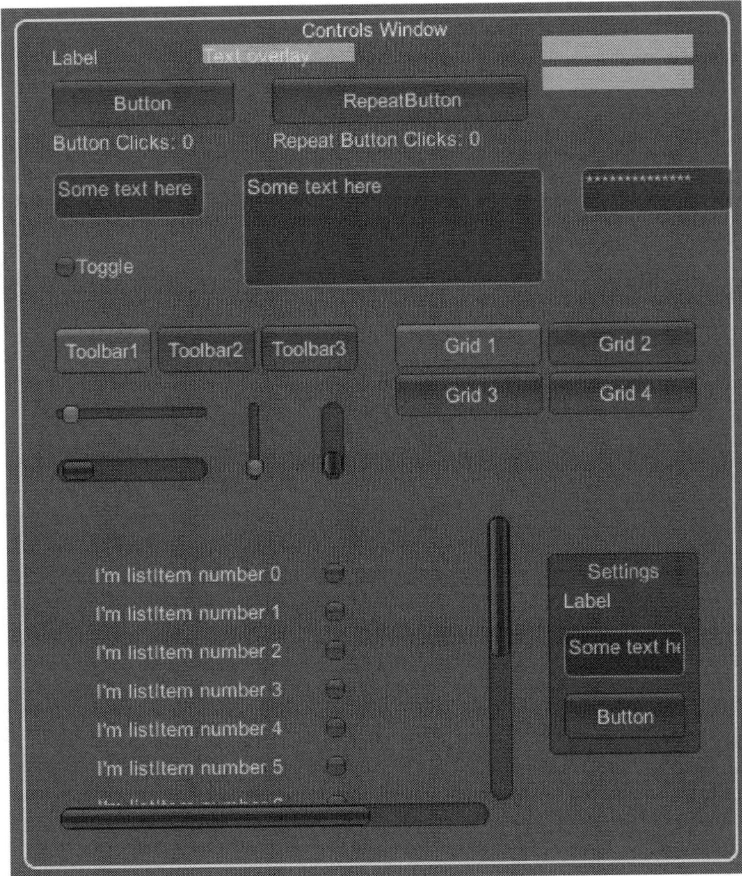

GUI styles and skins

Recognizing that not everyone likes plain backgrounds and the same font throughout their projects, Unity provided options to define a style for the layout and general look and feel of the legacy GUI system, these are defined as **GUIStyles**.

> These styles can either be applied globally using a **GUISkin** (see **GUISkin** in the following section), or they can be applied individually to each control (as detailed in the previous screenshot).

Each style has options to define:

- A `Name`
- A texture or text color for the different states of the control it's attached to (`Normal`, `Hover`, `Active`, and `Focused`)
- The border, margin, padding, and overflow sizes for the control (for each edge)
- A `Font` (with suitable size, style, alignment, word wrapping, and rich text support options)
- A text clipping size
- Image position within the control
- Offset settings for the content within the control
- A fixed width and height
- Stretching options for the width and height

I recommended configuring a public `GUIStyle` property in a class and then modifying it in **Editor Inspector** when setting up a `GUIStyle`, for example:

```
using UnityEngine;
[ExecuteInEditMode]
public class GUIStyles : MonoBehaviour {
  public GUIStyle;
  void OnGUI() {
//Create a label using the GUIStyle property above
    GUI.Label(new Rect(25, 15, 100, 30), "Label",
      myGUIStyle);
  }
}
```

You can also configure a `GUIStyle` in code, however it's not recommended as the editor is just better at it.

It is worth noting that having too many different GUIStyles all over the place can become very inefficient and hard to maintain. If you find you are using a lot of **GUIStyles** then I'd recommend you create a single script attached to a common object (say **Main Camera**) in your scene with all your GUIStyle's defined and have each script take `GUIStyle` references from there.

When you attach the preceding script with the `GUIStyle` property to a GameObject in your scene, it will look like this in **Inspector**:

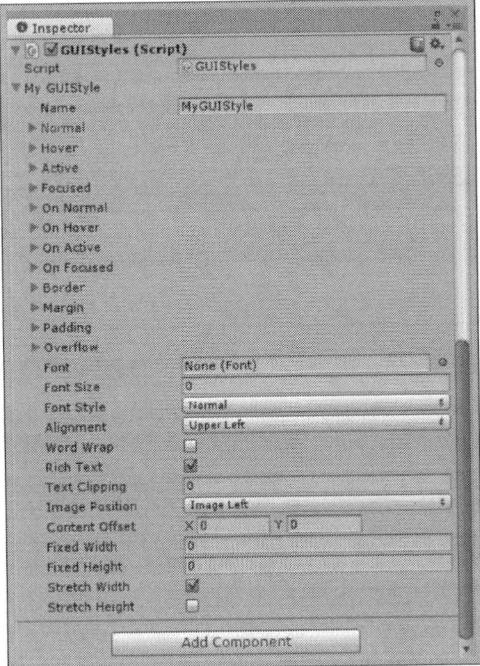

Note that the first time you open it in the editor you will get `NullReferenceException` in the console window; this is just because you haven't configured **GUIStyle** yet.

If you don't want to apply a style to each and every control directly, you can then optionally create **GUISkin**, which contains all the styles for each control type. This is then applied using the `GUI` class prior to drawing any controls.

A **GUISkin** also has some additional options that apply to the GUI, which include:

- Setting whether a double-click action selects
- Setting whether a triple-click action selects
- The color of the cursor
- The cursor flash speed
- The default selection color
- Custom styles (an array of `GUIStyle` properties you can then reuse on controls)

To demonstrate, click on the **Create** button in the `project` folder view and select **GUISkin**, which will give you a new **GUISkin** asset in the project view. By selecting it, you will see the following window in **Inspector**:

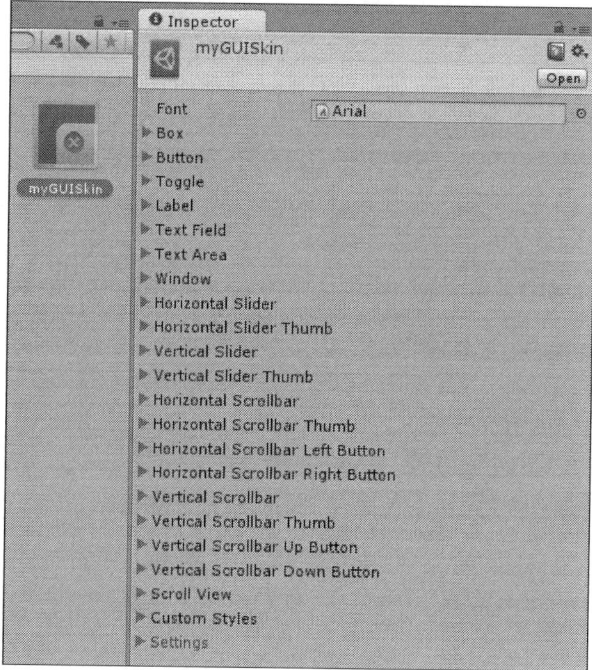

As you can see, it contains all the options for altering the style globally for each control. To use `GUISkin`, create a new script called `GUISkins`, then replace its contents with the following:

```
using UnityEngine;
[ExecuteInEditMode]
public class GUISkins : MonoBehaviour {

  public GUISkin MySkin;
  void OnGUI()
  {
    GUI.skin = mySkin;
    GUI.Label(new Rect(25, 15, 100, 30), "Label");
    //Draw the rest of your controls
  }
}
```

Then attach the `GUISkins` script to **Main Camera** in your current scene (disabling any other scripts currently attached) and drag the **GUISkin** you have created and apply it to the **My Skin** property of the script in the inspector:

By setting the skin at the beginning of any GUI drawing, any and all controls drawn will now use your custom skin instead of the Unity default. If you wish, you can use several skins by just changing the skin before drawing more controls.

For some of the best examples of **GUISkins**, try installing the Unity Extra GUI Skins asset (`http://bit.ly/UnityExtraGUISkins`), which is a collection of skin samples built by Unity themselves (and it's free).

> Note that if you want to reuse your own skins in other projects (or sell more skins through the asset store), then you can export them using Unity's **Export Package** option under **Assets** in the menu. For more details, check out `http://docs.unity3d.com/Manual/HOWTO-exportpackage.html`

Here's an example of what the GUISkins asset gives you:

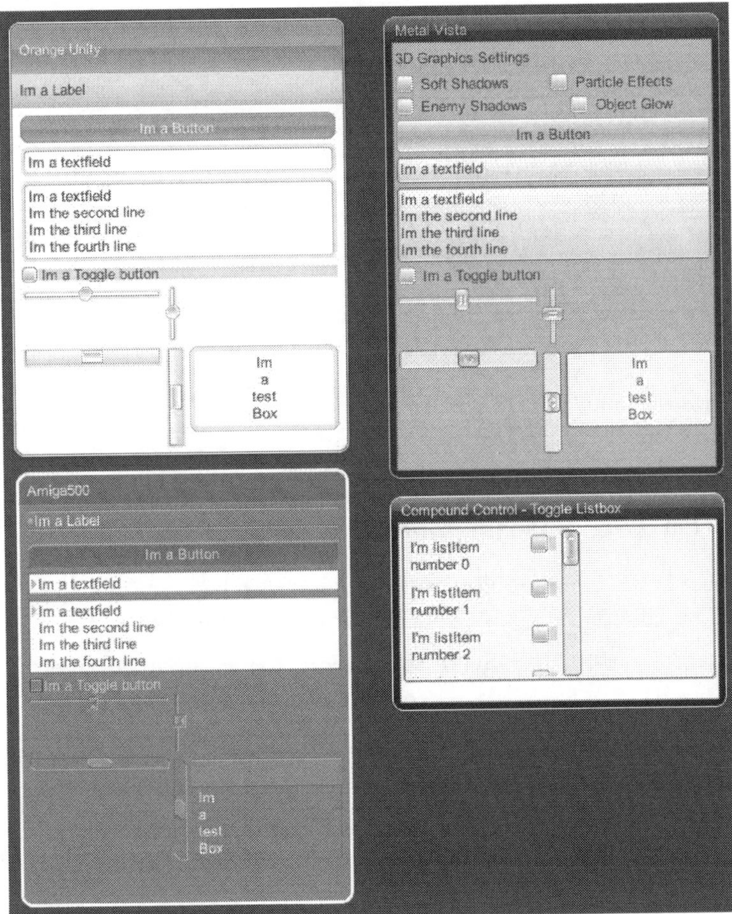

GUI events and properties

To support events in the legacy GUI area, Unity added an entire event handler specifically for GUI interactions. This class is aptly named the **Event** class.

Remember, this section refers to the legacy `GUI Event` classes, which has nothing to do with the new **UnityEvent** system introduced in the new **Unity UI** system. See *Chapter 6, Working with the UI Source,* for more details of the **UnityEvent** system.

These events center on user and device input, varying from:

- **Event types**: Is it a key event, mouse event, and so on
- **Event values**: Which key pressed, mouse button pressed, and so on
- **Event summary information**: Modifier keys, mouse movement delta, and so on

To access the events you simply need to query the `Event.current` property to get the current `Event` state. (The `Event` state updates when there is a change, until then you will get the last/previous state.)

The logon example earlier shows an example for using events, where we detect if the user has pressed a key and if that key is the *Enter* key as shown in this script:

```
if (Event.current.isKey &&
    Event.current.keyCode == KeyCode.Return &&
      GUI.GetNameOfFocusedControl() == "PasswordField")
  {
    CheckUserPasswordAndRegister();
  }
```

Along with the events, the GUI class also provides some additional properties you can query or set in the `OnGUI` method, namely:

- `enabled`: Is the GUI enabled and displayed on the screen. Can it be used to turn on or off controls that are to be drawn to the screen.
- `changed`: This returns true if any controls' values have changed since the last call of `OnGUI`.
- `color`: This is the global color tint for the GUI layout.
- `contentColor`: This is the global text color tint for the GUI.

- `backgroundColor`: This is the global background color tint.
- `depth`: This is the depth order for the current `GUI` script. This is useful if you have GUI elements in more than one script and want to layer them.
- `matrix`: The 3D transformation matrix for the current GUI.

All of these elements can be used to override all controls or individual controls by setting them in between controls.

Layout controls

If you prefer not to hand draw the position of every single control in your GUI, Unity does offer some automatic layout controls from the `GUILayout` class.

The Layout controls (using GUILayout instead of just GUI) have the same set of controls as the normal `GUI` class (hence I'm not going to describe them all over again), the main difference is that you do not need to specify a `Rect` area to draw the control, as it will just be drawn at the first suitable location; any further controls added will be laid out appropriately with enough spacing between the controls.

You can also control the spacing and even if you want, any empty space between the controls using the **Width**, **Height**, and **Spacing** properties (Space/FlexibleSpace) of `GUILayout`, following the same rules as for **GUI** controls (setting up the `GUILayout` before drawing a control).

If you don't want the layout to take up the maximum space for a control, you also have the settings for Width (MaxWidth/MinWidth) and Height (MaxHeight/MinHeight).

The main differences are as follows:

- BeginGroup becomes BeginArea
- Horizontal and vertical groups (sub groups)

BeginArea

Instead of defining **Groups**, you define **Areas**. Apart from the name, they behave exactly the same. This is the only layout control that takes a `Rect` parameter to specify where you want to draw the controls (excluding Windows of course); all `GUILayout` controls are then aligned to **Area** in the same way they are in **Group**.

It's recommended that when using `GUILayout` controls that you place them in an Area for the best effect.

Horizontal and Vertical layout groups

To control the layout of controls, you can define a set of controls to draw in a particular direction, either horizontally or vertically. You start these in the same way as areas by setting a `GUILayout.BeginHorizontal()` and `GUILayout.EndHorizontal()` command. Like the Area, you can specify additional content for the new sub-area such as text or textures.

The Asset Store

Several packages on the Unity asset store have tried to build a more fluent UI creation system. They have met with varying success and all suffer from one underlying issue, they weren't built by Unity and don't have access to some of the underlying runtime and rendering components of the Unity editor and player. This results in some performance issues (but in some cases they are actually faster than the legacy GUI, especially on mobile platforms) and (in some cases) hacky workarounds. All in all, most have done incredibly well without access to Unity's innards.

With the release of the new Unity UI system however, I would recommend checking the state of many of the `GUI` assets out there as several (quite understandably) have bowed their heads and are dropping off the store. The main package is still ongoing is NGUI (`http://bit.ly/UnityAssetStore-NGUI`), but it does have a hefty price tag to it. With it though are a multitude of supporting assets to make its adoption easier and offer integration into several other assets.

Enter Thunderdome

Now that you've seen what Unity has had available for so long with the legacy GUI (and if you have experienced it you will undoubtedly shudder at this point), it is a very welcome relief that the UI system has received such an overhaul in Unity 4.6. It has been a long time coming and very much anticipated!

Note that this section is just a preliminary overview so you know what's coming. Each section will be described in depth in the following chapters.

Recognizing the need for change, Unity set upon the path of redesigning the GUI system from the ground up. They have looked at what games have needed, what the community has built (even with the limitations and restrictions of not having access to Unity's core) and then sprinkled some fairy dust and hey presto, the new **Unity UI** system was born.

It has been a long, hard road with many bumps in the way, but the journey has begun (I say begun because the **Unity UI** journey does not end with Unity 4.6; it will continue to evolve into Unity 5 and beyond like many other components).

With a keen eye on the future, the new **Unity UI** system delivers on several core points, namely:

- **Extensibility**: Each and every control is a script and you can create new scripts to derive from them and create your own controls.
- **Uses sprites**: The new Unity UI system is predominately built on top of the new sprite system introduced in Unity 4.3. It has also however extended the sprite system with some new features as well.
- **Tight integration with GameObjects**: Each control is a GameObject in its own right with the same capabilities as any other game object including the ability to add further components and/or scripts.
- **Exposed events**: Each control has its own events which you can attach to and extend upon.
- **Tight integration with rendering and update loops**: Because they are GameObjects, you can even override the default rendering and updating of a control.
- **Animation**: Each control can be fully animated using the new Animator dope sheet and Mecanim. Some controls (such as the button) leverage Mecanim to do state-driven control. There are even animation specific events.
- **Screenspace AND WorldSpace**: Finally UI can be drawn in 3D in a performant way that doesn't involve hacking the project together or having to use PRO-only features.
- **FREE**: Unity UI comes as standard as part of the free license version of Unity (indie developers rejoice).
- **Open source**: Unity has made the source for the UI system open source and available for anyone to look at and even offer fixes / new suggestions, to coders delight.

New layouts

The layout features begin the story of the new **Unity UI**; they set the stage and ultimately define where controls will be drawn, in which direction they will be drawn, and also how they fit within a certain area.

Rect Transform

Introduced in 4.3 with the new Sprite functionality, the **Rect Transform** component provides a defining region for any 2D element within the Unity system. However, like most things in 4.6, it has received significant updates allowing more control over the area it manages as shown here:

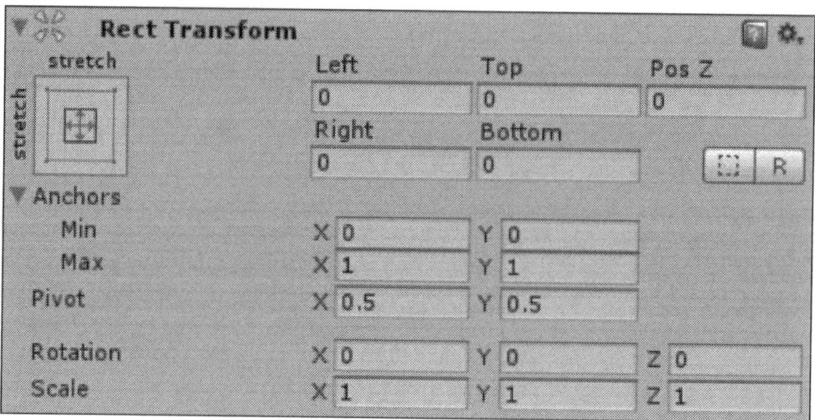

It also sports a new button in the editor (called the **Rect Tool**) to edit and manage **Rect Transform** from the scene view, as shown in the following screenshot:

The Canvas

At the core of all **Unity UI** drawings, is the new **Canvas** control. It acts as the paint board for your **Unity UI** controls (and even other canvases), once rendered the canvas is drawn to the relative point in your scene.

Thanks to vast improvements this canvas can be drawn in basic 2D overlay mode (same as the legacy GUI system), in 2D camera space (adding perspective), or even directly in 3D world space like as any other traditional 3D object (such as a rendertarget for UI) as shown here:

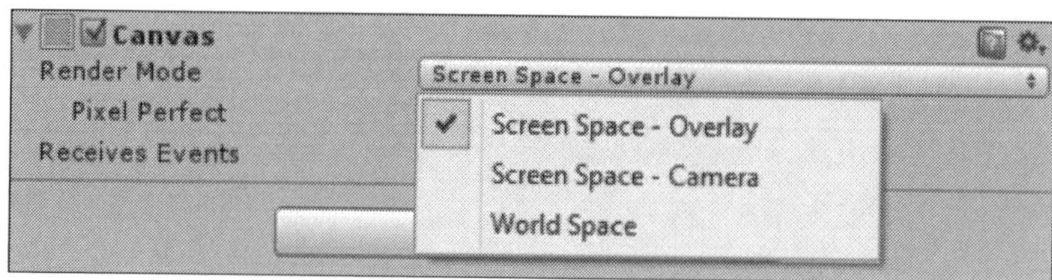

Groups

In the legacy GUI, groups were defined by the controls themselves;
if you wanted to orientate multiple controls together in a particular fashion,
you simply couldn't.

With the new **Unity UI** system, you can define several layout groups.

Horizontal Layout Group

A **Horizontal Layout Group** displays items in a horizontal line:

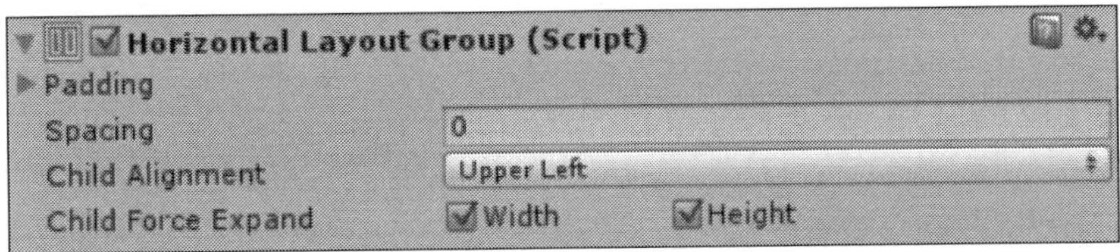

Vertical Layout Group

A **Vertical Layout Group** displays controls in a vertical line:

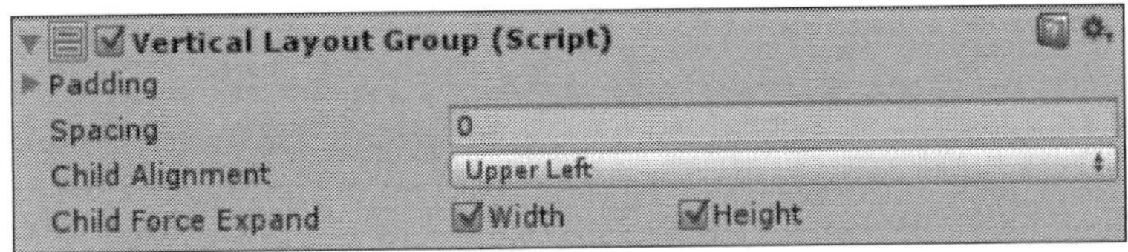

Grid Layout Group

A **Grid Layout Group** lays out controls according to a grid-based pattern of rows and columns:

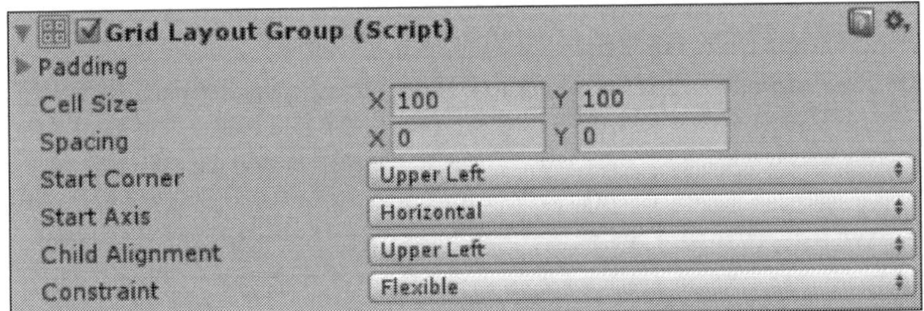

Toggle Group

A Toggle Group manages arranges toggle controls in to a group where only one can be active at a time (Like a Multiple choice selection where only one option can be chosen).

Canvas Group

A **Canvas Group** allows you to generically group child UI controls together and affect several common properties from the group, for example, the **Alpha** value of all child items:

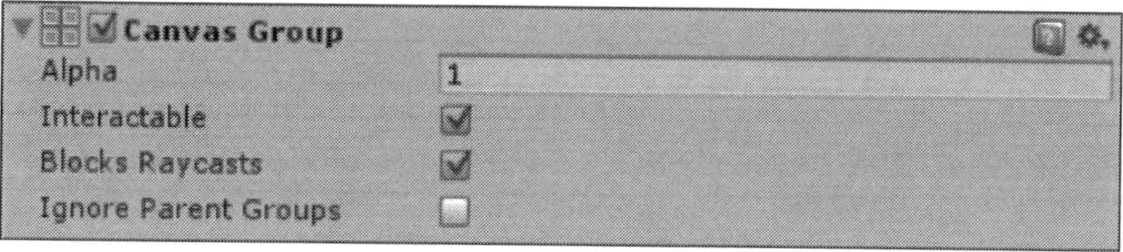

We'll cover these in more detail in *Chapter 2, Building Layouts*.

Masking

Recognizing the need for generic masking capabilities within the new Unity UI system (the ability to hide portions of UI within a certain region), they created a new Mask component. This can be added to any GameObject and any child objects outside the bounds of the parent GameObject would not be drawn, either partially or fully.

The **Image** control (highlighted later in the chapter) also includes an additional masking feature, when the `Image Type` property of an image is set to **Filled**; it gives several additional masking options to gradually bring the image into view. Just for reference now, we'll go into this in a lot more detail later.

New controls

Something old, something new, something borrowed, something blue.

Obviously when we look at a GUI, there is only so much that is really needed and Unity has recognized this. Starting with a fresh slate, they have looked at what it means to create a stunning UI and what you need to build one.

So with this fresh start, here are the new **Unity UI** controls:

Control	Description
Selectable (only available in the component list)	The selectable component is the base object for anything that needs interaction, and it basically turns any other component into a button. Note that it cannot be used on the same GameObject with something that is already selectable (button, toggle, and sliderbar).
Panel	This is a highlighted region, similar to the old **Box** control, mainly used to define groups when additional components are added. When **Rect Transform** alone is not enough. (Actually it's an Image control with a preset image and set to full screen)
Text	If text is your aim, then this control is for you. It gives you text options like font, color, font style, and overflow. Can also be set to resize text to fit the container it is in.
Image	This is a basic image that can either use a sprite or material to display to the screen along with an optional color tint.
Raw Image	This is an alternate image display component that takes a texture instead of a sprite or a material and can define a color tint. Additionally has options to set the UV coordinates for the displayed image.
Button	If you need a big red (color optional) button to press, then this control is for you. The button has received the biggest overhaul by far with so many options it will likely take a chapter on its own to explain. It also includes a new **UnityEvent** framework that allows you to create behaviors that can affect other objects or scripts directly from the editor. You can even set different colors for different states of the button, swap out images, or if you wish, use Mecanim and the new animation system to animate the button between states.
Toggle	Switch it on, switch it off. The toggle takes the button behavior and extends it as a prime example of what extensibility features are in the new UI framework. It adds additional properties to the button framework to identify the checkbox graphic and a grouping option should you want to group checkboxes (using a Toggle group).
Scrollbar	It slices, it dices, it even slides as well. Your typical scroll bar with a handle, fully customizable with options to control the direction, minimum and maximum values, step size, and number of steps to slide between. Also includes the event system used for buttons for when the value changes.
Slider	This is a more advanced version of **Scrollbar** with fill options (for a filling cereal bar) so you can build the fanciest health bar with ease.

New UnityEvent system

Unity has always lacked a good and robust event system. Sure there are the `SendMessage` and `BroadcastMessage` functions, but these are really slow and can be expensive.

The new **UnityEvent** System is built around providing and handling all events with a scene, primarily for the new UI system; but like everything else in Unity 4.x, it is built to be extensible, and you can enhance your own components and scripts to expose themselves automatically to the event system and derive new events when things happen.

A note about UI events in the new Unity UI system: the interaction events all rely on raycasting to detect clicks, touches, hovering, and so on. It is very fast and efficient. However, if you build a new UI component that cannot react to raycasting, then it won't be recognized or respond to such interaction events.

Control extensibility

One very cool feature of the new UI system is that practically every component is a script, meaning it can be used as the base for any new scripts you create. You can either use them as is or even extend them further.

In *Chapter 6, Working with the UI Source*, we will cover the coding behind all these components including a walk through the open source library. I'll even throw in a load of examples and reusable components from the community and myself.

Animation

A core tenant of the new UI system (since it is built upon the core of the new 2D sprite system) was animation. Every single control or component of the new Unity UI system is able to be fully animated.

Not only that, but it also gives different modes for how properties can be animated, from static fixed values to dynamic values that will alter and update with the controls behavior.

Even the Asset Store has you covered

Through the dark of the *beta* process, which many developers participated in. Several worthy asset creators worked feverishly to update their craft to make use of the new UI system ready for release. Some existing projects were greatly enhanced and even some new toolkits.

> Note that these recommendations are from my own experiences through the beta evolution of the new UI system. I've worked with (and against at times) a lot of things described in this section.
>
> I most certainly am not being paid to highlight these, they are just the best out there solving very unique gaps or limitations of the new UI system to date (however, Unity isn't sitting still, so these teams better keep up!).
>
> No doubt I'll mention more of them on my blog as I find them.

I'll point these out again in some of the chapters where you will get the most use out of them or where they are relevant.

The most notable assets at the time of writing are the following.

TextMeshPro ($65)

This is a fantastic text management system that helps to bridge the gaps and the limitations in Unity's aging text rendering system. Unity themselves have noted on several occasions they want to rip out the text system and replace it with something better, until that happens, the best asset to help with text generation from within Unity (not just getting an artist to build lots of text assets) is **TextMeshPro**.

TextMeshPro has been around for quite a while now and has run with the leaders to get it updated for the new UI system but the author didn't stop there. TextMeshPro has gone far and beyond its humble text rendering beginnings to add such features as improved alignment/indentation and rich text support, even adding vertex animation for the generated text! (Just check out `http://bit.ly/TextMeshProAnimation`.)

You can find TextMeshPro on the asset store here: `http://bit.ly/UnityUITextMeshPro`.

GUI Generator ($40)

Building clean and efficient UIs in Unity have always been a strain (just look at this chapter!), this is where GUI Generator comes in, starting with the old GUI, then adapting to also handle NGUI and now the new Unity UI system. It's a quick and advanced tool to clean up the look and feel of your UI (no, it doesn't build your UI for you, it styles it!).

It also has many built-in effects you can add to your UI to make it stunning. Like TextMeshPro, the author has been working hard through the *beta* to get this great tool updated to handle the new UI elements and skin them to great effect.

You can find GUI Generator on the asset store here: `http://bit.ly/UnityUIGUIGenerator`.

MenuPage ($10)

Not every asset for the new UI has to be a big beast of a tool meant to save you hours, sometimes you just need something to get you off the ground and using the new UI with great effect. This is where MenuPage comes in.

Put simply it's a new asset on the store aimed at building menu systems using the new UI system automatically. They are fully configured, laid out effectively and offer some advanced features such as fading, transitions, and much more.

What's even better is that all the source code is there and is fully documented/commented, so you can learn from some of the best coders out there purveying their wares.

You can find MenuPage on the asset store here: `http://bit.ly/UnityUIMenuPage`.

Summary

So now we have a deep appreciation of the past and a glimpse into the future. One thing you might realize is that there is no one stop shop when it comes to Unity; each feature has its pros and cons and each has its uses. There may still be cases when it is just easier to use the Unity legacy GUI to achieve an effect (still using the basic `GUI.DrawTexture` for a splash screen for example, although even that is very easy with the new UI system) provided you take the performance concerns on board with mobile devices. It all comes down to what you want to achieve and the way you want to achieve it; never dismiss anything just because it's old (except for `GUIText` and `GUITexture`, they are just really really old...)

In this chapter, we covered the following topics:

- The history of Unity legacy GUI
- Detailed walkthrough of the legacy Unity GUI
- Whistlestop tour of the new **Unity UI** system and what we can expect from this title

In the next chapter, we will start with the underlying framework and guts behind the new GUI system, namely:

- The new **Rect Transform** control (not just for Unity UI)
- The new **Rect Transform** component (and why it's great)
- The **Canvas** control
- What Unity have done for scaling and resolution for UIs
- The all new and improved Event messaging system for the Unity UI system, complete with new shiny raycasting features and helpers

It promises to be a fun ride, and once we are through that, then in *chapter 3, Control, Control, You Must Learn Control* we can move on to actually building some UI and then placing it in your game scenes in weird and wonderful ways.

Now stop reading this and turn the page already!!

2

Building Layouts

As we start to look deep into the crystal ball, we gaze upon our first sights of the new **Unity UI** system. In a breath of fresh air, **Unity UI** has appeared to aid the weary UI developer, who just wants their UI their own way.

We start with the beginnings of Unity UI and the foundations that it builds upon, most notably the Sprite 2D system that was introduced with Unity 4.3. However, **Unity UI** takes these simple beginnings and takes a bold leap forward. Almost every underlying part of the new sprite system has been improved and stretched to build something that is sensible and just works. In those areas, where it does not stretch enough, there is a base framework for extensibility; don't like it the way Unity has put it together, then do it your own way.

The following is the list of topics that will be covered in this chapter:

- The new Rect Transform
- The Unity UI canvas
- Layout and grouping systems
- Unity Events and the new EventSystem

This chapter focuses on the fundamental framework and layouts behind the new UI system and as such doesn't cover the individual controls themselves. The controls will be covered in greater depth in *Chapter 3, Control, Control, You Must Learn Control*.

First we need to understand the sandbox before you can start building stuff in it.

The Rect Transforms

The idea for the **Rect Transforms** started back in Unity 4.3 timescales with the introduction of the new **Sprite** system, they were exposed through the sprite editor when you were editing spritesheets, where you had a rectangular area to identify the area on the spritesheet where your sprite texture would come from. This was then used as the basis for drawing all sprites, you just didn't get to see it.

The Rect Tool

Seeing the need for more control over how sprites were drawn in the scene gave birth to a new manipulation control in the Unity editor called the Rect Tool, which took its rightful place in the main toolbar as shown here:

In its default mode, this tool allows visual scaling of a sprite as you can see here:

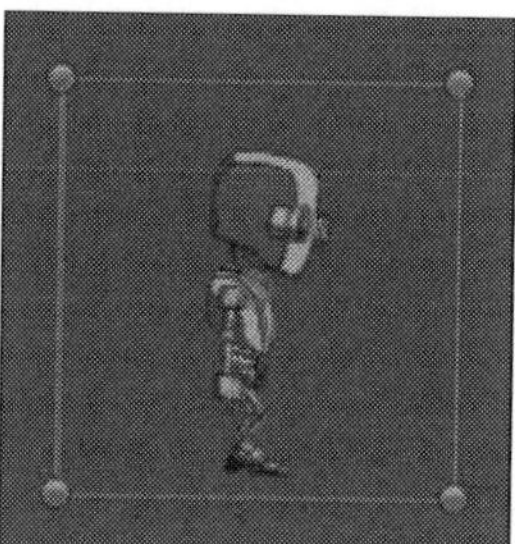

> If you cannot see the blue control points, you likely need to scroll the view in. At low zoom levels the controls are not displayed around sprites/objects.

You get the four control points (one in each corner) to scale the sprite in or out from that point and the central circle that forms the current pivot point.

> Note: If you hold down the `shift` modifier while moving any of the corner control points, it will scale the sprite uniformly, maintaining the aspect ratio of the sprite (equally on each side)

This tool in effect, was built to manage sprites introduced into a scene.

The Rect Transform component

Now the previous **Rect Tool** works just fine on all 2D and 3D objects and is a great extension to the Unity toolset; however, Unity also introduced the Rect Transform component specifically for the new **Unity UI** system, you can see it here:

> Note: If you add a **Rect Transform** to an ordinary sprite instead of a UI component, you will not get the full capabilities described here. The **Rect Transform** cannot update the **Sprite Renderer** component used by sprites alone, so it won't resize or be able to use advanced features such as the **Anchors**. Bear this in mind when tinkering. The primary reason for the new **Rect Transform** component is the new **UI** system.

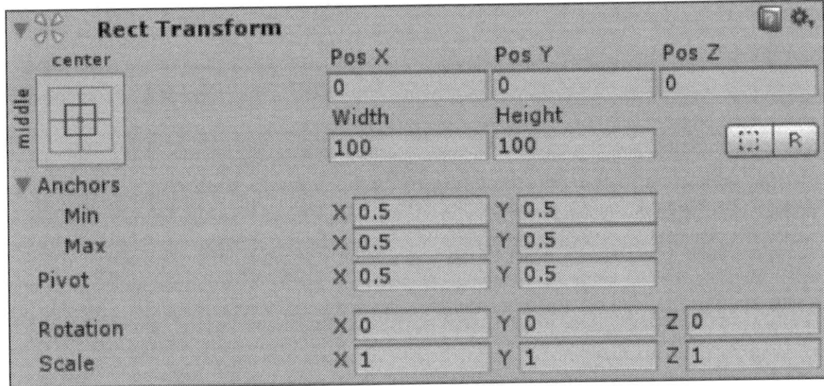

The Rect Transform with a fixed (non-stretched) anchor

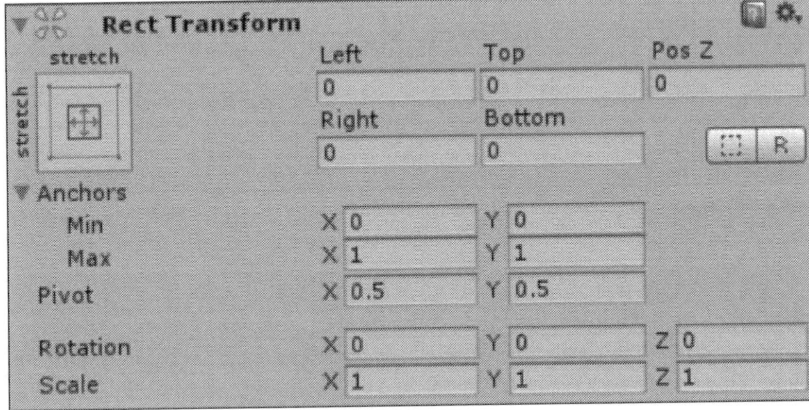

The Rect Transform with a stretched anchor

As you can see, it is quite different to the standard transform component we see on normal GameObjects; however, it does have the same `Rotation` and `Scale` parameters as the normal transform. Here's a quick breakdown of the new properties:

Note: The positioning values for the **Rect Transform** change based on whether the anchors are in a fixed (non-stretched) or stretched mode. For more details on anchoring, see *Chapter 4, Anchors Away*.

- **Pos X/Pos Y/Pos Z** (when in non-stretched mode): These identify the **X**, **Y**, and **Z** position of the **Pivot** of the **Rect Transform** before any scaling or rotation.
- **Width/Height** (when in non-stretched mode): These identify the width and height of the **Rect Transform** area.
- **Left/Top/Right/Bottom** (when in stretched mode): These values replace the above properties when the **Rect Transform** uses stretched Anchors; they identify the offset positions of the Rect Transforms Pivot point from the border of the parent **Rect Transform**.
- **Blueprint mode**: This changes the selection corners for the **Rect Transform** to an un-rotated and unscaled box. The base Rect selection area is identified by the preceding parameters.

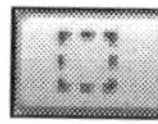

- **Raw mode**: By selecting this toggle, any changes to pivot or scale will not also alter the position and size of the **Rect Transform**.

- **Anchors**: This controls the layout behavior of the **Rect Transform**; this will be covered in more detail in *Chapter 4, Anchors Away*.
- **Pivot**: This designates the **pivot point** for the **Rect Transform**, this is where the **Rect Transform** will rotate around.

The **Pivot** of a **Rect Transform** can only be edited for UI components, not to be confused with a **Sprite** pivot point, which is set in the **Sprite** import settings.

- **Anchor Point** (the graphic in the top-left hand corner): This is a graphical way to alter the anchor points for the Rect Transform (see *Chapter 4, Anchors Away*).

The **Rect Transform** component is included with all Unity UI objects added to the scene instead of the regular Transform component and forms a core part in the layout of all **Unity UI** controls.

> If you add a **Rect Transform** component to any GameObject, it will automatically replace the **Transform** component. If you remove the **Rect Transform** component it will revert back to the standard **Transform** component.

With UI components, the **Rect Tool** also reacts to the control modifiers in the toolbar, depending on what they are currently set to, as you can see in the following screenshot there are two modifier buttons, each with two settings:

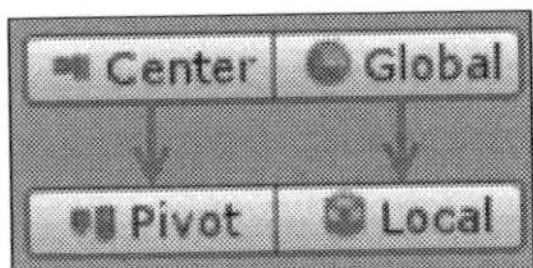

When you have the **Rect Tool** selected, these toggles behave as follows for a UI component:

- **Center**: The central pivot point of the Rect selection area acts as an anchor; holding the mouse down on it moves the Rect around the screen.
- **Pivot**: With this option active, holding the mouse down on the pivot point of the selection Rect moves the pivot point around the object, thus altering the pivot point for the object (the point at which the object is rotated/scaled around).
- **Global**: When in global mode, the selection area for a Rect Transform surrounds the entire object including any rotated space. If the Rect is rotated, the selection area stays un-rotated and sizes up to encompass all the used space by the Rect.
- **Local**: When in local mode, the selection area is tight to the Rect Transform area with rotation; if rotated, the selection area is also rotated.

> Remember, the **Pivot** point of a source image and the **Pivot** point of the **Rect Transform** are two separate things; altering the **Pivot** point of the **Rect Transform** does *not* alter the **Pivot** point of the source sprite/image.

Scaling the Rect Transform

A minor but important point to keep in mind with the new **Rect Transform** component when scaling: when you scale the **Rect Transform** it is done proportionally to the objects **Pivot** point.

With the **Pivot** point in the center, the scaling will happen proportionally across the entire **Rect Transform**. Move the **Pivot** point to a corner and the scaling will be apportioned from the corner where **Pivot** is.

Something to bear in mind if you're scaling is delivering some weird results.

This is in effect the same with **Rotation**, as any **Transform** will rotate around its **Pivot** point. The same is applied for Scaling an object, it gets scaled by its **Pivot** point.

The Canvas

As we start to take our first steps with the new **Unity UI** system, we are welcomed by one of the first cornerstones of Unity's new implementation, the **Canvas**.

Put simply, the **Canvas** (as the name suggests) is your drawing board for all new UI elements. The legacy GUI system had the **GUILayer** component attached to a specific camera. The new **Canvas** however, has a separate component in its own right that can (by default) overlay the current rendering scene (as with the legacy GUI), It can be attached to a specific camera with its own perspective, or even be embedded in the 3D scene like any other 3D object.

As with many things, you can have more than one **Canvas** per scene and can even nest Canvases within each other if you so wish.

Whenever you attempt to add any new UI control to a scene, Unity will automatically add a base **Canvas** GameObject into the hierarchy and make your new UI control a child of the new Canvas. Any new UI elements not parented to a Canvas will *not* be drawn to the screen.

If you drag a **Unity UI** control from a **Canvas** and parent it to any other object in the scene that is not a child of a **Canvas** object, it simply is not drawn and is ignored. This includes if you drag it to the top of the Unity project hierarchy.

Unity will also add an **EventSystem** to the scene, if one does not exist already; this is explained in detail in the following **Event System** section.

To try it out, open a new scene in your project and either:

- Create a new `Canvas` by selecting to the **Create** | **UI** | **Canvas** option in the hierarchy window, or
- Create any `UI` component by selecting to **Create** | **UI** | **Go Wild** (select any control) option in the hierarchy window

If you then select the **Canvas** in the project hierarchy, you will see the following in the **Inspector** window with the default **Screen Space - Overlay Render Mode**:

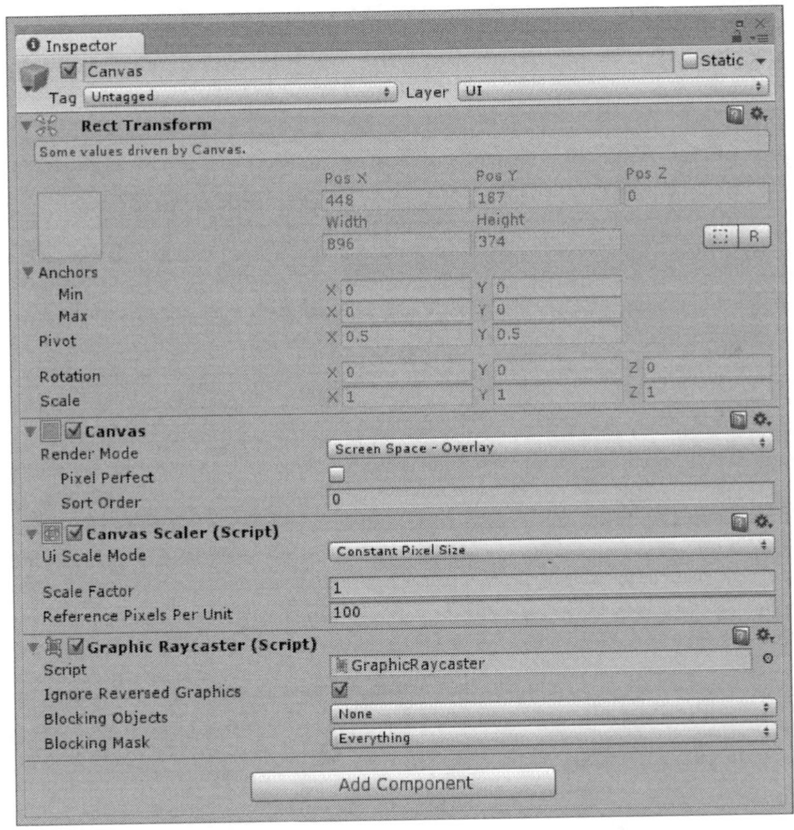

The default Canvas, with Screen Space – Overlay selected

You can then change the Canvas Render Mode to either the Screen Space - Camera option as shown here:

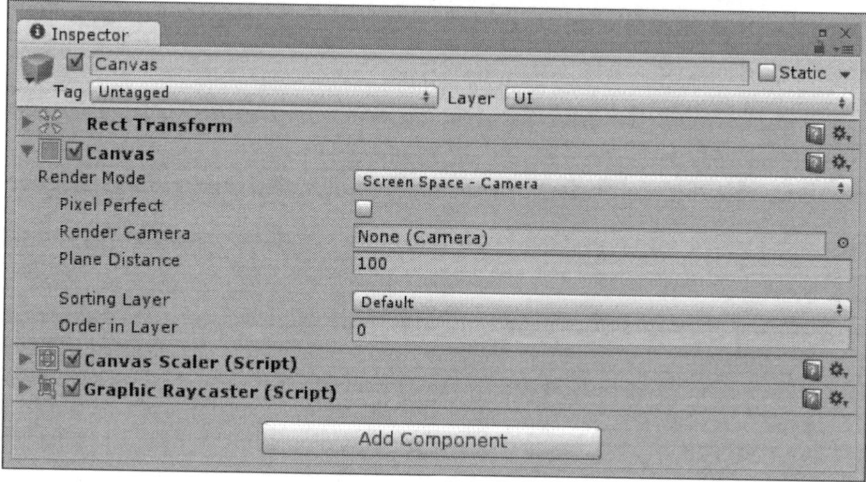

A canvas with the Screen Space – Camera render mode selected

Or select the World Space Canvas Render Mode as shown here:

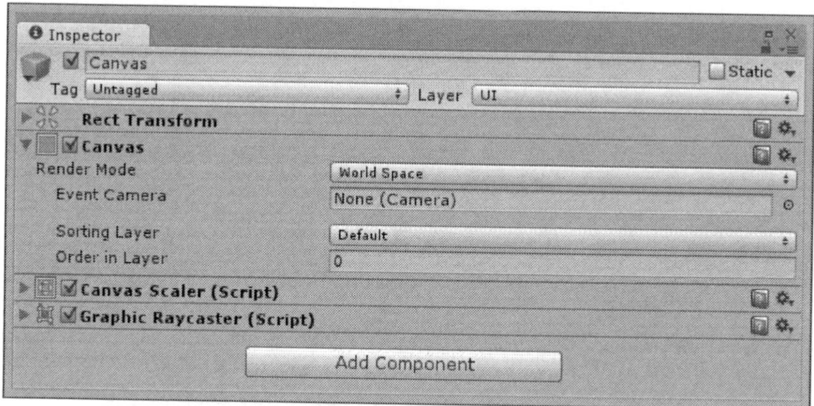

A canvas with the World Space render mode selected

Let's first walk through all the options we have shown below:

> We'll discuss each of these in more detail in specific sections of this chapter and in some cases, other chapters. There's a lot to go through so these are just the highlights mentioned here.

- **Rect Transform**: The base **Rect Transform** for the **Canvas**, which is set (by default) to the size of resolution for the platform/screen resolution you have selected. You will note that the **Rect Transform** for the base **Canvas** is read-only for **Screen Space** Canvases, as it is driven by the platform resolution to be full screen and cannot be altered. However, you can also create child Canvas elements, whose size can be modified. A **World Space** canvas **Rect Transform** can be altered as it is a free spirit.
- **Canvas**: The main **Canvas** component has several different modes in which it operates and drastically changes how it is drawn in a scene. The following options change based on which **Render Mode** you have selected:

Note, we'll cover the differences between **Screen Space - Overlay**, **Screen Space - Camera** and **World Space** in more detail later in *Chapter 5, Screen Space, World Space and the Camera.*

    - **Render Mode**: The **Unity UI** Canvas has three distinct rendering modes, these are **Screen Space - Overlay**, **Screen Space - Camera**, and **World Space**. Between them we have the ability to project our **Unity UI** canvas wherever we want, within either a 2D or 3D scene, even embed the canvas as a separate 3D element in a 3D scene (far surpassing the old legacy GUI). We'll discuss these in more detail in *Chapter 5, Screen Space, World Space and the Camera.*
    - **Pixel Perfect** (*Screen Space canvases only*): This is a high-quality option for those times when you need pixel perfect rendering of the 2D UI elements; by default this is turned off as there is a significant performance hit from enabling it. By turning this feature on, it will cause the entire canvas and its children to be recalculated and redrawn (as opposed to just the elements that have changed).
    - **Sort Order** (*Screen Space – Overlay only*): If you have multiple **Screen Space – Overlay Canvases** in the scene, what is the drawing order for this **Canvas**. Lower orders will be drawn below others, higher orders will be drawn on top.
    - **Render Camera** (*Screen Space - Camera only*): This selects the camera on which the canvas should be drawn to; this allows the setting of a different perspective and view for the canvas over the **Main Camera**. The result is then drawn with the **Main Camera** depending on the Render Camera's Depth.
    - **Plane Distance** *(Screen Space Camera only*): Dictates how far away from the **Camera** the **Canvas** should be drawn, also known as drawing distance (perspective depth).

  - **Event Camera** (*World Space only*): This identifies which camera should be used to render and receive events on (same as the **Render Camera** for **Screen Space - Camera**).
  - **Sorting Layer** (*Screen Space – Camera* and *World Space only*): When the Canvas is used with other Sprite Rendering components in a scene (such as the 2D rendering system and Sprites), this sets which **Sprite** Sorting Layer the canvas renders on.
  - **Order in Layer** (*Screen Space – Camera* and *World Space only*): The draw order on the selected Sprite **Sorting Layer**.

- **Canvas Scaler** (the **Script** component): Defines how the canvas resolution and positioning units are measured. For more details, see the *Resolution and scaling* section later in this chapter.
- **Graphics Raycaster** (the **Script** component): This component is part of a new Raycasting framework delivered with the new **UnityEvent** system. (See the following *UnityEvent system* section later in this chapter). Events and human interaction are derived through a new and efficient **Raycasting** system (which the **Graphics Raycaster** is one implementation of). This provides hit tests from the user's current input position through the Unity UI layer and feeding back information to the **UnityEvent** system. The settings here provide configurations to drive how the raycast functions will react; they are as follows:

  - **Ignore Reversed Graphics**: If a **UI** element is reversed (seen from the back), then this setting will define if a raycast hit will qualify as a hit or not and generate an event (basically does what it says on the tin).
  - **Blocking Objects**: Allows you to block raycast hit tests from 2D, 3D, **Everything** or **None** (allowing hit tests from everything).

Note: By default, raycasts will pass though the UI layer in to your scene, so this setting can be very useful. But you can also control this behavior with a Canvas Group (see the **Canvas Group** section later in this chapter).

  - **Blocking Mask**: Allows you to restrict the rendering layers that raycasts will operate on: you can select multiple layers, a single layer, or all layers.

The Canvas Renderer

In order for a GameObject to render visuals on to a **Canvas**, a GameObject has to have a **CanvasRenderer** component attached to it. By default, all built-in UI controls will add this component and you cannot remove it unless you remove the UI control first.

If you build your own **UI** components that render to the **Canvas**, don't forget to add a `[RequiresComponent]` for the **CanvasRenderer** if you want it displayed.

> If you build your own **UI** controls based on one of the existing ones, the **CanvasRenderer** will be added automatically by default. Isn't inheritance brilliant (sometimes)!
>
> If you build your own **UI** components that render to the **Canvas**, don't forget to add a `[RequiresComponent]` for the **CanvasRenderer** if you want it displayed.

Canvas Groups

The **Canvas Group** component is a simple little component that can change the behavior of a **Canvas** in very subtle ways; put simply, it will group child components together and allow you to group alter certain properties, namely:

- The **Alpha** value (to allow group fading), which fades all UI components that are the children of this group.
- Whether or not a set of child controls receives events or they are blocked (Interactable).
- Whether or not the group **Blocks Raycasts** to the scene behind the canvas.
- Should the group ignore settings from parent **Canvas Groups** (if you have nested groups) allowing you to override settings by checking the **Ignore Parent Groups** property.

It's all very simple as you can see here on the component itself, which has been added to an empty GameObject:

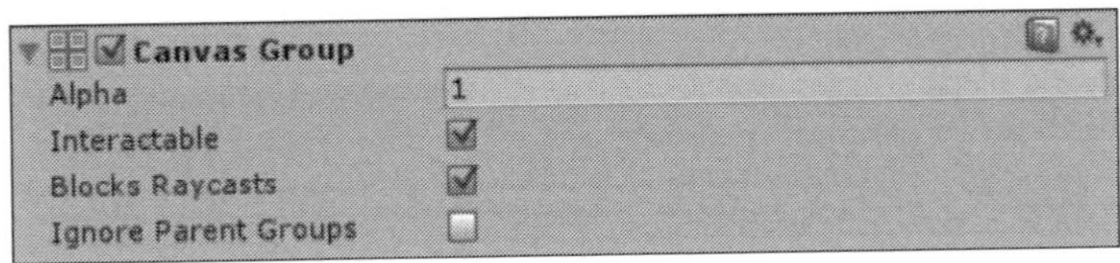

Automatic layouts and options

You can obviously place **UI** components within the **Canvas** and place them (if you wish), but there are those situations where you need to be able to either group or order elements together, such as:

- A list box
- A grid
- A scrollable area

In the legacy GUI system, this was done with separate controls that had layout options built-in. For the new **Unity UI** however, this has been broken up into a more component-based system with new grouping components, these can be attached to any GameObject to organize the elements attached to that GameObject as children.

The types of groups you can create are:

- **Horizontal Layout Groups**
- **Vertical Layout Groups**
- **Grid Layout Groups**

Groups don't have to be static top level elements; like with anything else in the new system, everything is flexible. Want a **Horizontal Layout Group** within a **Vertical Layout Group** within a **Grid Layout Group**, then knock yourself out, as there are no limitations (well other than common sense, it still has to look good doesn't it).

Horizontal Layout Group

With the horizontal layout, it will automatically place child GameObjects side by side (columns) within the group's **Rect Transform** area. For example, we can create a simple horizontal list (like what could be used to list a selection of in-app purchase items) by creating the following:

1. Create a **Canvas** in the scene (**Create** | **UI** | **Canvas**).
2. Right-click on the new **Canvas** and add an empty GameObject (**Create Empty**).
3. Rename this new **GameObject** to **Horizontal Layout Group**.
4. Select the **HorizontalLayoutGroup** GameObject object and add a **Horizontal Layout Group** component by clicking on **GameObject** by navigating to **Add Component** | **Layout** | **Horizontal Layout Group** in the **Inspector** (or just searching for it when clicking on the **Add Component** button).

5. Set the **Width** of the **HorizontalLayoutGroup** GameObject to `300` (*3 children = 3 x 100* width children as it will auto resize its children **Rect Transforms**).
6. Right-click the **HorizontalLayoutGroup** GameObject and add three child. Image controls (UI | Image), I named them **Child1**, **Child2**, and **Child3**. (**UI** | **Image**).
7. Set the **Source Image** of each child to a **Sprite** of your choice (I borrowed the Unity 128 x 128 logo as an example, which is included in the book sample assets download).

This would result in the following view:

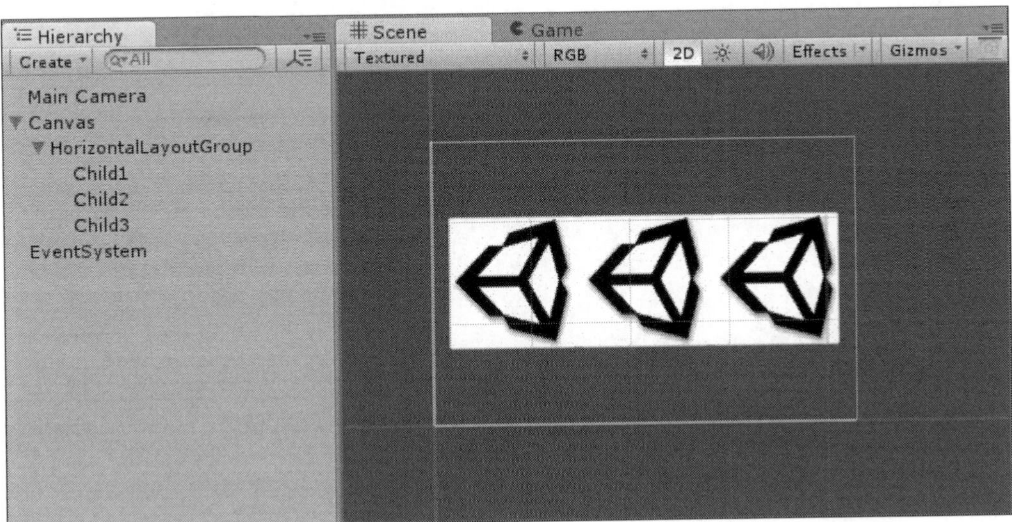

An example showing 3 sprites arranged horizontally by the layout group

The resulting view shows three child Unity logos arranged side by side organized by the **Horizontal Layout Group** component automatically.

This is a very basic example, but we will cover more advanced layouts later in the book.

Note: By default, the layout group will resize the child elements to fit within the area defined by the group's **Rect Transform**, to alter this you will need to either resize the group to fit its content or use **Layout Element** or **Content Size Fitter** components described in the sections that follow.

The three 128 x 128 Unity logo's in this example got resized down to 100 x 100.

When we look at the **Horizontal Layout Group** in the **Inspector** window, we see the following:

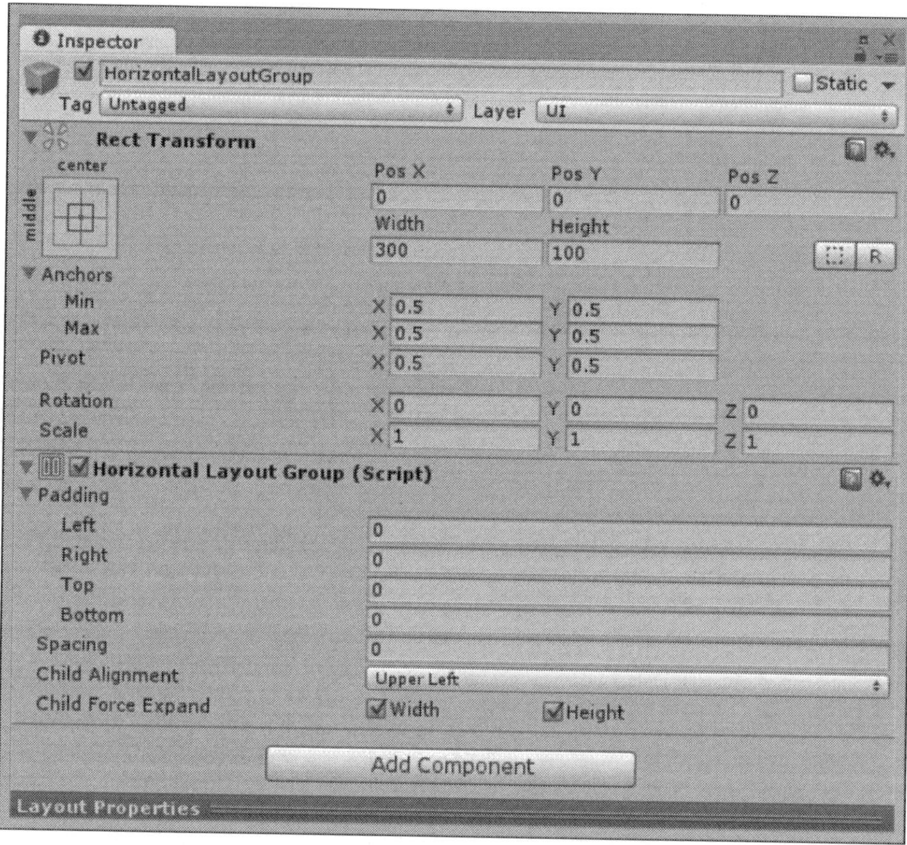

Within the **Horizontal Layout Group** component itself, we have **Padding** options to alter the area surrounding the child elements of the group. This allows you to have a wide border within the group surrounding the laid out elements within.

You can also set the spacing in between each of the child elements with the **Spacing** property, leaving a gap equally between each child (if you want finer control, then you need to use **Layout Element** component to manually control a child elements size see the **Layout Element** section later in this chapter).

Additionally, you can align the the children within the group, however, this setting only takes effect if you also use some of the additional layout options with a **Layout Element** component.

Finally, there are two **Child Force Expand** options (**Width** and **Height**) to force all child elements within the group's borders to take up the maximum space possible for each child (evenly distributing that space between its children). These settings also override the **Maximum** settings for all child settings if you have applied **Layout Elements** (see section later in this chapter)

> The default for the **Child Force Expand** settings is *on*, so keep this in mind if you are using any of the layout options described later as it will render some of them **invalid**.

Vertical Layout Group

With the **Vertical Layout Group**, as the name suggests we tile the child components vertically into separate rows. Everything else is pretty much the same as the **Horizontal Layout Group**.

You can even use the same previous example, switching the **Width** and **Height** values, then using **Vertical Layout Group** instead of **Horizontal Layout Group** component, which would result in the following screenshot:

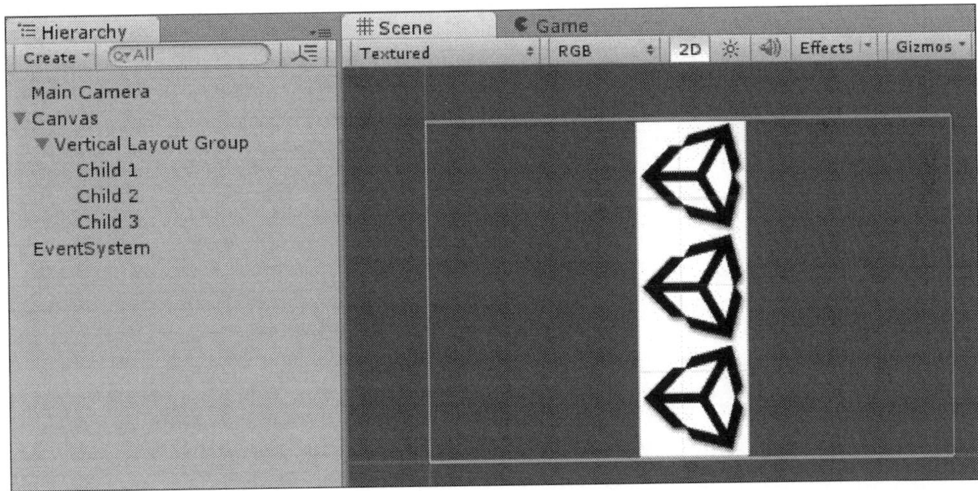

An example showing 3 sprites arranged vertically by the layout group

Looking at **Vertical Layout Group** in the **Inspector** window, we also see familiar options:

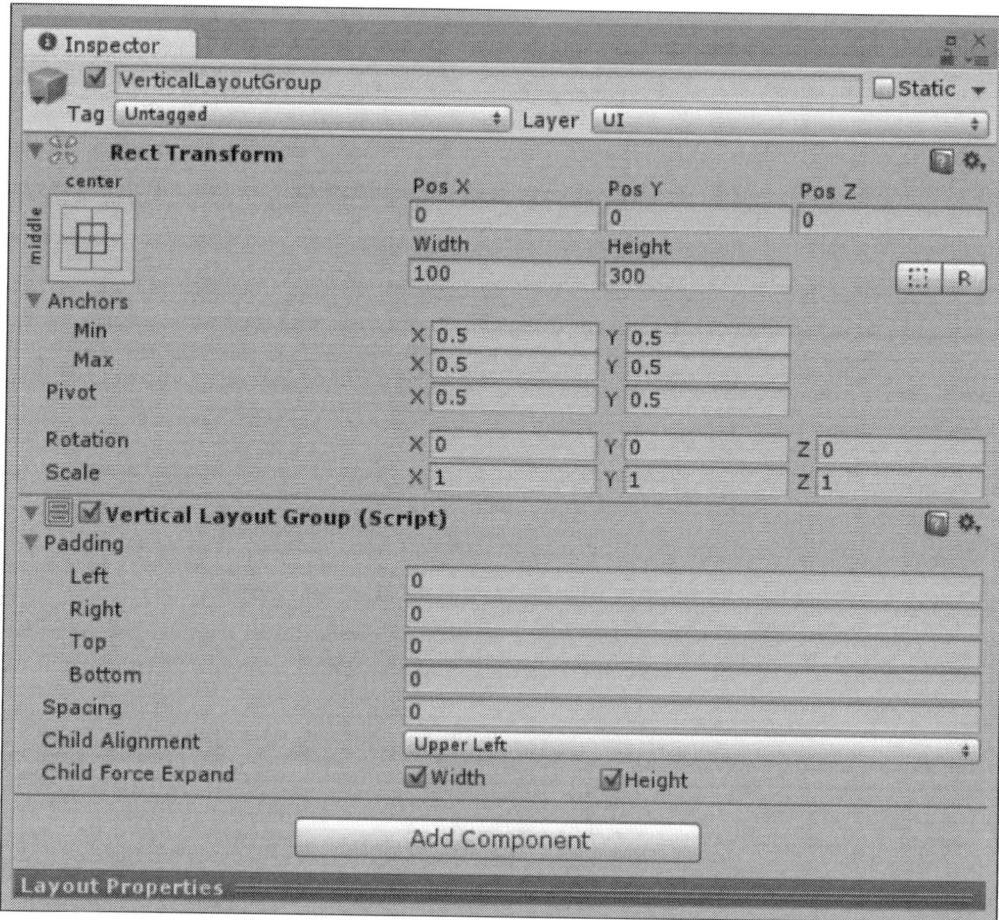

So we have the same **Padding**, **Spacing**, and **Child Alignment** options as with the **Horizontal Layout Group** and the same restrictions apply to child elements.

Grid Layout Group

The **Grid Layout Group** is slightly more advanced than the horizontal and vertical layout groups, giving you more flexibility and control over how the child elements are drawn within a grid formation.

Creating the **Grid Layout Group** is done in exactly the same way as the vertical and horizontal layout groups but selecting the **Grid Layout Group** component instead. Setting the **Width** and **Height** to `200`, and adding 4 children instead of 3. This would result in the following screenshot:

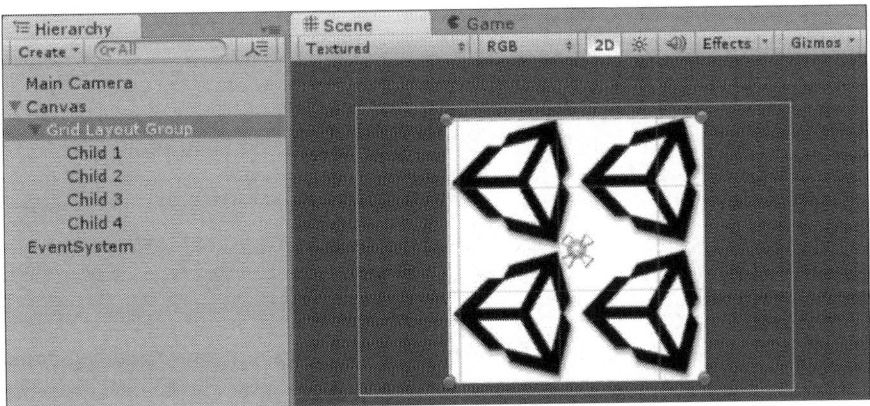

An example showing 4 sprites arranged in a 2x2 grid by the layout group

When we look at the **Inspector** window, the flexibility we have becomes more evident:

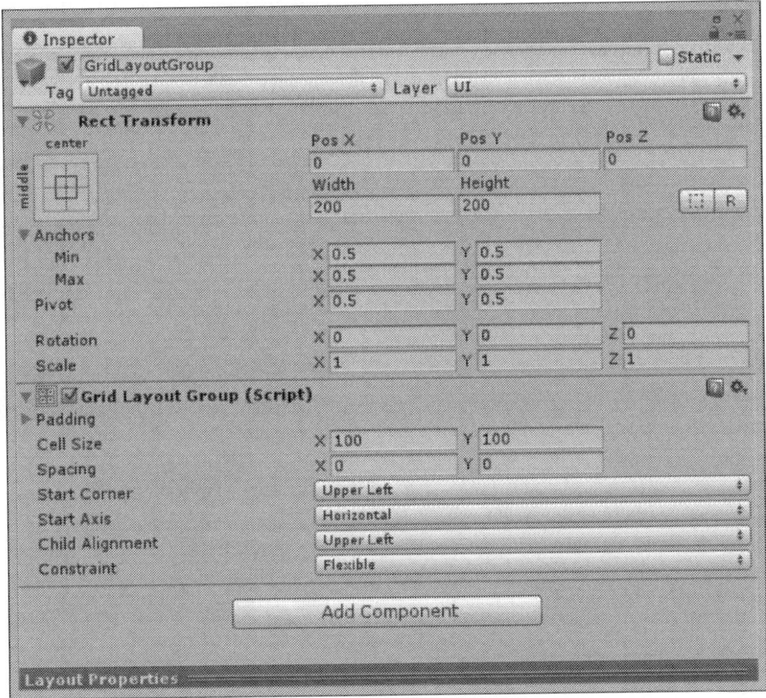

Again, we have the familiar **Rect Transform** to set the Grid's layout area and the same **Padding** options as the other layout groups.

The rest of the options open up some new possibilities for how children of the grid should be arranged; all these settings will determine how many cells will appear within the **Rect Transform** of the grid and how they are laid out. They are elaborated here:

- **Cell Size**: This defines the interior cell size of child elements; this will also resize the content to the defined size unless overridden by the **Layout Element** component (see **Layout Element** section later in this chapter). The control will automatically try to fit as many child elements within its grid based on the cell size and the size of the group **Rect Transform**. If the grid cannot fit a new cell in, then it won't attempt to. (A fine balance to work out from how big you want your cells to the size of the group itself.)
- **Spacing**: As with the other layout groups, you can define spacing in-between child elements; the main difference with the **Grid** contents is that you can set separate spacing for both vertical (**Y**) and horizontal (**X**) children.
- **Start Corner**: A nice little effect sets which is the first cell within the grid that children are drawn from (the start point). You can choose from any of the four corners of the grid, defined as **Upper Left**, **Upper Right**, **Lower Left**, and **Lower Right**. (No, you cannot start in the middle! That would just be silly.)
- **Start Axis**: Along with the **Start Corner**, you can also define the flow for the cells by drawing in a horizontal direction first (starting from the **Start Corner**) or you can draw in the vertical direction first. If we set the **Start Corner** to **Upper Left** the child controls would flow in the following order:

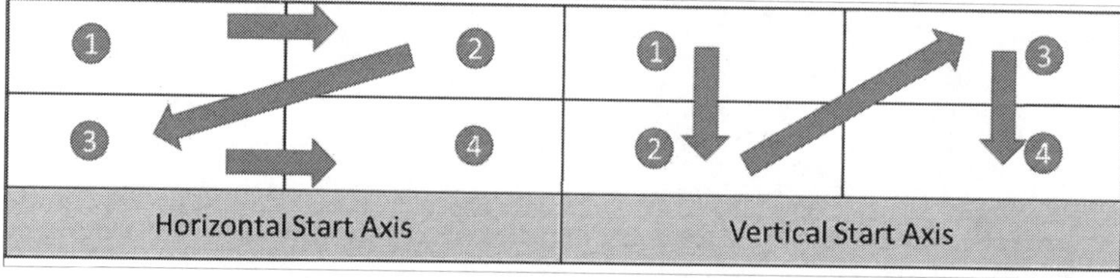

- **Child Alignment**: If the child elements have been configured with a **Layout Element** (later in the chapter) component, then you can align them within the grid cells around any of the edges or the middle.

- **Constraint**: We could all use a little constraint and the **Grid Layout Group** is no different. If you want to limit the number of rows or columns, the grid will show that you can set this property to either **Fixed Row Count** or **Fixed Column Count**, which will open up an additional **Constraint Count** property for you to provide the constrained number. The default is **Flexible**, which is basically unconstrained.

Unlike the vertical and horizontal groups, which resize the content to fit the entire layout group area, the **Grid Layout Group** will actually overflow and draw any additional cells that don't fit in the Group area below the group, filling up more rows. If you don't want this behavior, then you will need to either set a **Constraint**, add a **Mask** component or limit how many child elements you add.

It will still resize the original image, however, to fit your defined Cell sizes by default.

For more details about the Mask component, see the **Mask** section later in this chapter.

Layout options

The default behavior of the Layout Group components is good for most situations but for others you want to add a finer level of control. For these situations, Unity has provided several layout overrides to constraint the use of controls within a group or as a standalone **UI** element:

- **Layout Element**
- **Content Size Fitter**
- **Aspect Ratio Fitter**
- **Scroll Rects**
- **Masks**

All of these components can also be used on most **UI** controls as well as to alter their behavior when presented on the canvas; the layout groups are just the default use for these controls.

Layout Element

Most **UI** controls implement **Layout Element** properties internally but to expose these for manipulation, you need to add the **Layout Element** component (**Add Component | Layout | Layout Element**) to a child of a layout group as shown here:

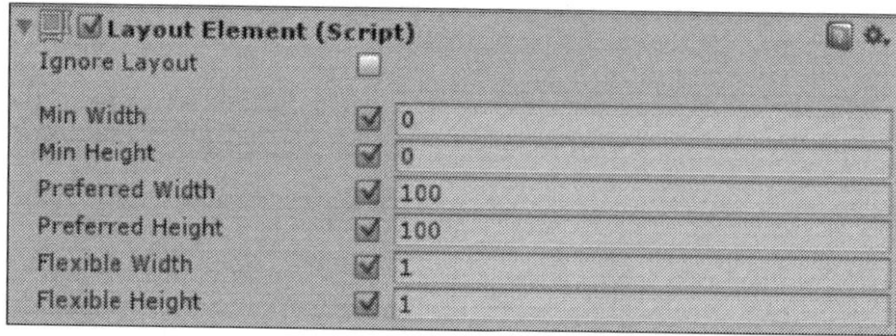

Through each of the settings we can define:

- **Ignore Layout**: Added the override and then changed your mind? Then you can turn it off with this handy toggle. Most likely for use in scripts or animation where you want to alter the layout properties of a UI element at runtime but don't want to keep changing the settings. It does not reset the properties set in the **Layout Element**.
- **Min Width**: The minimum width property defines the smallest width that the **Rect Transform** for the child element in a layout group will scale down to. If the layout group's **Rect Transform** width is reduced, the control will scale down until this width property is hit and will not scale the width down any further. In the following example, the topmost element has a **Min Width** set to `100` and is not resized, whereas the bottom most element has not and as such has been scaled down:

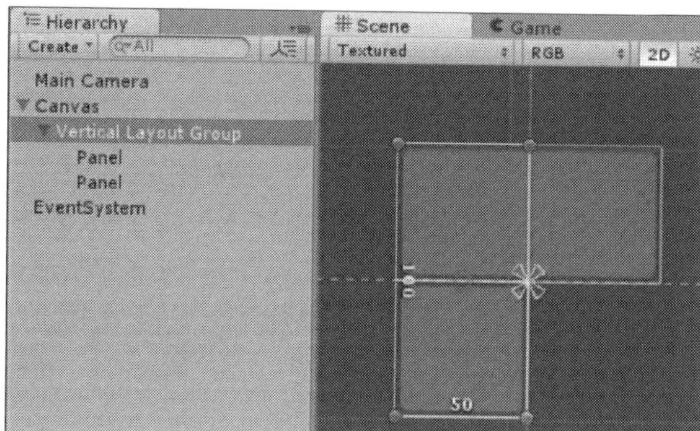

The top most child element overrides the layout and remains larger

- **Min Height**: The minimum height property defines the smallest height that the **Rect Transform** for the child element in a layout group will scale down to. If the layout group's **Rect Transform** height is reduced, the control will scale down until this height property is hit and will not scale the height down any further. In the following example, the leftmost element has a **Min Height** set to `100` and is not resized, whereas the right-hand element has not and as such has been scaled down:

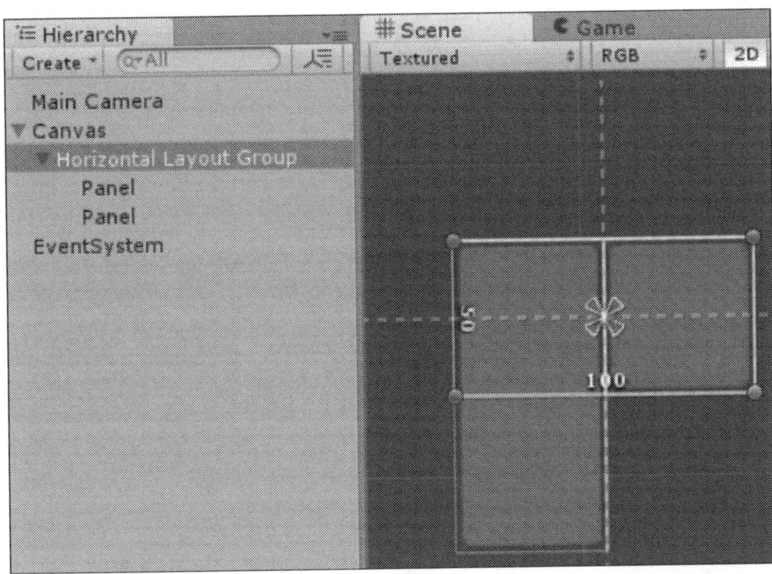

The left most child element overrides the layout and remains larger

- **Preferred Width**: The preferred width property defines the largest width that the **Rect Transform** for the child element in a layout group will scale up to. If the layout group's **Rect Transform** width is increased, the control will not scale up any more beyond this value. Its width however, will scale lower than this value.

> Note: If you have left the default options on the group for **Child Force Expand**, it will override any preferred settings of the **Layout Element**, forcing the UI element to take up the maximum space available within the group.

   - In the following example, the topmost element has a **Preferred Width** set to `50` and its width is smaller than the bottommost element, which has not been set. With the parent **Rect Transform** set to `100`, the topmost element has not scaled up past its maximum to match its parent:

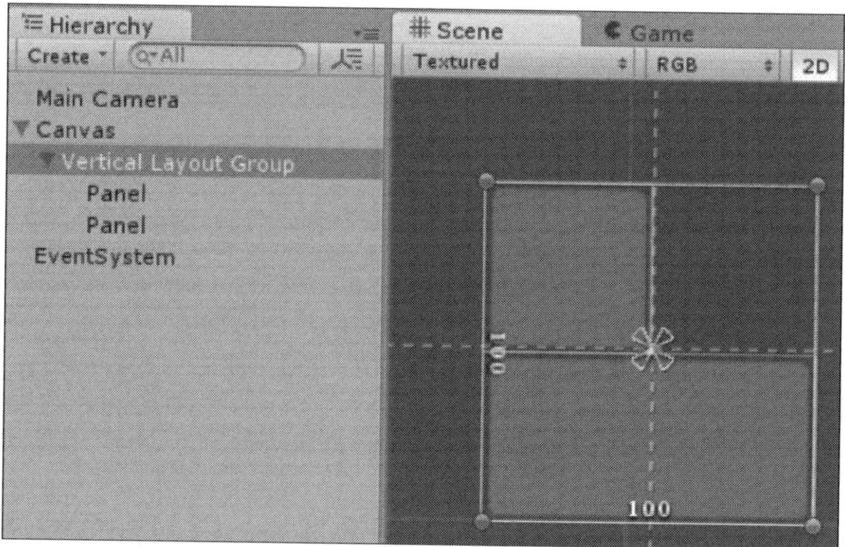

The topmost child element overrides the layout and does not grow bigger

- **Preferred Height**: The preferred width property defines the largest height that the **Rect Transform** for the child element in a layout group will scale up to. If the layout group's **Rect Transform** height is increased, the control will not scale up any more beyond this value. Its height however, will scale lower than this value.

> Remember, if you have left the default options on the group for **Child Force Expand**, it will override any **Preferred** settings of the **Layout Element**, forcing the UI element to take up the maximum space available within the group.

- In the following example, the leftmost element has a **Preferred Height** set to `50` and its height is less than the rightmost element which has not been set. With the parent **Rect Transform** set to `100`, the leftmost element is not scaled up past its maximum to match its parent:

The leftmost child element overrides the layout and does not grow bigger

- **Flexible Width**: The flexible width property can be best be described as a width percentage of the containing group's **Rect Transform**. This is defined as a number between `0` and `1` to indicate the percentage.

Remember, if you have left the default options on the group for **Child Force Expand**, it will override any flexible settings of the **Layout Element**, forcing the UI element to take up the maximum space available within the group.

- In the following example, the topmost element has a **Flexible Width** applied at `0.8` (80 percentage) and its width is smaller than the bottommost element, which has not been set:

The topmost child element overrides the layout and only takes u 80% of the available width

- **Flexible Height**: The flexible height property (same as the width) can be best be described as a height percentage of the containing group's **Rect Transform**. Defined as a number between `0` and `1` to indicate the percentage.

Remember, if you have left the default options as the group for **Child Force Expand**, it will override any flexible settings of the **Layout Element**, forcing the **UI** element to take up the maximum space available within the group.

  - In the following example, the leftmost element has a **Flexible Height** applied at `0.8` (80 percentage) and its height is less than the right-hand element which has not been set:

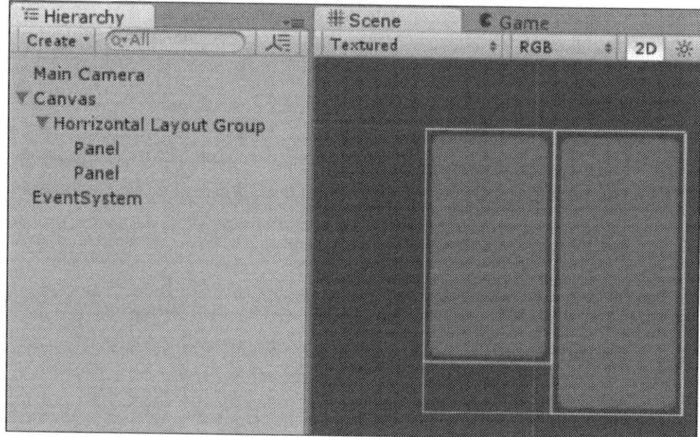

The leftmost child element overrides the layout and only takes up 80% of the available height

Content Size Fitter

Seeing the need to constrain the **Rect Transform** for a layout group's based on its content (instead of fitting the child elements to the group, which is the default) Unity created the **Content Size Fitter** component. When attached to a layout group, the **Content Size Fitter** will automatically manage the bounds of the **Rect Transform** for the group so that it will resized based on the dimensions of its children.

For the **Content Size Fitter** to function, it needs to have child controls that support minimum or preferred layout size settings such as text or an image (or any other control deriving from the `ILayoutElement` interface). It can also be used with other layout groups.

By default, these settings are used automatically based on the native controls setting of the **Min** and **Preferred** sizes; however, these can also be overridden by adding a **Layout Element** component manually, to child components to define the **Min** and **Preferred** size of the content.

When you add the **Content Size Fitter** to a GameObject, you get three options per axis:

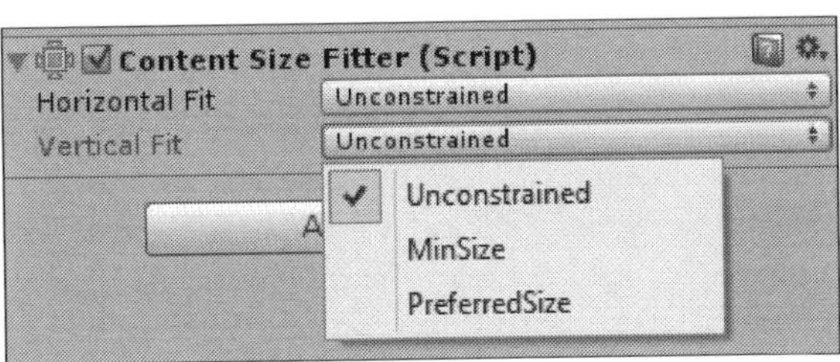

The options provide the following capabilities:

- **Unconstrained**: Do nothing, the **Content Size Fitter** does not control this axis
- **MinSize**: This lays out the content and restricts the **Rect Transforms** width or height to the minimum values of the GameObjects content and/or children
- **PreferredSize**: This lays out the content and restricts the **Rect Transforms** width or height to the preferred values of the GameObjects content and/or children

Using the **Content Size Fitter** becomes especially important when you are working with content sized to the target platforms resolution and if you have additional background images/layouts on a parent GameObject or dynamically sized content.

As an example, let's create a text chat window that will automatically grow and shrink based on the text within it:

1. Add a Canvas to the scene (**Create** | **UI** | **Canvas**) or use one that you already have.
2. Right-click on the **Canvas** and select to **UI** | **Image** – this is our text window background.
3. Right-click on the **Image** and select to **UI** | **Text** to add a **child text** component.

Note that the text size now overlaps the **Image**.

4. Select the **Image** in the **Hierarchy** and in the **Inspector** click on the **Add Component** button and then select **Layout** | **Vertical layout Group**.

Note that the **Text** has now positioned to the top-left of the **Image** and its **Rect Transform** now fills the **Image's Rect Transform**. This shows by default the child resizes to the parent.

5. Still with the **Image** selected, click on **Add Component** and select **Layout** | **Content Size Fitter**.

Note that there is no actual change yet as the defaults for the fitter are **Unconstrained**.

6. Change the **Horizontal Fit** of the **Content Size Fitter** to **Preferred Size**.

Note, that the **Image Rect Transform's** width has reduced to match the **Text** width of the **Text** component.

For fun, you can extend on this example and set the **Vertical Fit** and add some additional child **Text** controls and end up with something like the following:

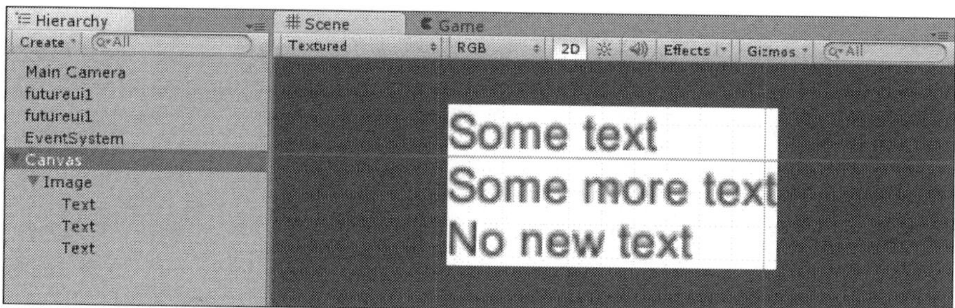

As you can see, the parent **Image** (thanks to the **Content Size Fitter**) now resizes to fit the latest child instead of the other way round.

Aspect Ratio Fitter

The **Aspect Ratio Fitter** was one of the late entrants to the UI framework and is certainly one of the fringe cases you can use to organize your UI. In effect, this layout tool will resize the UI of a **Rect Transform** according to an **Aspect Ratio**.

> Bear in mind, this is the aspect ratio of UI elements and not the aspect ratio of the screen resolution. The final resolution of the screen has no impact on GameObject managed by the **Aspect Ratio Fitter**.

If you add the **Aspect Ratio Fitter** component to a UI GameObject navigating to **Add Component | Layout | Aspect Ratio Fitter** we see the following:

From here the **Aspect Ratio Fitter** has several different modes:

- **None**: This does nothing at all and if you try to change the **Aspect Ratio** property, it will just reset it to its previous value. It literally does nothing (why even add the component unless you are going to animate something with it maybe?).
- **Width Controls Height**: In this mode, the **Aspect Ratio** will alter the **Height** of the **Rect Transform** it is attached to based on its **Width**. So, *Height = Width x Aspect Ratio.*
- **Height Controls Width**: In this mode, the **Aspect Ratio** will alter the **Width** of the **Rect Transform** it is attached to based on its height. So, *Width = Height x Aspect Ratio.*
- **Fit In Parent**: This mode will resize a **Rect Transform** within the bounds of its parent based on the **Aspect Ratio**.
    - When the **Aspect Ratio** is less than `1` (but greater than `0`), it will make the **Width** of the **Rect Transform** a percentage of the **Width** of the Parent, as shown here:

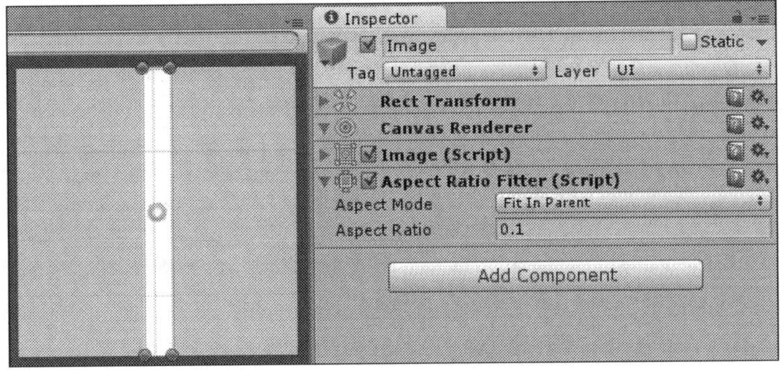

Rect Transform drawn based on aspect ratio width

- When the **Aspect Ratio** = `1`, the **Rect Transform** of the GameObject will match the parent **Rect Transform** area
- When the **Aspect Ratio** is greater than `1`, it will make the **Height** of the **Rect Transform** proportional to the parents **Rect Transform** based on the **Aspect Ratio**, as shown here:

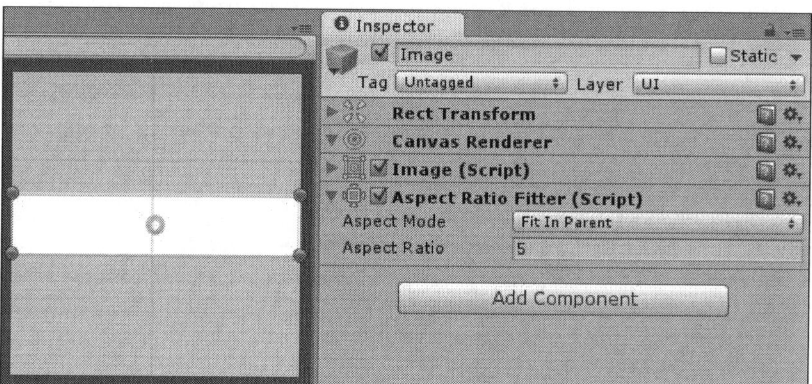

Rect Transform drawn based on aspect ratio height

- **Envelope Parent**: The **Envelope Parent** mode is the same as the **Fit In Parent** mode with one obvious exception, instead of working within the parent **Rect Transform**, it applies its logic to be outside the parent **Rect Transform**. So instead of working inwards, it work outwards from the parent. The effects of the **Aspect Ratio** are the same, just in reverse.

I personally struggled for the use case behind the **Aspect Ratio Fitter** but there must be one. For the best use of this **Fitter**, I suggest you play with the settings if you find a need for this style of fitter.

Scroll Rect

When a layout group needs to be larger than the display can handle is where **Scroll Rect** comes in. This provides the user with an area that they can interact with that gives the scrolling capability to the selected Rect Transform content, for example:

1. Add a **Canvas** to the scene (**Create** | **UI** | **Canvas**) or use one that you already have.
2. Right-click the **Canvas** and select **Create Empty** to add an Empty GameObject to the **Canvas** as a child.
3. Rename the new **Empty** GameObject to **ScrollRectArea**.

4. Set the **Width** of the **ScrollRectArea** to `300`, this will form the area of the screen the user can interact with.
5. With the **ScrollRectArea** selected and add a **Scroll Rect** component to it by navigating to **Add Component | UI | Scroll Rect**.
6. Add another **Empty** GameObject as a child to the **ScrollRectArea** and rename it to **Content**.
7. Set the **Width** of the **Content** GameObject to `1000`, which is several times larger than the **ScrollRectArea** and larger than the screen width (make it bigger if you wish).
8. Select the **Content** GameObject and add a **Horizontal Layout Group** by navigating to **Add Component | Layout | Horizontal Layout Group**.
9. Add several **Images** as children of the **Content** GameObject and set them to different colors or apply different source images to tell them apart.
10. Finally, select the **ScrollRectArea** GameObject and drag the newly created **Content** GameObject from the hierarchy to the **Content** property of the **Scroll Rect** (or select it using the discovery button to the right of the **Content** property of the **Scroll Rect** component).

This should result in the following display:

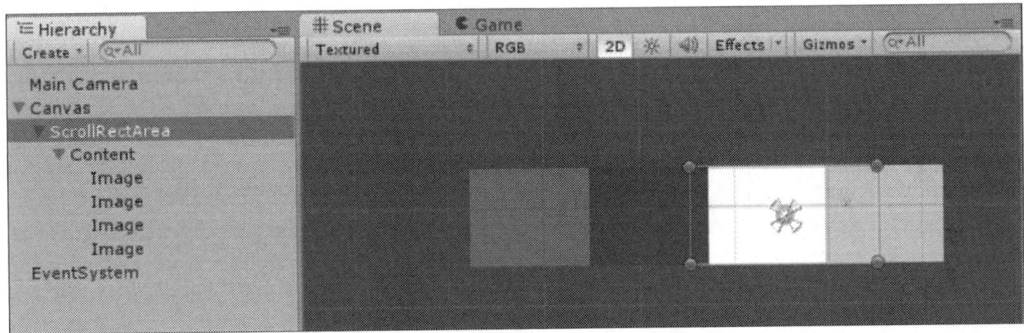

When run, the user can swipe or click and drag within the **ScrollRectArea** (identified with the **Rect Tool** selection area), which will move the **Content** area in the direction of the user's movement but not beyond the viewable area of the Scroll Rect control's **Rect Transform**.

We'll make a bigger example with the Scroll Rect in *Chapter 3, Control, Control, You Must Learn Control*

If we look at the **Scroll Rect** in the **Inspector**, we will see the following:

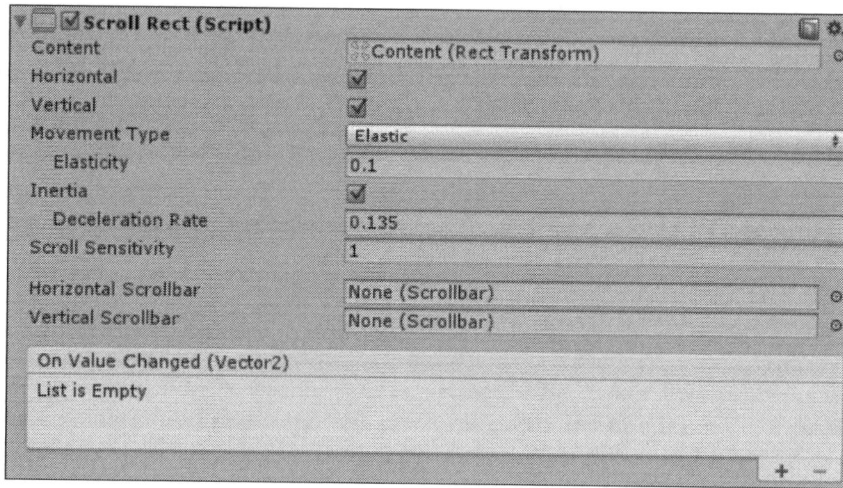

From the previous screenshot we have:

- **Content**: This defines the **Rect Transform** that contains the content to be managed by the **Scroll Rect**; it doesn't have to be a **Layout Group**, it can be any other **UI** control that needs a scrollable area. It should have dimensions larger that the **Scroll Rect** to work properly.
- **Horizontal/Vertical**: These options allow you to enable or restrict the scrolling direction for the **Content** area. Useful if you want just a vertical or horizontal swiping area.
- **Movement Type**: With the **Movement Type**, you can control how the user interacts with the scrollable area:
    - **Unrestricted**: Moves and keeps on moving without restriction (even off the screen where you cannot get hold of it again)
    - **Elastic**: Moves with an elastic motion, which snaps back if it goes beyond the scrollable area
    - **Clamped**: Moves in a fix motion within the scrollable area, and stops as soon as it hits the edges
- **Inertia**: Applies a physical force to the scrollable movement, both how fast it moves initially and how quickly it slows down. You can also set a **Deceleration Rate** for how fast the scroll slows down.

- **Scroll Sensitivity**: Scales the input from scroll devices such as a mouse wheel or track pad scroll.
- **Scrollbars**: As well as the normal grabbing of the scrollable area, you can also attach scrollbars to the **Scroll Rect** to give a visual indication of how large the area is, both **Horizontally** and **Vertically**.

To apply **Scroll Bars**, simply add them to your scene like any other **UI** component and then drag your relevant **Vertical** or **Horizontal Scrollbar** to the relevant property in the **Scroll Rect** component. More on this later in *Chapter 3, Control, Control, You Must Learn Control.*

So the **Scroll Rect** provides us a way to scroll over larger content than we can see on the screen, as shown here:

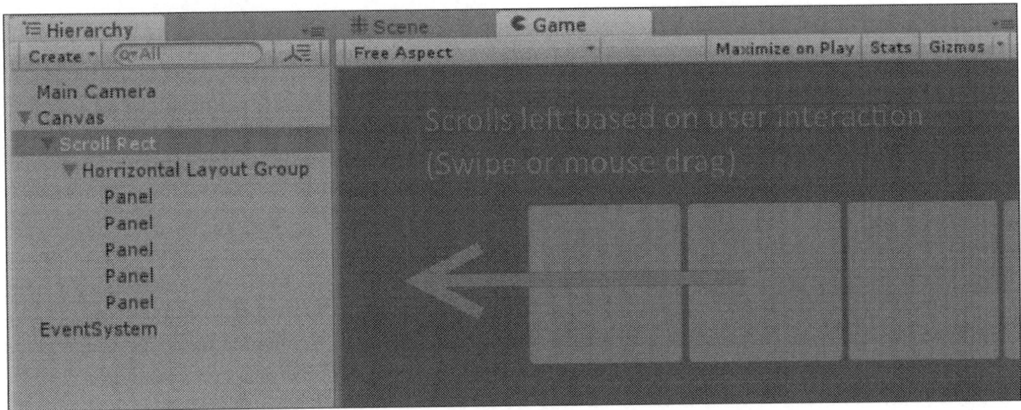

A basic Scroll Rect example

If you want to also restrict the visible area of the **Scroll Rect**, then we also need a **Mask**.

Masks

A welcome addition to the **Unity UI** arsenal is the **Mask** component. In short, it limits the drawing of child components to the **Rect Transform** of the GameObject it is attached to. It is very basic and very easy to use.

Note: The **Mask** requires an **Image** or other **Visual** component in order to mask the child area. Having a **Mask** on its own without an additional component that uses the **Canvas** layout won't work and will not mask the area.

If you add a **Mask** component to the **ScrollRectArea** GameObject from the previous example (and an **Image** component without setting a **Source Image**, as the **Mask** requires a **Graphic** component), then it would only show the **Content** area within the bounds of the **ScrollRectArea** GameObject's **Rect Transform** as seen here:

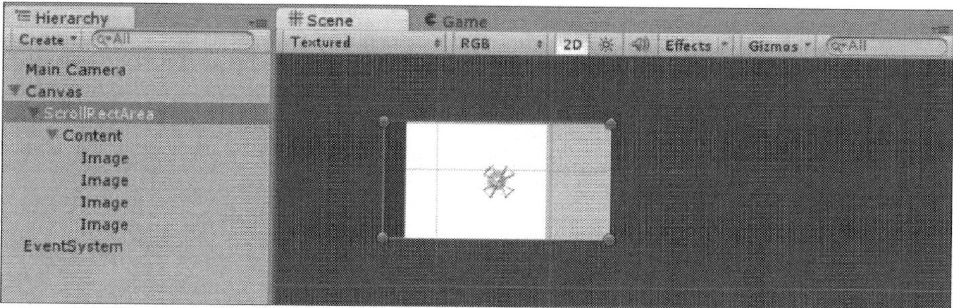

Resolution and scaling

Since there has been a **UI** and the need to display on more than one type of screen (basically since the days of arcade when you knew what you were running on), there has always been the challenge how to best design and implement a good **UI** that will work on any resolution, especially in Unity!

We will just cover the basics in this section, and full examples will be given in *Chapter 4, Anchors Away* when we cover building responsive layouts with **Anchors**.

To answer this call with the new **Unity UI** system, Unity has created a resolution scaling component that is attached to a **Canvas** by default in order to control the resolution-based drawing of the GameObjects and components within; this component is called the **Canvas Scaler**.

The **Canvas Scaler** has several modes of operation that alter how the **Canvas** is scaled when drawn to the screen:

- **Constant Pixel size**
- **Scale with Screen Size**
- **Constant Screen Size**

The **Canvas Scaler** script shows some interesting ways to write a script that alters the resolution of a **Canvas**; if you wish, you can extend the existing script or create your own. Extensibility to the max! (See *Chapter 6, Working with the UI Source* for further details on viewing the **Unity UI** source.) However, you can only use one script at a time, else your display will be completely messed up.

Constant Pixel Size

With the **Canvas Scaler Ui Scale Mode** set to **Constant Pixel Size**, we see the following in the **Inspector**:

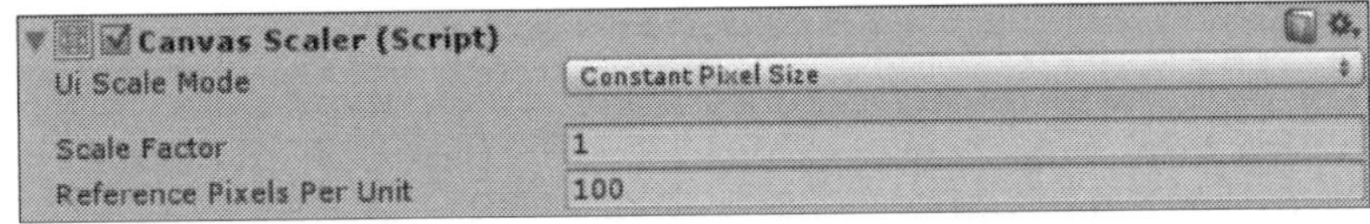

The **Constant Pixel Size** setting basically means no resolution control at all; the **Canvas** is simply drawn as is without any resolution management.

The only available options are the **Scale Factor**, which alters all three transform scale components (**X**, **Y**, and **Z**) by the same value and the **Reference Pixels Per Unit** setting, which sets the **Pixels Per Unit** setting for the **Canvas**.

The **Pixels Per Unit** setting defines how many in game units an object takes up (how big it is in relation to your other GameObjects). This is then used by the **Reference** value that decides how many pixels are in `1` unit, `100` pixels in this case makes `1` game unit of width and height.

For more information on this, check the Unity documentation here: `http://docs.unity3d.com/Manual/class-TextureImporter.html`

Scale with Screen Size

With the **Canvas Scaler Ui Scale Mode** set to **Scale with Screen Size**, we see the following in the Inspector:

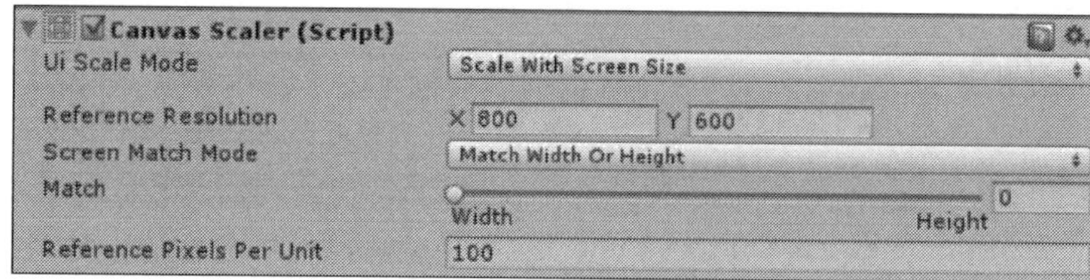

With this setting, we create a virtual space to match an expected resolution.

When the **Screen Match Mode** is set to the **Match Width Or Height** mode, you can specify how the width (**X**) and height (**Y**) of this virtual space is to be proportioned when drawing to the screen, to either favor the width, the height, or a balance:

- If the physical resolution you output to is lower than the expected virtual resolution, then all components within the **Canvas** will be scaled down, keeping the same proportions based on the matching value.
- However, if the physical resolution is larger than the expected virtual resolution, the canvas and its children will be scaled up to match the proportions of the controls based on the matching value as they are laid out on the canvas.

The two other **Screen Match Mode** option are different and will do an automatic Best Fit to scale the **Canvas**:

- **Expand**: This will scale down your **Canvas** to ensure it always draws the reference resolution within the output screen size
- **Shrink**: An odd settings but can be valuable, this will shrink your **Canvas** by scaling it up and cropping it to fit the output screen

> In all cases, it is the **Scale Factor** of the canvas and its children that is altered. So, you can write your own version of this **Ui Scale Mode** to alter the **Scale Factor** of GameObjects in your own way if you wish, or just to customize it. See *Chapter 6, Working with the UI Source* about working with the source code.

In all cases, it really is about tinkering with the options with the **Scale With Screen Size** (or **Reference Resolution**) **Ui Scale Mode**. Play with the settings over multiple resolutions until you get a look and feel that is just right for you.

Constant Physical Size

With the **Canvas Scaler Ui Scale Mode** set to **Constant Physical Size**, we see the following in the inspector:

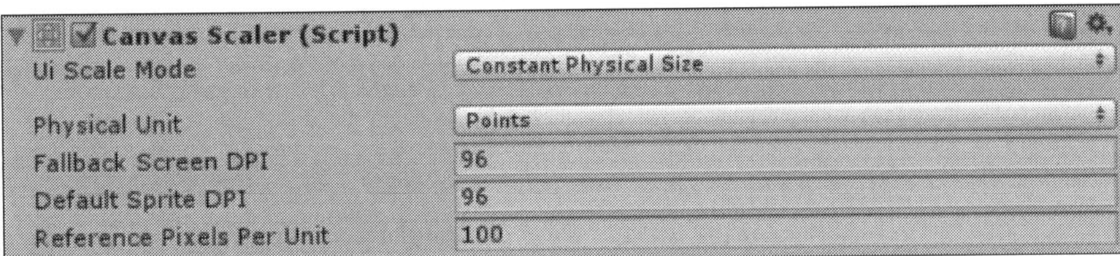

While the **Scale with Screen Size** works by scaling the **Canvas**, the **Constant Physical Size** lets you organize elements on a canvas according to your own positional coordinate preferences. You can specify the units used to proportion or place child elements within the bounds of the **Canvas** based on your own preset proportions.

This allows you to draw using a **DPI** (or units per inch) appropriate to the drawn resolution rather than to an actual physical resolution or world space coordinates.

For example, by setting the Unit to Points and **Default DPI** to `96`, you are specifying that the **Rect Transform** bounds within the **Canvas** is `96` **DPI**.

The available units of size are:

- Centimeters
- Millimeters
- Inches
- Points
- Picas

I had to look up what Picas were and yes, it is a real measurement ☺, the first three measurements are quite self-explanatory, and for Picas and Points I found this helpful article: `http://support.microsoft.com/kb/76388`

Unlike the **Scale with Screen Size** option though, the **Constant Physical Size** option does not scale; it is an exact measurement of size that will be reflected on the target device.

The UnityEvent system

The second most important improvement to Unity (in addition to the new **UI**) is an all singing, all dancing new event system.

This section is just a UI overview of the new **UnityEvent** system; for a more code intensive overview, see *Chapter 6, Working with the UI Source* (it's all about the code, about that code, no tuples - a little Meghan Trainor reference for you, now that song that is likely stuck in your head as well!! ☠).

At its core, it is not much more than a weak reference manager, marshalling calls between the input and raycasting systems and exposing these calls as events that any delegate or control can attach to. It's also much, much more, with its extensive extensibility framework.

For more information on what *Weak Referencing* is and what it means to you, check out this great Code Project article on it: `http://bit.ly/WeakReferencing`.

Raycasting

At the heart of the new **Unity UI** user interaction system is the use of **Raycasting** to determine what UI component the user is interacting with, either via movement (am I over a UI control?), direct interaction (click, hold, drag, release, and so on), or combinations thereof.

Raycasting is a method of drawing a line from a single point to another and determining whether anything got in the way or got hit by drawing that line (known as a ray). It can either be two arbitrary points, or (as in most cases) a line from the user's touch, click, or hover through the scene to see whether they are interacting with anything.

For more details, check the Unity page on **Raycasting** here: `http://docs.unity3d.com/Manual/CameraRays.html`.

In most cases, raycasting is done to a single layer in your scene (the interactable bits) to improve performance and only interact with interactable things on that layer.

With the UI system, these are generally UI controls on the UI layer (the default for Unity UI controls) but this behavior can be altered if you wish.

By default, **Unity UI** adds a **Graphic Raycaster** (a new graphics-based raycasting component) to a **Canvas** that provides a robust and performant raycasting system for the graphical canvas (as highlighted earlier), this provides user interaction with graphical elements of the UI system.

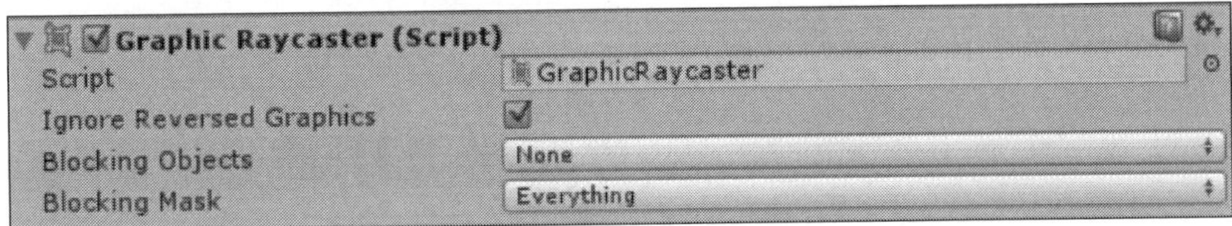

Unity also provides some other *out-of-the-box* raycasting components, including:

- **Physics Raycaster**: This performs raycast tests on 3D models and 3D collidable objects, such as models/meshes
- **Physics 2D Raycaster**: This is the same as the Physics raycaster but limited to 2D sprites and 2D collidable objects
- **Base Raycaster**: This is a high-level base implementation to create your own raycast systems

All of these systems rely on an **Event Camera**, which will be used as the source for all raycasts and can be configured to any camera in your scene—which camera will depend on your needs.

Input modules

The other input to the Event system is the hardware interaction for touch, mouse, and keyboard inputs. Unity has finally delivered a framework in which these are now abstracted and (more importantly) implemented in a more consistent manner.

For other inputs, you will have to build them yourself or keep an eye on the community for new possibilities.

With this new abstraction, it would be relatively easy to drop in an input module for a Gamepad, Wiimote, or even the Kinect sensor or Leap controller.

Once built, you simply attach it to the Unity **EventSystem** for the scene and off you go.

The input modules that Unity provides out of the box are as follows:

- **Standalone Input Module**: This is your basic keyboard and mouse input, tracking where the mouse is and what mouse/keyboard buttons are pressed.
- **Touch Input Module**: This is a basic touch input system handling touches, dragging, and position data. It effectively fakes a mouse in its implementation.
- **Pointer Input Module**: This is a higher level class providing the base functionality for both of the previous modules, only accessible through code.
- **Base Input Module**: This is a base level input system that is used to create new implementations in code, providing all the raw framework to handle just about any input interaction.

If you want to support more than one input mode, then not to worry. Each input module is complementary and adds to the whole input system, so if you want more just keep adding them to the **EventSystem** GameObject in your scene, as shown here:

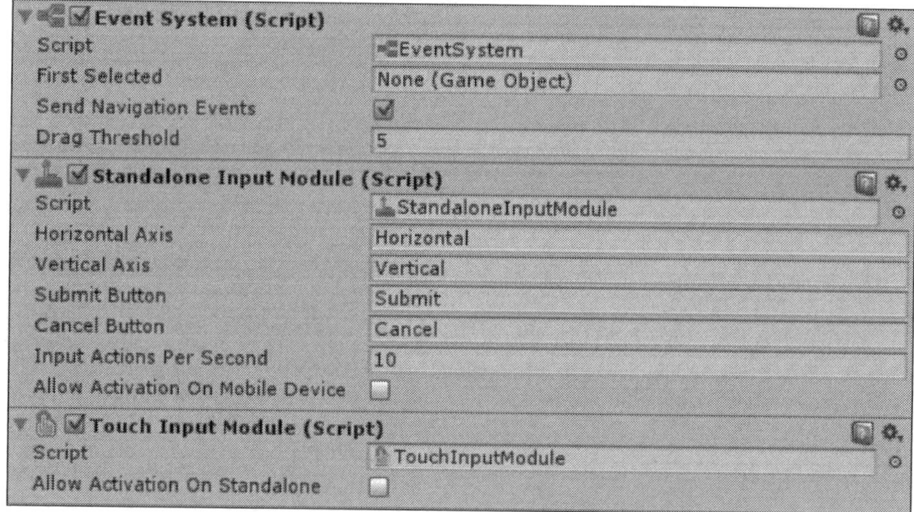

An **Event System** configured with both Keyboard/Mouse and Touch input

Input events

We'll cover Event triggers further in *Chapter 3, Control, Control, You Must Learn Control* with the implementation of the new **Unity UI** controls, but it is worth going over the basics here first.

At the core of Unity's new input event system, there are several interfaces that describe all the different types of events the base implementation is able to handle:

I say base events because the system is fully extendable and you can create your own events should you wish.

- **PointerEnter** (`IPointerEnterHandler/OnPointerEnter`): This is similar to the `onTriggerEnter` or `OnCollisionEnter` interfaces. It denotes the point when a cursor enters the region within a **Unity UI** control.
- **PointerExit** (`IPointerExitHandler/OnPointerExit`): Like `onTriggerExit` or `OnCollisionExit`. It denotes the point when a cursor leaves the region of a **Unity UI** control.
- **PointerDown** (`IPointerDownHandler/OnPointerDown`): This is fired when a **Mouse** button or **Touch** is held down; it fires for each frame where the button/touch is held.
- **PointerUp** (`IPointerUpHandler/OnPointerUp`): This is fired when a Mouse or Touch is released from being held (Not on release of click).
- **PointerClick** (`IPointerClickHandler/OnPointerClick`): This is fired when the user releases the mouse click or a touch on the same GameObject it was pressed on. (If the user hasn't moved the pointer off the GameObject.)
- **Drag** (`IDragHandler/OnDrag`): This is fired when a draggable object is held and movement has started in any direction (Movement delta increased).
- **Drop** (`IDropHandler/OnDrop`): This is fired when a draggable item has been moved and the mouse or touch has been released, finishing the movement.
- **Scroll** (`IScrollHandler/OnScroll`): Fired when a scroll wheel on a mouse or controller is used.
- **UpdateSelected** (`IUpdateSelectedHandler/OnUpdateSelected`): This is fired whenever the contents of a control are updated, such as a text field.
- **Select** (`ISelectHandler/OnSelect`): This is fired when an object or toggle is selected and focus is achieved, for example, when navigation occurs between Interactable GameObjects/Controls.
- **Deselect** (`IDeselectHandler/OnDeselect`): This is fired when an object or toggle is deselected and focus is lost. For example,when navigation occurs between Interactable GameObjects/Controls.
- **Move** (`IMoveHandler/OnMove`): This is a continuous event that is fired while a draggable object is being moved (Constant delta increase).

With these events, it is possible to write a script to enable any GameObject (even non-**Unity UI** related) to react to these events as they are generated from the Unity **EventSystem**, for example:

```
using UnityEngine;
using UnityEngine.EventSystems;
public class eventHandler : MonoBehaviour, IPointerClickHandler {
  #region IPointerClickHandler implementation
  public void OnPointerClick (PointerEventData eventData)
  {
    //Do something with a click
  }
  #endregion
}
```

The `#region` syntax is extremely useful for creating readable script files. It allows you to collapse or expand the code within a `#region/#endregion` block.

Check here for more details on using `#regions` to keep your code files clean: `http://bit.ly/RegionSyntax`.

This provides us with a base implementation to add click behavior to any GameObject in a scene. More on this later

Remember, for the events to be managed and captured, you will need the appropriate **RayCast** system attached to the camera that renders the GameObject. For example, if you attached the previous script to a 3D model, you would need to add the **Physics Raycaster** to the main 3D camera and the 3D object would need some sort of 3D collider such as **Mesh collider**.

Event Triggers

Not to be outdone by the previous weighty code-based approach for using input events from the **UnityEvent** system, there is also a just-as-powerful graphical system to add events to GameObjects using **Event Triggers**.

A configured Event Trigger with two events and a single action for each

Some of the new **UI** controls natively implement the **Event Trigger** behavior using the interfaces described previously, but it is also provided separately should you have the need to extend anything else with such a capability from **Editor**. (Although Unity recommends using code or the built-in controls.)

It is worth noting that although the **Event Trigger** component exists, Unity recommends you build your own scripts, mainly for performance reasons. The **Event Trigger** component is bound to *all* events and *receives all* events by default. It then decides which to act upon based on the component's configuration, so it's not as performant as your own specific script. Keep this in mind and only use the **Event Trigger** component if you really, really need it.

In short, the **Event Trigger** allows you to:

- Create an event hook in the inspector (Shown as `PointerClick` and `PointerExit` in the preceding screenshot)
- Attach the result of that event to another GameObject
- Select a property, script, or other attribute on the target object to manipulate (shown as the `Image.sprite` property or the `RectTransform.BroadcastMessage` method)
- If applicable, provide a value or input to the target call

What's even better is that you can attach as many different actions on the result of the event. So if you wished, you could update several different GameObjects or several different properties of a target GameObject on the result of a single event.

We'll cover this in more detail in *Chapter 3, Control, Control, You Must Learn Control* when we cover the specific controls that implement this behavior, just a taster for now.

Summary

That's a lot of framework theory and understanding you have gone through here and we still haven't actually built any real UI. Fear not, as from here we start building with a vengeance.

The previous concepts are really important to understand going forward as they are the foundations of the new Unity UI system.

In this chapter, we covered the following topics:

- The new **Rect Transform** system
- Many ways to layout your controls
- Knowing how to proportion your canvas for multiple resolutions
- An overview of the new Event system and its involvement in **Unity UI**

So we have a canvas and the ability to put stuff in it, so let's rock on with the next chapter and throw some paint on that canvas.

3

Control, Control, You Must Learn Control

So far we've covered a lot of theory; we waded through the legacy GUI system and then watched a nice presentation on the foundations of the new Unity UI system. If you managed to stay awake so far, be prepared for a shot of UI adrenaline.

It's time to shake things up a bit and have a bit of fun with the new controls and see just what we can do with them out of the box. Mind you, this is still in the same old 2D full screen graphics you have been used to, but later on, in *Chapter 5, Screen Space, World Space, and the Camera*, we will blow your socks off by putting what we create into different perspectives and even enter the 3D realm fully.

So as we venture forth, let us free ourselves from the shackles of the past and begin anew, with a fresh canvas and a dream to paint.

Here is a list of topics that will be covered in this chapter:

- All the base controls of the new UI framework
- Some interesting examples using the new controls
- A walk through the new control navigation system

Be warned, there is a lot to cram in here so this is a really long chapter. Time to dig in and get started!

Overview

In *Chapter 1, Looking Back, Looking Forward,* I gave you a rundown of all the new controls available in the new UI framework, namely:

- The **Text** control
- The **Image** and **RawImage** controls
- A **Button** control
- A **Toggle** control
- The **Scrollbar** and **Slider** controls

It may not sound like much (compared to the larger array of controls in the legacy GUI), but as you'll discover, it's all you really need as a base (especially when you combine them with all the other features of the new UI).

Beyond that, Unity also provides you with a fully extensible framework used to craft your own controls with events, structures, and design patterns to enable just about whatever you can dream up. You can even use another component called the **Selectable** component, that can be added to just about any other GameObject (on a Canvas) to enable user interaction.

Enough preamble, let's play.

Note: If you draw a **RectTransform** with a negative width or negative height, then UI controls will not be drawn. You can rotate the control in whichever direction you wish to alter how it is drawn in the scene (including reversed, as UI controls are two-sided textures) but the base **RectTransform** must always be drawn in a positive direction.

A word on code

Starting simple, we'll just play around with the controls in this chapter through the editor, with some code where it adds value to explain things.

We'll delve into building and using the controls through code in later chapters, including building controls with the event interfaces.

It's also worth noting a bit of best practice with project setup (something I went into in great depth in my previous book). To keep things clean and organized in the sample project accompanying this book, each type of object in the project is organized into its own folder, for example:

- Scenes
- Sprites
- Scripts

That way you can always find what you need and know where it will be.

Setting up the project

As with the previous chapters, you can either set up a new project to test the following examples or keep using the same project (or even use the sample project contained in the code download).

If you are setting up a new project, it can be either 2D or 3D (it makes no difference to the UI system).

However, if you are setting up in 3D, remember that images will be imported as **Textures** by default, so you will need to change them to **Sprites** after importing them.

A warning on the built-in images

Throughout this chapter, we will refer to the selection of built-in images that come bundled with Unity and are used as the default image for a lot of the UI control templates.

At the time of writing, these images are bundled as separate images and not on a combined spritesheet. Because they are separate images, they will need separate draw calls per control/image to render them to the screen.

If you use your own images and batch them together in a single spritesheet, your UI screen will be a lot more performant and use fewer draw calls.

Dealing with text

The first control/component we deal with is the **Text** control. This is used as the basis for all text drawing for all controls.

[You can find the examples shown here in the *Scenes\01-Text Control* scene in the bundled sample code.]

[As you will see, each control is reused by most other controls in a truly modular approach. This is a nice clean break from the Legacy GUI in which all controls were concrete implementations.

However, some may not like this approach and may prefer to build their own UI controls in the old way, as single controls. With the source now available to all, the choice is up to you.]

Whenever and wherever text is displayed in the new UI system, the **Text** control is implemented behind the scenes or added as a child component/control to the control you are adding.

[**The Unity Text System**

At the time of writing, the actual text drawing is still using the legacy text drawing system; this isn't ideal and can cause graphic artifacts on the screen when the text is scaled. This is due to be replaced in a later version of Unity, most likely not until Unity 5, but it could also be included in the later 4.x series.

If you need a more advanced **Text** drawing in your project or would like a few more text effects, then you can check out **TextMeshPro** on the **Asset Store**, `http://bit.ly/UnityUITextMeshPro`.

Its author, Stephan Bouchard, has been hard at work, updating this awesome tool to work in hand with the new UI framework, so from day one, you will be able to implement this in your project with awesome effects.]

Getting started, we can add a **Text** control to our scene (either create a new scene or reuse an existing one) by using any of the following approaches:

- From the Menu: **GameObject** | **UI** | **Text**
- From the project **Hierarchy**: **Create** | **UI** | **Text**
- From the project **Hierarchy**: Right-click | **UI** | **Text**

Additionally, because all of the new **UI** controls are also components, you can add a **Text** control to any other GameObject on a **Canvas**, either from:

- The Menu: **Component** | **UI** | **Text**
- The **Inspector**: **Add Component** | **UI** | **Text**

In all cases, this will result in the default view of the **Text** control/component on your **Canvas** in the **Scene** view as you can see here:

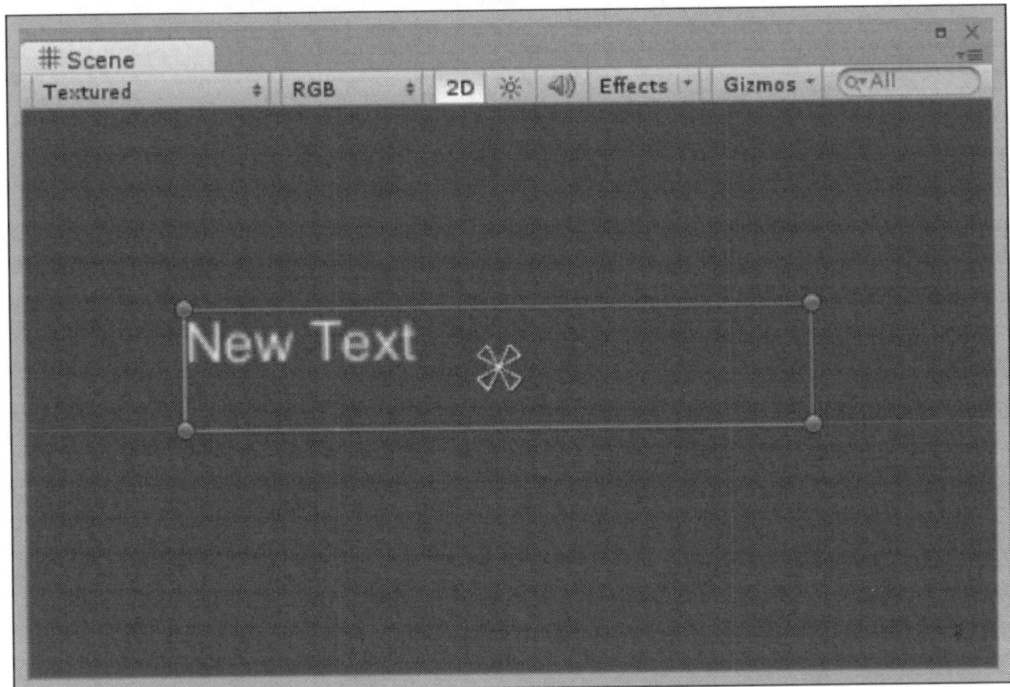

A new Text control added to a scene with the color set to white to make it more visible

> The border around the text is just the selection box around the control. **Text** controls do not have a border, they are just text.
>
> There's no need to add a **Canvas** if you don't have one already; all UI controls will automatically add a parent **Canvas** and an **EventSystem** to your scene, if you don't have one already.

> The **default color** of the text on the control is now **Black**. This was changed in the beta due to popular demand. I have simply changed it to white in the previous example to make it more visible.

If we then look at the **Inspector**, we can see the following:

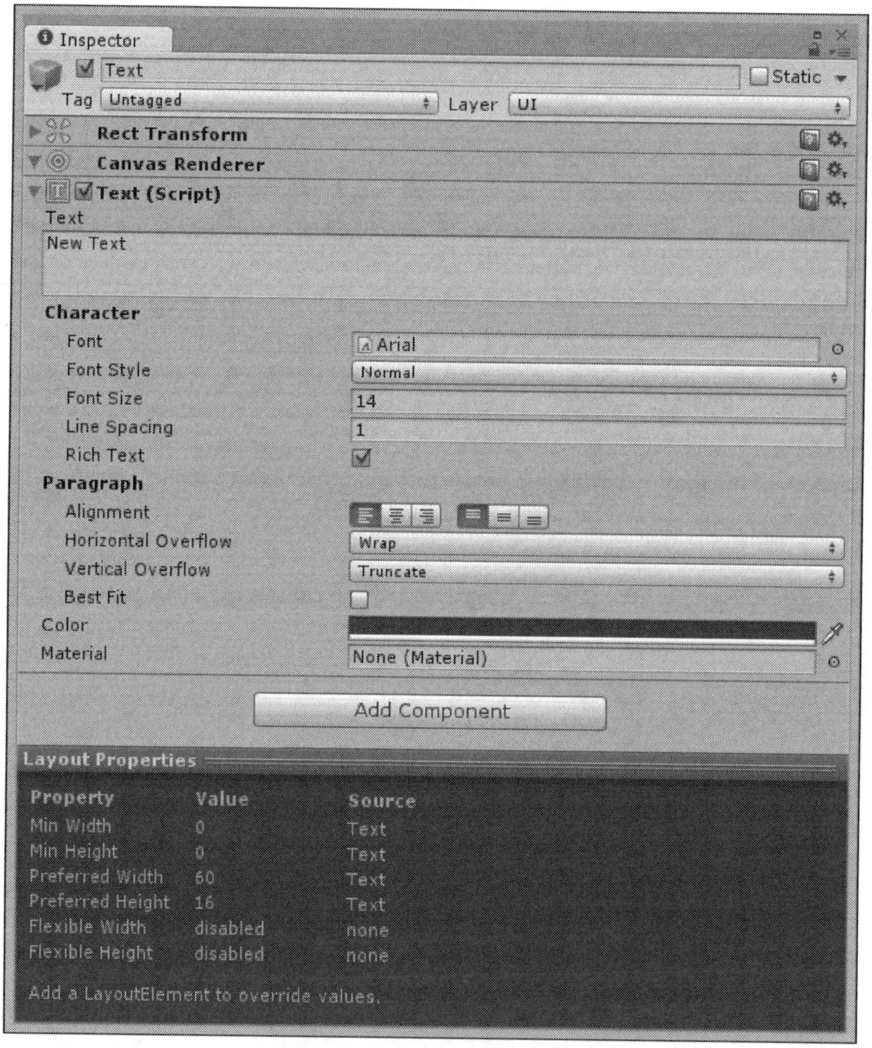

This gives us several familiar text style properties to configure how the text is drawn and presented on the screen.

Walking through the **Text** component properties, we have the following:

- **Text**: This is the text to be displayed on the screen.
- **Font**: This decides which font to use from the list of imported fonts in your project. By default, only **Arial** is supplied.

Unity supports a wide range of Font types and many can be imported using Font Definition files and you can even create your own.

You can read more about Fonts in Unity at `http://bit.ly/Unity3DFonts`.

As the font system is not changing in Unity 4.x, it isn't covered in great depth in this book.

- **Font Style**: This decides whether the text will be in **Bold**, **Italics**, ***both***, or just **Normal**.
- **Font Size**: This decides the size of the font to be displayed (see the previous note about the font system).
- **Line Spacing**: This decides the spacing in-between font lines. By default all text controls are multilined.
- **Rich Text**: This **Text** control enables rich text drawing capabilities (same as with legacy GUI, as detailed in *Chapter 1, Looking Back, Looking Forward*, in the Rich Text formatting section).
- **Alignment**: This decides where the text is placed within the bounds of the text control, such as left/right or top/bottom, and so on.
- **Horizontal Overflow**: If the text is too big for the control to display, this controls how the text should continue overflowing the control bounds. This can be set to **Overflow** (continue on same line) or **Wrap** (continue the next word on a new line).
- **Vertical Overflow**: Like the **Horizontal Overflow**, the **Vertical Overflow** controls how far down the screen the text will flow. This can be set to **Overflow** (continue lines vertically) or **Truncate** (no further characters displayed).

If text doesn't fit vertically (either due to line breaks or wrapping) and **Vertical Overflow** is set to **Truncate**, the lines that don't fit will be entirely removed even if they fall a fraction outside the Text control area. Only lines that completely fit within the box will be displayed in this mode. (Courtesy of Adam Dawes, one of my excellent reviewers.)

- **Best Fit**: This allows the text to resize the font to ensure it fits within the bounds of the control. It also allows you to set minimum and maximum font sizes if you want to constrain the scaling.
- **Color**: The base color of the font (which can be overridden by Rich Text formatting features), the default color of text is **Black**.
- **Material**: The default material the text should be rendered with. Note that this does not include Font atlases; these are not supported in the base **Text** control (but you could extend it). This is also used to assign shaders.

A simple FPS control

The simplest text example that is used in most games is an FPS counter, so first let's create a script for that. Start by creating a new `C#` script in your project called `FPSCounter` and replace its contents with the following:

```
using UnityEngine;
using UnityEngine.UI;

[RequireComponent(typeof(Text))]
public class FPSCounter : MonoBehaviour {
}
```

We start off with the expectation that the control has a **Text** component attached to the GameObject using the `RequireComponent` attribute, we also add the brand new `UnityEngine.UI` namespace that holds all the new **UI** functionality.

Next, we'll add some simple properties to track the FPS for our script:

```
private Text textComponent;
private int frameCount = 0;
private float fps =0;
private float timeLeft = 0.5f;
private float timePassed = 0f;
private float updateInterval = 0.5f;
```

Nothing too fancy, and now we need to capture a reference to the **Text** component used by the GameObject (always try to use strict references and not to keep looking up the **Text** component reference on each use), we do this in the `Awake` function as follows:

```
void Awake()
{
  textComponent = GetComponent<Text>();
```

```
    if (!textComponent)
    {
    Debug.LogError
     ("This script needs to be attached to a Text component!");
      enabled = false;
      return;
    }
}
```

Because we are using the `RequireComponent` attribute, we don't actually have to have to put the error test for the component in the script; however, it is a good practice to get into and will avoid nasty bugs appearing, when you least expect it, when you reference other components from scripts!

Lastly, we need an update loop to calculate the `FPS` and set the `Text` variable on the **Text** control:

```
void Update()
{
  frameCount += 1;
  timeLeft -= Time.deltaTime;
  timePassed += Time.timeScale / Time.deltaTime;
  //FPS Calculation each second
  if (timeLeft <= 0f)
  {
    fps = timePassed / frameCount;
    timeLeft = updateInterval;
    timePassed = 0f;
    frameCount = 0;
  }
  //Set the color of the text
  if (fps < 30) { textComponent.color = Color.red; }
  else if (fps < 60) { textComponent.color = Color.yellow; }
  else { textComponent.color = Color.green; }
  //Set Text string
  textComponent.text = string.Format("{0}: FPS", fps);
}
```

If you now add a **Text** control to your scene and then add the script to it, (you can just add the script to a GameObject and it will automatically add the **Text** component, thanks to the `RequireComponent` attribute), you will then get your basic **FPS** output as shown here:

You could also use rich text to draw the text, if you so wish, if you have it enabled in the **Text** settings.

Adding interaction with input

Displaying text is all well and good, but what about when you need the player to enter some text? Using the native platforms input features is OK but it breaks the illusion of the world within by breaking out of the game and showing a bulky platform input box.

To give a better look and feel, Unity have provided a base text **Input** component, which is best used when combined with the **Text** control (The **Input Field** control will add a Text component by default) along with an **Image** component as a background. (Although you can add it to any other UI control if you wish.)

When you add an **Input Field** control, navigate to **Create** | **UI** | **InputField** in the **Hierarchy** window (or from the multitude of options as detailed at the start of this section) you will see the following additional options in the **Inspector** window:

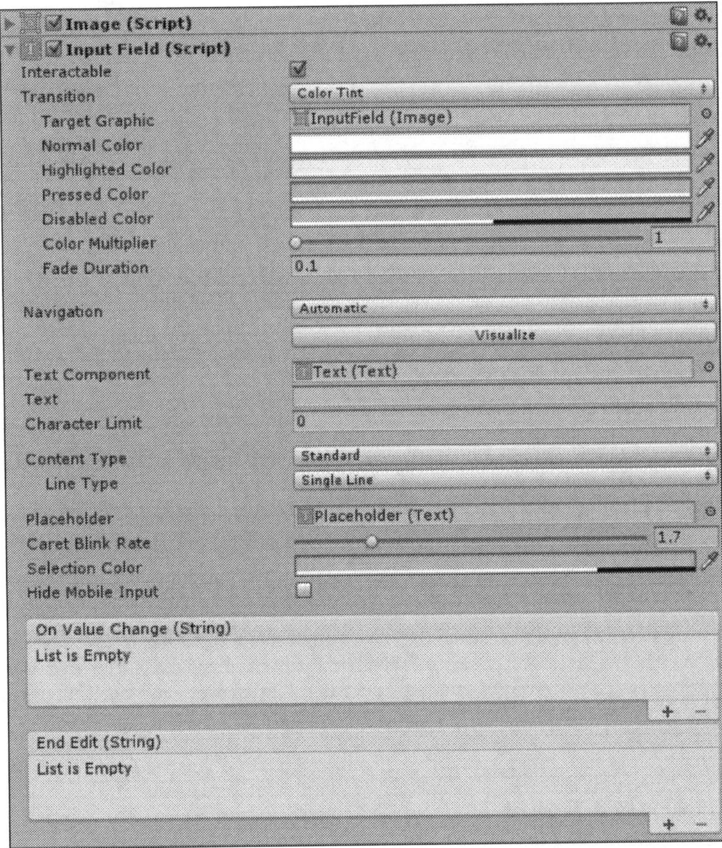

This control went through many iterations until it arrived at this final design with a lot of debate to boot.

As you can see, there are a multitude of different options, from the primary **Text Component** field, which holds the entered value (for which you can supply a default value and a limit on the number of characters the user can enter), to the **Placeholder Text** field, which is only displayed until the user enters a value (useful as it separates default values from actual user data). By default, adding the **Input Field** control also adds two child **Text** components for the **Text** and **Placeholder** properties.

The control also provides a multitude of configurations for the **Input Field** through the **Input Type** property, each with their own configurable elements:

- **Standard**: Single or multiple lined
- **Autocorrected**: Single or multiple lined with word prompts (depending on the platform it runs on, does not function in editor)
- **Integer Number/Decimal Number**: Only numbers
- **Alphanumeric**: Only letters and numbers; no special characters
- **Name**: Letters only, and first characters of each word are uppercase
- **E-mail address**: Complete with e-mail address text validation
- **Password/Pin**: Hashed out entry with either all characters or just numbers

Additionally, there is a custom option where you can mix and match the option above you build your own style of input control.

Several other options are available as well from setting the blink rate of the Text caret (blinking line showing where you are typing) and the color of the text when the user highlights/selects it.

We'll discuss the **Transition** options when we go over the **Button** control and the **Navigation** option in the **Navigation** section.

Shadows and effects

In any modern UI framework, there are always options to apply effects to content, whether it is with shadows, gloss, or blur. Usually, this is done with shaders but it's tricky at the best of times and without adequate experience, very time-consuming.

To this end, Unity has all over implemented a modular effect component system that can modify the vertexes (points in 3D space) of the content being drawn before it is passed to the rendering system.

All UI content when drawn to the scene through the Canvas renderer is batched into quads for fast and easy rendering. This results in a simple way to alter the makeup of these quads for effects before rendering occurs, quickly and efficiently. This also means it will work for any platform regardless of what type of graphic system it is.

Unity provides several of these effects out of the box in 4.6, one of which provides a shadow effect on the UI GameObjects it's attached to. It gives the best effect on **Text** components. It can only be used, however, on any GameObject that uses the **Canvas Renderer** in the new UI system (for example, the new UI controls).

You don't have to stop there either; all effects are based on the `IVertexModifier` interface, which allows you to create your own effects as well. Just look at the source code for the UI system for additional details on building these effects from the provided implementations (see *Chapter 6, Working with the UI Source*).

To use these effects, simply add the required component (for example, **Add Component | UI | Effects | Shadow**) to the GameObject you want affected. The **Shadow** component when added, looks like the following in the inspector window:

As you can see, the **Shadow** component gives you a couple of options to set the color of the shadow (only color, not material) and how far out from the GameObject the shadow should extrude. Here is what it looks like when the **Shadow effect** is applied:

Along with the **Shadow effect**, Unity is also shipping two other Effect components out of the box, these include:

- **Outline**: An extension of the **Shadow** script, which provides a customizable outline for the text instead of just an offset shadow.
- **Position As UV1**: Provides UV1 data for shaders about the **Text**. A bit more of an advanced case that was requested quite strongly in the beta. This also serves as a great example for how to build other effects that use the vertex data of UI elements.

As stated, if that's not enough for you, then flex your coding skills and make some more effects of your own, to share (you should always share if you can), or even sell them if they are fancy enough. I'd expect a fair few of these to turn up after release.

Bring on the images

Next up is the **Image** control/component, which is the basis for all textured drawing in the new **UI** framework (even if you just want a colored box).

The **Image** control is also very important for any input where you want the player to interact with any UI GameObject as it forms the **Hittable/Interactable** area for the Raycasting system. This determines what point of the screen a user is touching/clicking and then uses the Image and its bounds (through the **Graphics Raycaster**) 3to determine which control the user may be interacting with.

Don't forget, there are also other Raycaster systems such as the Physics and Physics2D raycasters if you want to test against 3D data, or you can build your own based on them.

When we add the Image control to our scene, we get the default view in the inspector as follows:

Note: The **Image Type** property will not appear until you have assigned a **Sprite** to the **Source Image** property, allowing you to just use it as a simple or transparent background for basic images or **Masks**.

Walking through this control, the common options we have are:

- **Source Image**: This is the sprite image to displayed within the bounds of the **Rect Transform**.

Note: Other than color, none of the other options will do anything unless an image has been selected. Without an image, it just acts like a colored box.

There is a pretextured **Image** control called a **Panel**. A **Panel** control is just an Image control with one of the built-in sprites that come with Unity preconfigured as the **Source Image**.

- **Color**: This is the tint color to apply to the sprite or the background color of the **Rect Transform** area.

Note, if your **Sprite** has black sections, then the color tint will not affect those parts.

- **Material**: If you wish to apply shaders to your UI controls, then you can apply a material with a shader attached to it.
- **Preserve Aspect**: If you want to uniformly scale the source image within the **Rect Transform**, then by clicking this option, the source image will remain in the same aspect as the original image no matter how much you stretch and twist the GameObjects **Rect Transform**. This option only appears for Simple and Filled **Image Types** (see the following section for the explanation of Image Types).
- **Set Native Size**: If you want to resize the **Rect Transform** of the GameObject to the original size of the selected image, then clicking on this button will do just that.

Image types

The other option on the Image control, the **Image Type** property, opens up a wrath of other options and capabilities. The options are:

- Simple
- Sliced
- Tiled
- Filled

Simple Images

As the type name suggests, this just presents the selected image or base color within the bounds of the **Rect Transform**. Nothing fancy, just draws the image, although you can use the shader material to affect how it's drawn and/or use **Effect** components to alter the GameObject presentation.

Sliced Images

Slicing (or 9 slicing as it is sometimes called) is a method where you can define a border within the bounds of your image, then that border will be preserved around the edges of the **Image** GameObject's **Rect Transform**. In layman's terms, it allows the border of an image to retain its aspect while the interior of the image will just be stretched to fill its area. This ensures the border will always look the same no matter the size of the image. (See *Chapter 5, Screen Space, World Space, and the Camera*, for a full example).

To define a border for an image, select it in your project's **Asset** view and then open up the **Sprite Editor** using the **Sprite Editor** button in the inspector window (which is now available for *both* **Single** and **Multiple** sprite images). When you open up the editor and click in the area for the selected sprite (selected by default for single images), you will see a **green** border surrounding the image at the top, bottom, left, and right-hand sides, as you can see in the following screenshot:

Note: The corner picking points and the green border only show up once you have added a border, either by dragging the four picking points surrounding the image or by manually altering the border dimension properties.

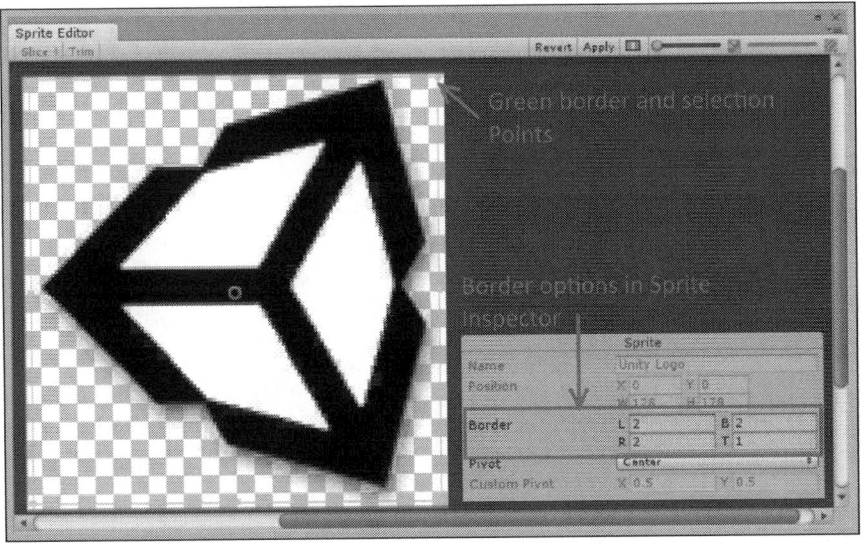

By adjusting this border zone, you can control which parts of the image will be scaled and stretched (the portion surrounding the border) with the size of the **Rect Transform**.

When using a sliced **Sprite** as the **Source Image** for the **Image** control, if you set the **Image Type** to **Sliced**, you will see the following in the **Inspector** window:

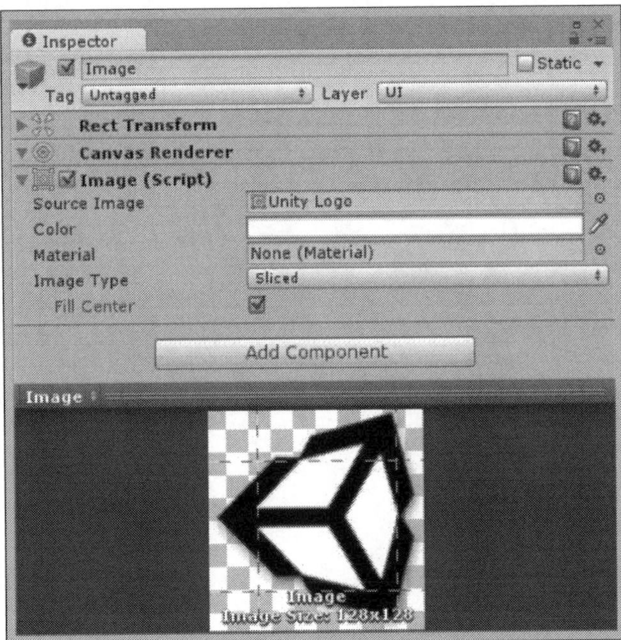

If your **Source Image** does not have a border set (a border with dimensions | 1), then you will get a warning when setting the **Image Type** to **Sliced**, informing you that the image cannot be used in this mode without a border.

As you can see, the preview window shows the border positions as well as an additional **Fill Center** option, which when checked will draw the entire image in the **Rect Transform** with non-uniform scale; unchecking it will remove the portion of the image within the border square.

Note: An image that has a border defined cannot be used for a **Tiled** image (see the following screenshot). Additionally, when you apply an image with a border to an **Image** control, it will automatically default to a **Sliced Image** type.

Tiled Images

Instead of scaling the source image, Unity also provides the option to tile an **Image** within the bounds of the GameObject's **Rect Transform**. By setting the **Image Type** option to **Tiled**, the image will then tile both horizontally and vertically from the bottom-left point of the **Rect Transform** as shown here:

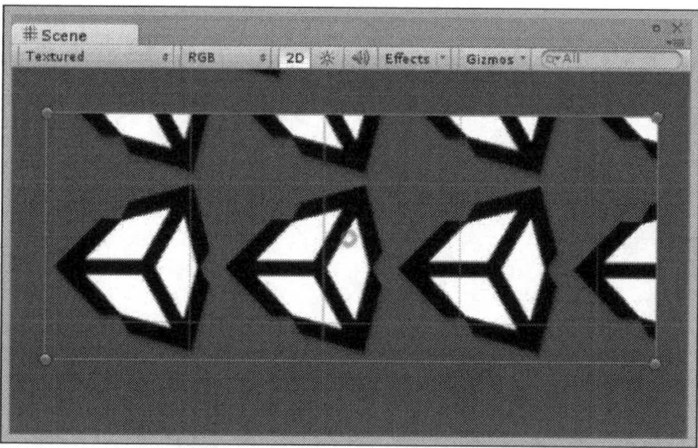

A limitation with the Tiled image at preset is that there is no way to alter the scale of the source image used; it will simply be drawn using its native size. Also if you use a **Sprite** with a border, the control will attempt to also draw the border tiled, which gives some very unpredicable results at present.

There isn't much more to say about the **Tiled** option. It does exactly what it says on the tin. If you want images to tile from a different corner, then you will need to rotate and flip the **Rect Transform** to put the desired corner where you wish.

Alternatively, you could create your own version of the Image control and override the **Tiled** feature to give it a little more flexibility. See *Chapter 6, Working with the UI source*, for more details.

Filled Images

The last **Image Type** option, the Image control is probably the most fascinating as it mixes masking elements with a gradual fill to offer a way to gradually introduce an image into the scene. When we set the **Image Type** to **Filled** we see the following in the inspector window:

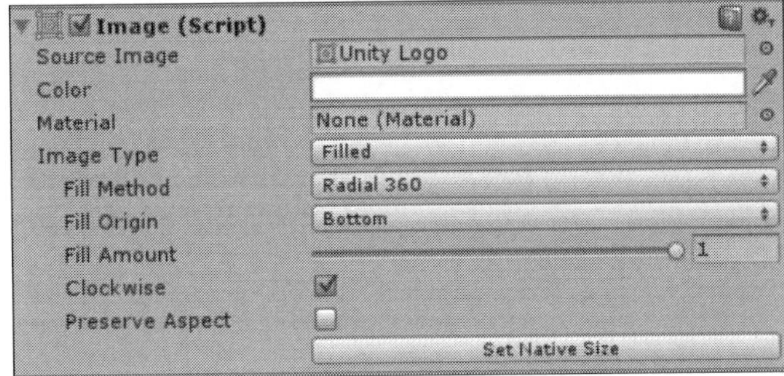

We see the familiar options as well as a few new ones, all of which you just have to play with to get the real sense of this option. They include:

- **Fill Method**: This allows you to set the way in which the image is filled in, from **Horizontal** or **Vertical**, to **Radial** in either a `90`, `180`, or `360` fashion (see the following screenshot with an example of a **Radial360** fill)
- **Fill Origin**: This sets the position where the fill should start from, be it **Top**, **Bottom**, **Left**, or **Right** depending on the type of fill you select

- **Fill Amount**: This is a simple slider that ranges from `0` to `1` to control the percentage of the image that is filled
- **Clockwise** (only available for Radial fills): If you don't like the direction the fill is facing, then flip it to the other direction; simple!

As an example of a **Radial360** fill, see the following progression by altering the **Fill Amount** property:

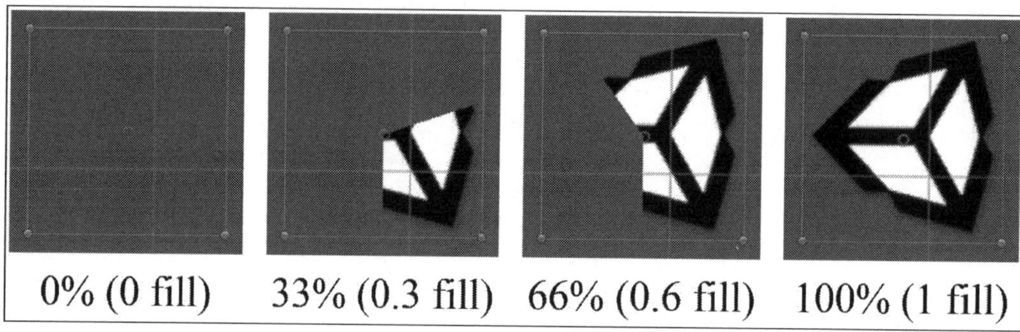

Adding animation to the mix

One good fact about the new **UI** system is that each and every part can be fully animated. To show this, let's build a simple animation logo using the **Filled Image** control.

Note: We will only be covering the basics of the Unity Animation system here as it's outside the scope of this title. I'd recommend picking up a good Unity 2D title to learn more about it. I'm sure I've seen one somewhere!

First off, let's build a quick animation to control our **Image**:

1. Create an **Image** control called `LoadingLogo` and apply a sprite to it, then set the **Image Type** property to **Filled**.
2. Ensure that the **Filled Amount** is set to `0`.
3. Create a new folder in your project called **Animation** and two sub folders called **Controllers** and **Clips** (you can skip this step if you wish, it's a standard thing for me).
4. Create a new **Animation Controller** by navigating to **Create | Animator Controller** from the project menu and saving it in the `Animation\Controllers` folder.

5. Double-click the new controller to open the **Animator** editor window.
6. Right-click in the **Animator** window and navigate to **Create State** | **Empty** to add a new state to the controller, then rename the new state **Start**.

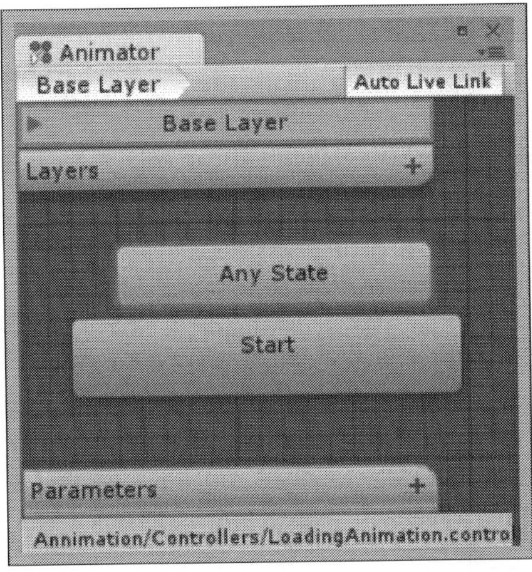

The Animator Controller with a new Start animation state

7. Return to your scene and add an **Animator Component** to the **Image** control by navigating to **Add Component** | **Miscellaneous** | **Animator**.
8. Apply the new **LoadingLogo Animation Controller** to the **Animator** component by dragging it from the project view to the **Controller** property.

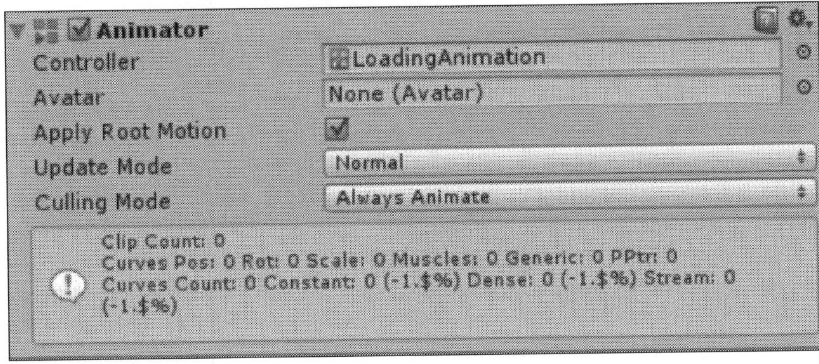

The configured Animator Controller on the LoadingLogo Image GameObject

9. Select the **LoadingLogo** GameObject and open the **Animator** window (**Menu | Windows | Animation**).
10. Create a new **Animation** clip (when prompted, save it to the `Animation\Clips` folder) by clicking on **Create New Clip** in the clip selection dropdown of the Animation Dope sheet and call it **LoadingAnimationClip**, as shown here:

Animation clip selector with Create New Clip option in drop down

11. Check whether the Dope sheet is set to record by clicking on the **Record** icon (the red dot in the previous screenshot) and set the time at `1` second by clicking on the **1:00** point on the dope sheet (a red line should now appear at that point).
12. Select the **Image** control and alter the **Fill Amount** to `1`. A new property should be added to the view, as shown in the following screenshot:

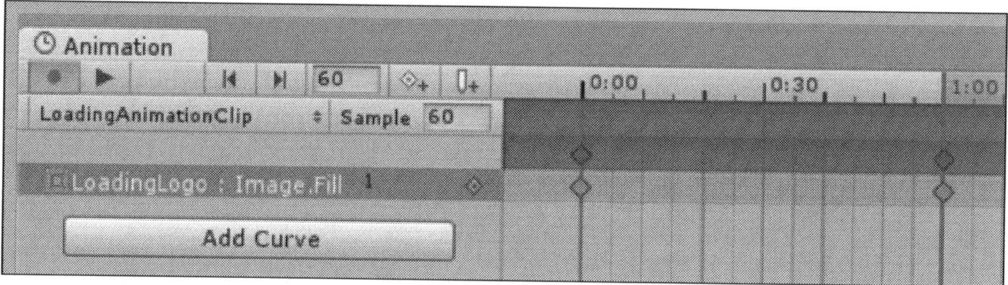

Completed Loading Animation clip

If you hit the play button on the **Animator** window, you will see the Image being filled gradually over time in the **Scene** view.

1. Now return to the Animator view and add a new **Bool** property called **Loading** by clicking on the **+** icon in the **Properties** box in the lower left of the screen and then selecting **Bool** and entering the name **Loading**.

2. Next, right-click on the **Start** state, select **Make Transition**, and then click on the new **LoadingAnimationClip** state (automatically added when we created the new clip previously) to create an animation transition between the two states, as shown in this screenshot:

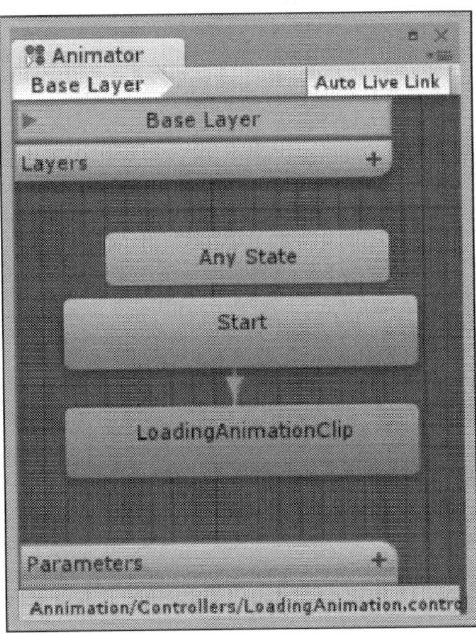

Animator controller with new LoadingAnimationClip and a transition created from Start to the new state

3. Select the new transition (the arrow) from **Start** to **LoadingAnimation** and in the inspector under the **Conditions** section, click on the drop-down, and select our new **Loading** property. Check whether the value is set to **true** (which should be the default). This simply means that when the **Loading** property is set to **true**, the animation should move (one way) to the connected state.

Setting the conditon for the Start to LoadingAnimationClip state transition

4. Finally repeat steps 14 and 15, this time creating the transition between the **LoadingAnimation** state to the **Start** state with the **Loading** condition set to **False**.

That finishes the animation part. We now have an end-to-end animation that will play the loading animation when we tell it we are **Loading**; it will also stop the animation when we tell it we are not **Loading**.

Now we need to tell the animation when the game is **Loading**. To do this we'll add a script to play the animation when the scene starts.

Create a new C# script called **LoadingAnimation** in the `Assets\Scripts` folder and replace its contents with the following:

```
using System.Collections;
using UnityEngine;

public class LoadingAnimation : MonoBehaviour {

  Animator loadingAnimation;
  // Get the Animator component on Awake
  void Awake () {
    loadingAnimation = GetComponent<Animator>();
  }

  // Start the loading animation by setting the animation
  // Loading property to true
  void Start () {
    loadingAnimation.SetBool("Loading", true);
    StartCoroutine(LoadLevel());
  }

  // A simple coroutine to wait 3 seconds and load the level
  IEnumerator LoadLevel()
  {
    for (int i = 0; i < 3; i++)
    {
      yield return new WaitForSeconds(1);
    }
    loadingAnimation.SetBool("Loading", false);
    //Application.LoadLevel("Main Menu");
  }
}
```

This is just a simple script that gets the reference to the **Animation** and starts it by setting the **Loading** property of the **Animation** to **true**, after 3 seconds it then stops the animation to load a level. (Which is commented out, as it's just an example.)

Attach this script to the **LoadingLogo** GameObject, and now you have a very simple **UI** loading animation, which will work with any of the **Filled Image Type** options.

A word on RawImage

Alongside the **Image** control is the **RawImage** control. The only difference between the two is that the **RawImage** uses a **Texture** instead of a **Sprite** as its **Source** (the **Texture** property in this case).

Apart from the advanced texture import settings, the big advantage here is that you could use this to display images downloaded from the Web (once you have downloaded it), since there are functions to turn a downloaded image stream into a **Texture**.

Don't push this button

As we venture into the interactive realm, we tackle the first of the combined controls, the **Button** control/component. In fact, the **Button** control is not a single entity but a combination of several different components under one banner. The **Button** is more of an example of what can be achieved by building/combining controls to do what you want more than anything else.

Like with the previous controls, you can add the **Button** from the menu or through the project **Hierarchy**, or using the component options (**Create** | **UI** | **Button**). When you add a **Button** control, what you actually get is the following:

- An **Image** control
- A `button` script that implements:
    - The **Selectable** control (covered later)
    - Several `Trigger` events
- A **Text** control (as a child)

A fairly well-built stack that draws in all the features it needs. In fact, let's look at the `Button` control in code:

Note: This is taken directly from the UI source as an example. If you add this in a project it will cause an error because there is already a **Button** control/class!

```
using System;
using System.Collections;
using UnityEngine.Events;
using UnityEngine.EventSystems;
using UnityEngine.Serialization;
```

```
namespace UnityEngine.UI
{
    // Button that's meant to work with mouse or
    // touch-based devices.
    [AddComponentMenu("UI/Button", 30)]
    public class Button : Selectable,
      IPointerClickHandler, ISubmitHandler
    {
        [Serializable]
        public class ButtonClickedEvent : UnityEvent { }
        // Event delegates triggered on click.
        [FormerlySerializedAs("onClick")]
        [SerializeField]
        private ButtonClickedEvent m_OnClick =
          new ButtonClickedEvent();
        protected Button() { }
        public ButtonClickedEvent onClick {
            get { return m_OnClick; }
            set { m_OnClick = value; }
        }
        private void Press() {
            if (!IsActive() || !IsInteractable())
                return;
            m_OnClick.Invoke();
        }
        // Trigger all registered callbacks.
        public virtual void OnPointerClick(PointerEventData
          eventData) {
      //Click handler for left click
        }
        public virtual void OnSubmit(BaseEventData eventData) {
            Press();
            // Submit handler
        }
        private IEnumerator OnFinishSubmit() {
            // Finish submit handler
        }
    }
}
```

As you can see, practically everything the **Button** implements comes from the **Selectable** control (see the following screenshot) or through direct implementation of the **EventSystem** interfaces. The main parts of the code (commented out, else this would take several pages) handle clicking on the **Button** and what should happen if the **Button** fires a **Submit** (finish) event for a form (granted, this is more for keyboard rather than mouse or touch).

When we look at the **Button** control in the **Hierarchy** and **Inspector** window, we see the following:

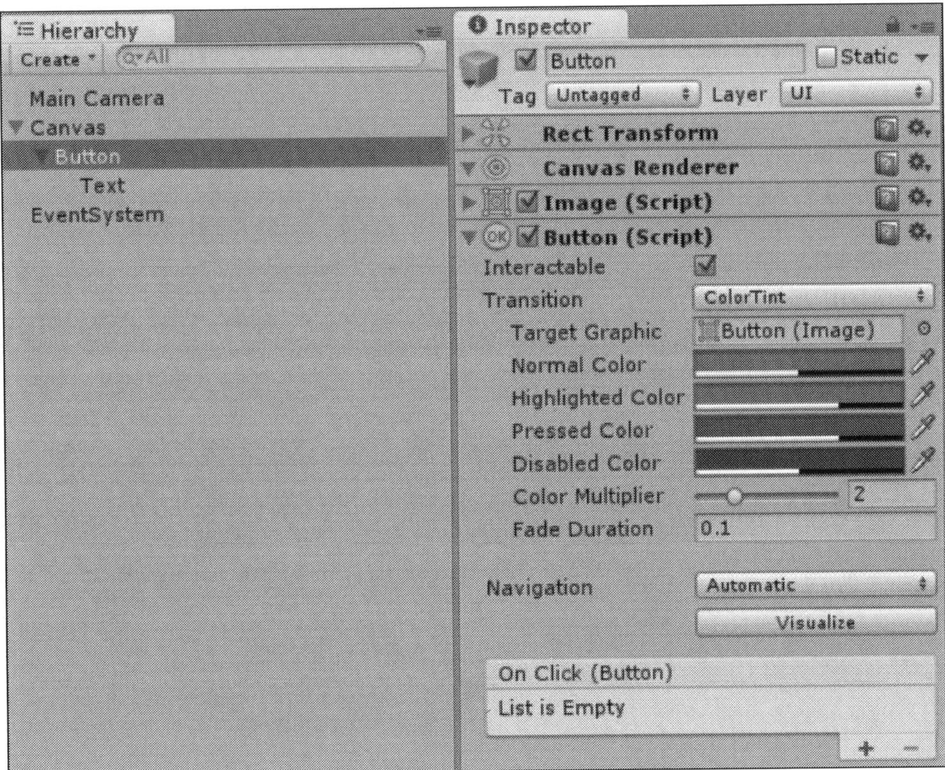

This shows the full implemented control in the editor, so let's look at these new components.

What makes it Selectable?

The **Selectable** component covers everything that is needed by a GameObject to react to inbound events from the **UnityEvent** system; it then offers several graphical actions based on these events.

Note: For the **Selectable** component to function correctly, it must have a component that will interact with the current raycast system in use. By default, it requires an **Image** component attached to work with the default Graphic's Raycaster. Other raycasters may be used if you wish; you would then need to attach the corresponding detection component (for example, a mesh with a physics collider for the Physics Raycaster) to the Selectable's GameObject.

The events that the Selectable control manages by default are:

- `OnPointerEnter`/`OnPointerExit` (hover/highlighted)
- `OnPointerDown`/`OnPointerUp` (pressed)

These provide input to the control from the **UnityEvent** system (either touch, mouse, or keyboard). If we look at just the Selectable component part of the **Button** control, we see the following **Transition** options:

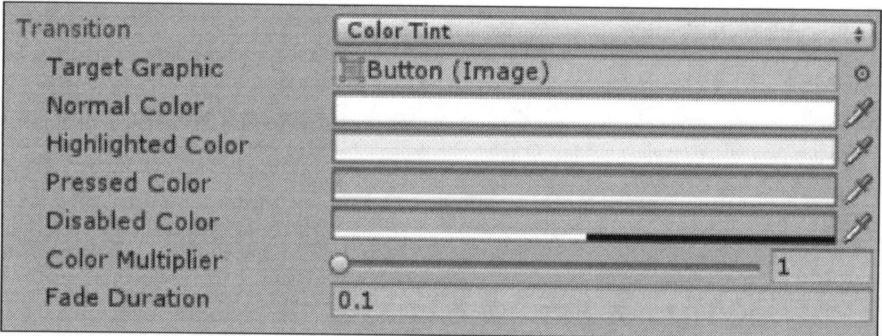

These **Transition** options provide us with several customizable options we can use to affect the visualization of **UI** components based on the current input state:

- Whether the pointer is on top of (hovering over) the GameObject (mouse only)
- Whether the GameObject is being pressed (mouse, touch, and keyboard)
- Whether interactivity on the control is disabled

The type of **Transition** determines the result of the previous events; they include:

- **ColorTint** (the default shown in the preceding screenshot): This changes the base tint color for the selected **Image** based on the control's state
- **SpriteSwap**: This replaces the target image with an alternate sprite based on the control's state as shown here:

- **Animation**: Instead of just some basic features as discussed previously, controls implementing the **Selectable** component also come with an option to do, basically, whatever you want to when the events occur by using the full power of the Mecanim animation system.

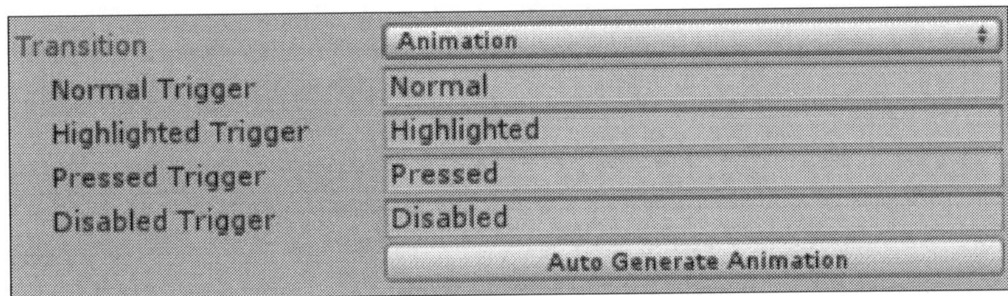

So based on the control state, the animation controller will activate an animation with the name supplied. To make things even easier, Unity has provided a handy button to generate the default animation states and a controller (aren't they nice).

[If you want to use the same animation on multiple buttons, just add an Animation Controller component to the additional buttons and then drag the controller you initially created to the new buttons.]

We'll cover the animation option in more detail in an example later.

- **None**: Basically don't do anything, be a really boring button if you really want to.

One really nice feature with the **Selectable** component is that it can be attached to any GameObject on a UI Canvas. So if you want text that reacts to touch, the mouse, or even an image (which is basically what the button is), then you can. You can even go wild and make your own version of the **Selectable** control with your own features.

> Remember, if you want to do anything with the Events that the **Selectable** component implements, you will need either an **Event Trigger** component (covered in *Chapter 2, Building Layouts*) or a script implementing the `Event` interfaces (like the button script), which we will cover next.

An event occurred, what do I do?

Next we come to one of my favorite additions with the new UI system, graphical event hookups.

The **Selectable** component listens, by default, to events, but the **Button** also needs to act on those events to do something else, turn on a light, activate a Hero's skill or even just exit the game (disabled by default of course). For this, the **Button** control also implements the `IEventSystemHandler` and `IPointerClickHandler` interfaces.

> These interfaces are just subcomponents of the **EventSystem**. The EventSystem automatically searches for components and scripts that implement these interfaces while it is running. The **Button** is similar to the **Event Trigger** component we covered in the previous chapter; however, it is designed to specifically handle only certain events and avoids the overhead of providing all types of events (just the click event, which is all the **Button** actually needs).

If we look at the **Event** portion of the **Button** control, we see the following:

Through this simple interface, we can attach the **Click** event from the **UnityEvent** System to just about anything else within the realm of the Unity Editor; this includes:

- Script methods (not statics)
- GameObject properties
- GameObject components

We'll cover more on what you can and can't use as parameters to script methods in *Chapter 6, Working with the UI Source*; for now just know you can only use base .NET types such as string, float, int, and bool or Unity types as parameter values.

Once you click on the **+** symbol, it adds an action to the list; every item in the list is then called or executed when the event occurs. Each action in the list looks like the following:

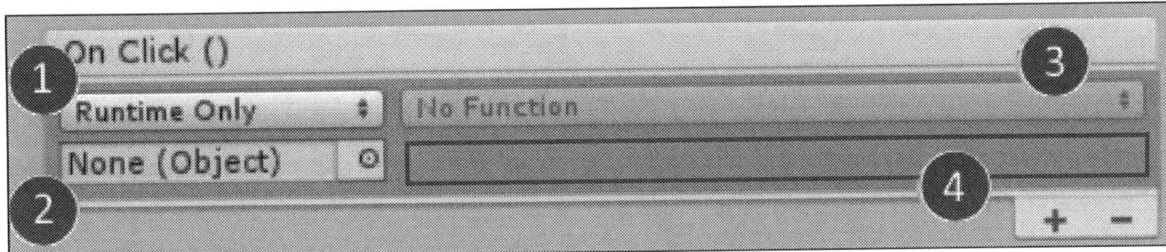

Looking closer at this action item in the list, we see the following:

1. **Runtime selector**: A simple little option with each event is that you can decide if you want it to also run in the editor or just in the game. As always, there is also the option to just turn off an Event rather than delete it and lose the setting.

The runtime selector when you select an editor option is effectively the same as using the `[ExecuteInEditMode]` attribute in scripts.

2. **Object selector**: Clicking on the **Object selector** brings up the standard object browse window, which allows you choose from items in the current scene or from the entire project (including the built-in Unity assets). Selecting an object will then enable the **Action selector**.

> The selection system actually allows you to select anything within the realm of your project if you wish but not instantiate them. This part I find particularly odd because such a global selection doesn't make sense. You can even select shaders, prefabs, and primitives. I guess at some point this feature will be expanded in later releases or the global filter reduced to only those actionable assets. Basically, not everything you can select is actually useful.

3. **Action selector**: Based on the object you have selected, you will have different options available to you in the **Action selector**. This basically gives you a list of all the components attached to the selected object and then within each you have a list of properties or methods that can be actioned or affected. For example, by selecting the **Button** GameObject itself, we see the following possible actionable components:

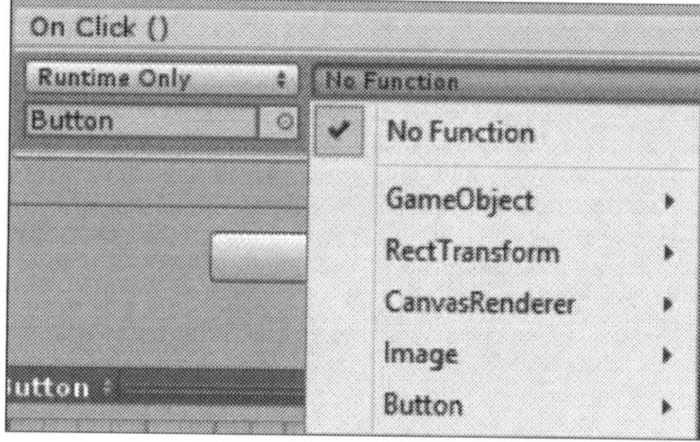

This shows each part of the Button's GameObject that we can select. The GameObject itself, the object's **Rect Transform**, and even the individual components of the Button (not children however, just the selected GameObject). After you select the **Button** component of our button, we can see the following list of properties and methods that we can affect:

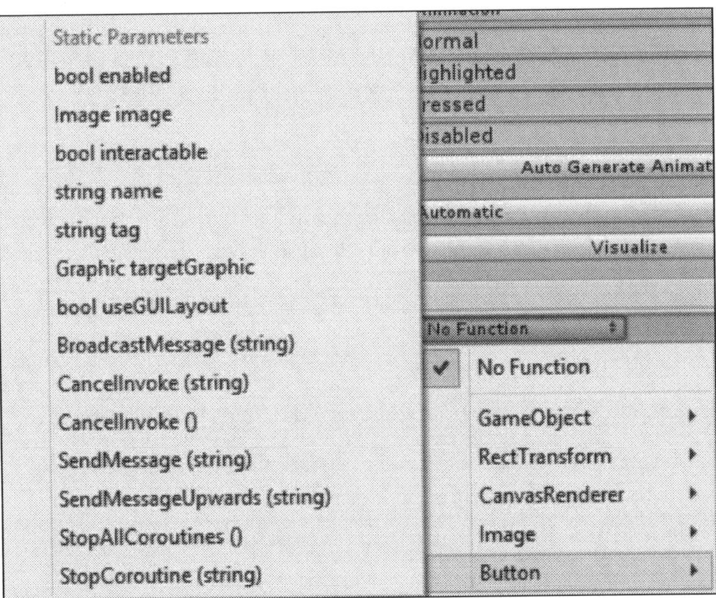

The list of public properties of the Button component on our selected GameObject that we can set

4. **Value selector**: The action you have selected will determine whether the **Value box** is enabled or not. If you have selected an editable property or a script method with a parameter, then it will be enabled so you can set the property or pass a single variable to the method. If the method does not require a variable, then it is disabled. The **Value** field is also type sensitive and will alter its look based on the type of variable/property required, a checkbox for a **bool**, an image selector for an image, and so on.

Note: Methods with multiple parameters and static methods/classes are not supported in the editor at the time of writing.

All this functionality gives a mountain of choice and a set capabilities directly from the editor with no coding required (although, to be honest, most things you would want the click to do will likely require a script attached to the object).

Note that the button only exposes the `Click` event (well it is a button after all); if you want to include more events to add actions to, then you will need to extend the base button control.

You are not limited to a single action (line in the event grid); if you want, you can have as many as you like! Just don't get too crazy.

To remove an action from the list, just select it by clicking on the specific row and then click on the - symbol.

The ultimate awesome menu

Putting together what you have learned so far, we can fashion some interesting concepts very easily, using a nice little free UI pack from `http://opengameart.org/content/ui-pack` and importing the spritesheets contained within. Using this artwork, we can construct a good looking menu UI, as shown here:

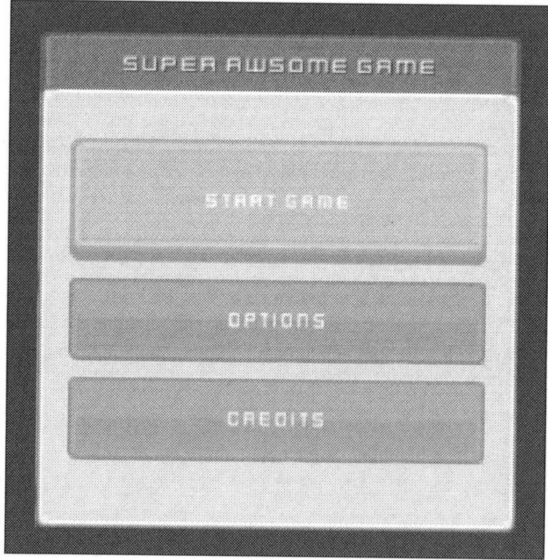

The previous example (like everything else here) is included in the sample project with the code download that accompanies this book.

Unfortunately, with this UI pack, you'll run into one of the slightly annoying features of the 2D sprite editor; most 2D spritesheets use the top-left for position `0,0` when configuring individual sprites. However, Unity's sprite editor uses the bottom left for position `0,0`.

Bear this in mind, when you use spritesheet configuration files (usually packaged with the spritesheet) to determine the configuration of the sprite position and size. The **X**, width, and height will usually be fine, however, the **Y** value will need some love. Just take the spritesheet height and take away the sprite's expected value and then take away the sprite's height to get the **Y** position for Unity. For example, the spritesheet height is `210`, the buttons generally have a height of `45`, so a **Y** position of `39` in the spritesheet configuration would translate to the **Y** position `126` in Unity. (It's just inverted). The UI pack above has one of these spritesheet configuration files packaged with it. Armed with the previous infomation you should import the three spritesheets and attempt to set them or use the example in the code download as a template.

If you are unfamiliar with the Sprite Editor, then I suggest watching Unity's own tutorial video on the subject at `http://bit.ly/Unity2DSpriteEditor` or picking up a nice 2D book (self-promotion mode enabled), I hear mine has been very popular — *Mastering Unity 2D Game Development, Packt Publishing*.

WIth the UI Pack spritesheets imported (Blue, Yellow and Grey), building this example menu is very simple with the following hierarchy:

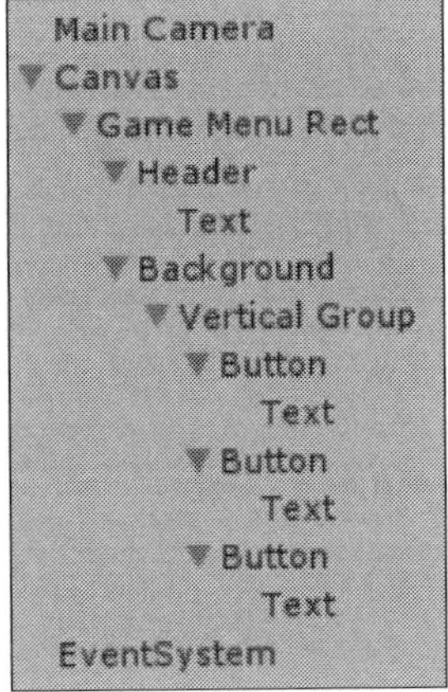

This is defined as:

- **Canvas**: A basic **Screen Space - Overlay** canvas
- **Game Menu Rect**: This is an empty GameObject for the area of the menu (**Width** `300`, **Height** `300`)
- **Header**: This is the header image using an icon from the blue spritesheet plus white text.
- The menu **Background**: This is an **Image** using a background sprite from the grey spritesheet.
- A **Vertical Layout Group**: This is positioned in the center of the menu background, also with a **Content Size Fitter** applied set to **Vertical Fit Preferred**.
- Three **Buttons**: These **Buttons** are set to sprite swap using a blue sprite for the normal, yellow for highlighted, another yellow for pressed, and a grey sprite for disabled. Additionally, because we are using a **Content Size Fitter** on the group, add a **Layout Element** component setting the **Preferred Height** to `50`.

Provided you set up your spritesheet correctly (either using sliced sprites or just basic images), you should get a nice basic effect. Hovering over the buttons turns them yellow, clicking on them just alters them slightly, and if you disable interactivity on a button it will turn it grey.

> Additionally, the UI pack comes with a `kenvector_future.ttf` **Font**. If you feel adventurous, then drop it in your Unity project and set the **Font** of the **Text** components to give it a different feel.

That's all well and good, but let's add a little bit more flair and leverage the extra layout bits we added:

1. Change the **Start Button** to an Animated button by setting the **Transition** property of the **Button** to **Animation**.
2. Click on the **Auto Generate Animation** button to create the default animation controller. When asked, save the controller in the `Animation\Controller` folder in your project (create it if it doesn't exist already). This will result in the following **Animator** being created for the button (it will also add an **Animator** component to your button **GameObject**). You can view the Animator at any time by double-clicking on the new animation controller file in the project view:

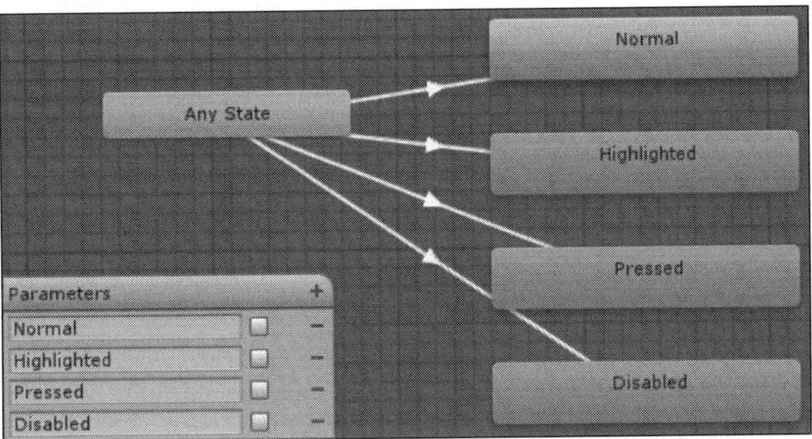

3. Select the **Button** in the project hierarchy and open the **Animation** window (navigating to **Menu** | **Window** | **Animation**); if you open the **Clips** dropdown, you should see there are four clips, one for each Button state.
4. Select the **Highlighted** clip and ensure the **Record** button is pressed (a red line should appear in the window and the **Play** controls at the top of the editor should turn red (be warned, anything you change now will be added to the animation!)
5. Change the **Source Image** of the button's image control to one from the yellow spritesheet (remember as we switched from the **Sprite Swap** to **Animation** mode, any options you had previously now no longer apply).

You don't need to set an animation position as it will automatically blend from the button's previous state.

6. Additionally, set the **Preferred Height** in the **Layout Element** component of the Button to `100` to stretch the Button.

With the new UI system, it's always better to control/alter the native sizes of a control rather than scale it; this allows the UI system to do the magic for us. Since the button is in a layout group, we cannot alter its size directly, which is why we are using the **Layout Element** and **Content Size Fitter** to our advantage. You can use scale if you wish, there is nothing stopping you if that's how you roll.

Turn off the Animation recording and play your scene. The Button when hovered over, will now resize as well as change color as shown in the first screenshot in this section.

Feel free to play with other animation clips for the other states; go wild and see what you can do. In the downloadable example that comes with this book, I made the button also rotate when clicked.

As noted, the complete sample is in the Code Download accompanying this title if you get stuck.

Which direction to travel?

There are times in life when you reach a fork in the road and need to decide which way to turn; here's where the Toggle control comes in, making a binary decision much more fun and snazzy (ok, maybe not).

There's not much one can actually say about a **Toggle** control, it's on or it's off, job done. Well almost.

The **Toggle**, like the **Button** control, is built from several other controls and components, as shown here when it's added to the **Scene**:

As you can see the **Toggle** is a slightly more complex setup, comprising several parts:

- The parent **Toggle** GameObject
- A child **Background** image for the **Toggle** box (a Unity base image)

- A child **Image** of the **Background** containing a **Checkmark** sprite overlaying the toggle box
- A **Label** offset to the right of the toggle box as a child of the **Background**

This system is completely flexible and you can modify it to your needs as you wish, the default Unity version is basically just a quick example.

Looking at the **Toggle** component that was added to the parent object, we can glean what is actually needed for the Toggle to function:

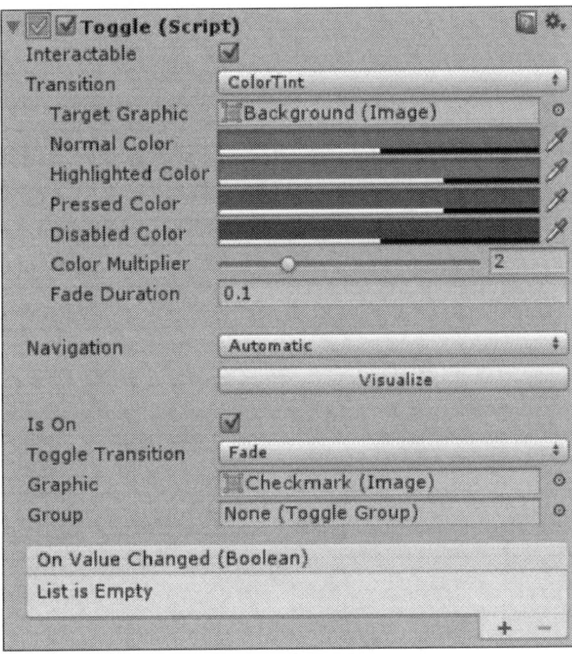

As we can see, the **Toggle** has the same **Selectable** component base as the **Button** control and an event handler; this time however, it is using the **On Value Changed** event instead of **Clicked**.

The **Toggle** specific options that are exposed (in the middle) give us a few capabilities:

- **Is On**: This determines the initial state of the **Toggle**, active/checked
- **Toggle Transition**: This controls how the toggle graphic enters and exits the view, blinkered on/off or fades in/out (default)

There are only two options at present for the transition, I would have liked to see more or at least a Mecanim hook-in here. Hopefully, it'll be extended in future updates. If not, then you can always do it yourself.

- **Graphic**: This is the sprite to use for the check image (*not* the checkmark GameObject as shown previously, which is the checkmark background), this is the image that is turned on/off by the **Toggle**
- **Group**: We'll cover this later, essentially, it allows for grouping of **Toggle** options together, only allowing a single item in a group to be checked at a time

So from the default setup that Unity gives you, all that is needed is a Toggle graphic and you're done, but as Unity shows, you should really think beyond that for a good UX.

Grouping toggles

As described earlier, in the **Toggle** control's properties, multiple toggles can be grouped together under a single group. The net effect of a toggle group means that only one **Toggle** within the group can be active (checked true) at a time. This is great for those multiple choice situations where there can only be one right answer.

Groups can be placed anywhere on the scene, the best option however, is to create a parent empty GameObject, add the **Toggle Group** component to it, and then place each toggle that is part of the group as a child of this parent GameObject. For example:

1. In a new scene, create a **Canvas** and add an empty **Empty GameObject** as its child. Name this new GameObject **Toggle Group Parent**.
2. Add the **Toggle Group** component to the **Toggle Group Parent** GameObject.
3. Add a **Toggle** control as a child of the **Toggle Group Parent** GameObject.
4. Select the **Toggle** and drag the **Toggle Group Parent** to the **Group** property of the **Toggle** component.
5. Set the **Is On** property to **False** (unchecked).

The **Toggle Group** script does *not* check or manage the initial state of the Toggles it manages, only the selection logic is handled. So if all Toggles are **on/checked** by default, then *all* will be on when the scene starts. Only after all but one have been unselected by the user will the script control the selection.

If you want one set as the default, then just be sure that only that one is checked by default.

6. Duplicate the **Toggle** GameObject a couple of times and reposition them in the scene.

If you run the scene, you will see that by default all the **Toggles** are unchecked, by clicking one **Toggle** it will be selected. If you then select another **Toggle**, then the previous **Toggle** that was selected is now unchecked as only one can be checked at a time.

You don't have to arrange the GameObjects this way, they can be anywhere in the scene. Just be sure to have your **Toggles** in the scene that you want grouped together and set the same **Toggle Group** GameObject as the **Group** property of each **Toggle**.

Dynamic event properties

In the **Button** control, you had an event that was a single action—click on this and do this; there was no additional information fed from the action to say anything about it.

With the **Toggle** however, it has a **Boolean** state, which means we have a potential input to use or pass to whatever action we wish to perform. These are referred to as **dynamic parameters** and are exposed as separate options when we try to select an action on a **GameObject**, as shown here:

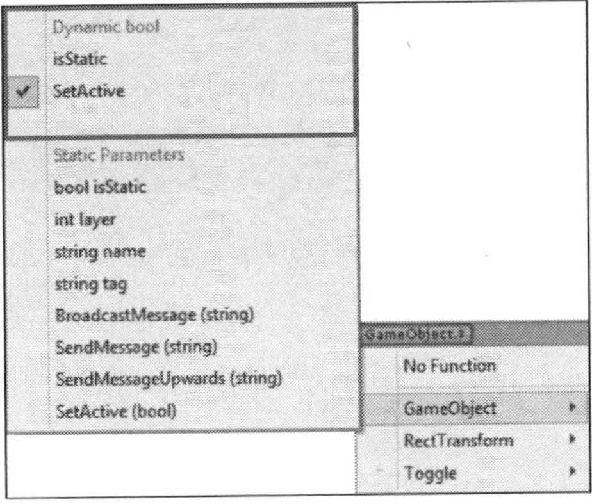

The Event handler with a Toggle selected showing Dynamic (top) values and Fixed/Static (bottom) parameters

These additional options are type specific to the value provided from the control, such as a **Boolean** from a **Toggle**. Other controls provide `floats` or `integers`, including the list of methods that accept the same data type as a parameter.

When you select these dynamic options, the Value field of the event action is disabled as the value comes from the control and not some user entered value.

This means it will use the current value or state of the control or property when calling a function or setting another property. For example, using the Boolean state of the checkbox to set the visibility of another GameObject on or off.

Sliding opportunities

As we almost get to the end of our built-in controls journey, we see more complex setup of controls that are again just combinations of what has come before with a simple script to manage a set of child components (instead of the bulky legacy GUI controls of the past).

You should see a pattern emerge now, that just about anything is possible and how you use even the built-in scripts is completely within your control.

As we can see, when you add the **Slider** control to our **Scene**, we get yet another default control makeup (you don't have to be bound by the default setup either):

For the Slider, Unity provides by default:

- A grouping parent GameObject for the slider, with the **Slider** component attached
- A **Background** for the entire control (unlike the **Toggle**, which was just the checkbox area)
- An empty GameObject used to provide a **Rect Transform** area for the **Slider** bar, with a child **Image** to fill the area using a default built-in sprite, the area is filled based on the **Value** property of the **Slider**
- An empty GameObject used to provide a Rect Transform area for the sliding handle and a child **Image** to denote the **Handle** itself

As we look to the **Slider** control itself, we see that these two lower child elements are the key parts of the **Slider**. However, their parent is just as important as it provides the bounds of how far the **Slider** can travel:

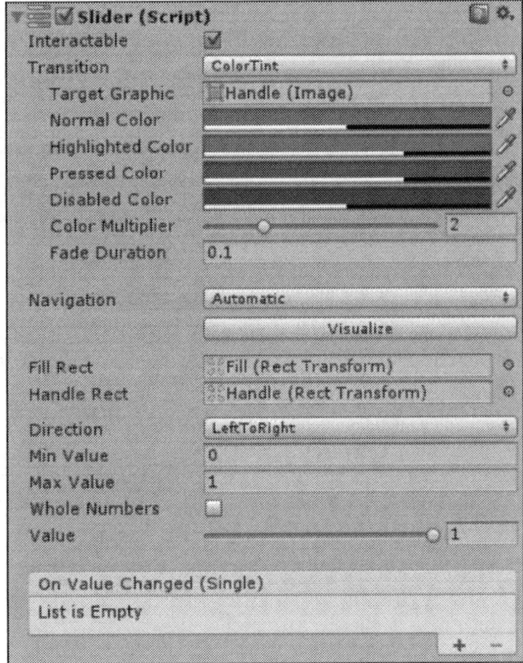

Again, we see the familiar base controls of the **Selectable** and **UnityEvent** controls, this time it is the **On Vaue Changed** event but with a data type of single (basically a float).

If we look deeper into the properties of the **Slider**, we can see the following:

- **Fill Rect**: This provides the graphical range for the **Slider** control, it translates the **Min** and **Max** values into graphical components on the **Canvas**. This is also Selectable to allow the user to jump to a position in the **Slider** range.
- **Handle Rect**: This provides the grabble handle for the user to drag the **Slider** through its range and also provides input to the **Fill Rect** for range calculations.
- **Direction**: This allows you to define the default direction of travel for the slider in either horizontal or vertical directions (no diagonal sadly, but you can always rotate the control J), giving you *left to right* or *right to left* options for example.

Note: You will have to resize the control if you want to switch from horizontal to vertical and vice-versa.

You don't rotate the control to switch from horizontal to vertical as it messes with the settings the control uses to render the control.

- **Min** and **Max Values**: This is the minimum and maximum values the **Slider** can range to, nothing more, nothing less.
- **Whole Numbers**: Given the base data type of the **Slider** is a `float`, it allows for fine incremental changes. However, there are those situations where you only need whole numbers or steps. Setting this option will cause the handle and the **Slider** value to jump up in increments, say for selecting pages/tabs on a form.
- **Value**: The all-important default value for the **Slider**, restricted to the **Min** and **Max** values you have set previously.

And that's all she wrote, there really isn't anything more fancy about the **Slider**, it just does exactly what it says on the tin. As with the other controls/components, you aren't restricted by Unity's default layout (the images don't even need to be visible), go wild and see what options you can come up with, slip slide away.

Ancient scrolls

As we enter the twilight of this chapter, we take a look at one last control, the **Scrollbar**.

> Personally I've always questioned the reason why the **Slider** and **Scrollbar** are separate controls They perform almost the same function with only a few key differences. Maybe it's for further modularization (the current **Scroll Rect** component will only use Scrollbar's and not Slider's) or ties back to the legacy GUI, or even to maintain consistency with other UI frameworks, who knows?

Where the **Scrollbar** differs from the **Slider**, is that it provides either a freeform movement along the range (such as the **Slider**) or a fixed step movement, allowing you to have fixed pages of content to view. It also has only one **Rect Handle** by default, as the GameObjects **Rect Transform** is used to set the bounds. Looking at the **Scrollbar** in the editor, we see the following:

As you can see in the **Hierarchy**, it looks very similar to the **Slider** but a little more cut down.

In the **Inspector**, we see a very similar story:

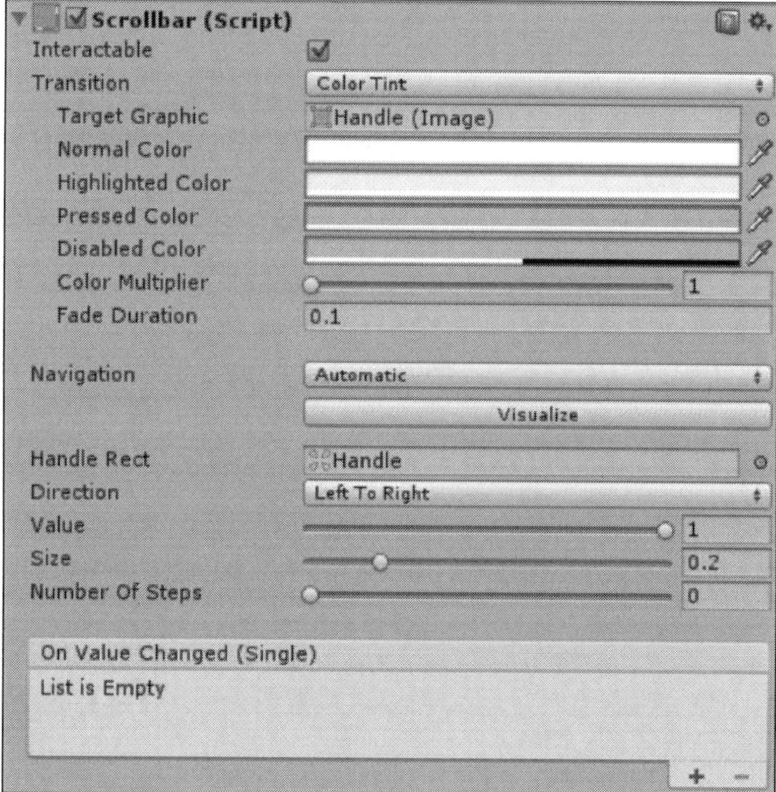

Here, for the **Scrollbar**, we have very similar settings, which work the same as the **Slider** with a few obvious exceptions:

- **Value**: This differs from the **Slider** as it can only move incrementally between `0` and `1`.
- **Size**: This setting alters the width (when moving horizontally) or the height (when moving vertically) of the Scrollbar's **Handle**. The control will then adjust its calculations for the values the control will expose.
- **Number of Steps**: If you want a fixed set of slots or steps, then by setting this option it will constrain the value's movements to this number (anything less than two does nothing!), If you set it to `6` then the value option will increase in 1/6th's across its scale from `0` to `1` for example, `0, 0.2, 0.4, 0.6, 0.8, 1`.

In the following example, we'll walk through one of the intended uses of this control with a **Scroll Rect**.

Scrolling, Rect'ing, and Masking, oh my

As a nice little example of what we have covered so far, let's throw together a couple of components to make a handy image viewer (yeah I know, it's not that game related but I thought it would be fun for a change), as shown here:

You will also find this example included in the Code Download that accompanies this title.

Building this example is (like most of the basic features of the new **UI** system) very easy; if we look at the project hierarchy for the completed example, we see this:

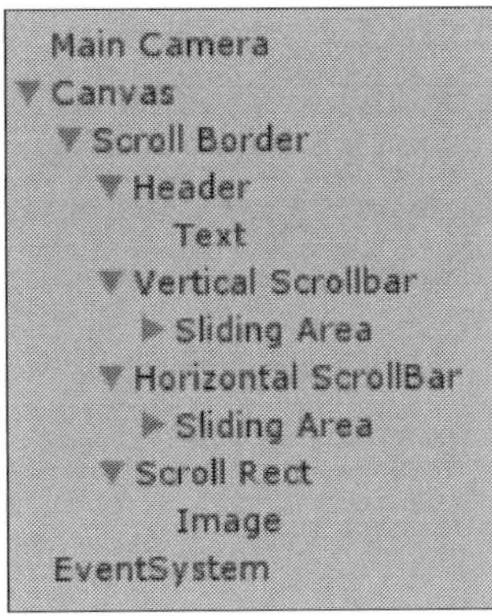

For this example, we create the following:

1. An empty GameObject for the boundaries of the **Scrollable** area. I also added an **Image** control (using one of the backgrounds from the UI Pack we used earlier) to have a border around the image area for effect. Name this GameObject **Scroll Border** and set its dimensions to 400x200.
2. Add an **Image** and a child **Text** control for the header positioned above the main **Scroll Border** (yes, you can place UI GameObjects outside of their parents').
3. Then add two **Scrollbar** controls to the right and bottom of the **Scroll Border**. Resize the **Scrollbars** to fit, don't rotate them! Then set the **Scrollbar Direction** appropriately for the Vertical or Horizontal nature of the bar. For example, I set the Vertical bar to **BottomToTop** and the Horizontal to the default **LeftToRight**.
4. Add an Empty GameObject called **Scroll Rect** as a child to the **Scroll Border** and resize it to the inner dimensions of the **Scroll Border**. (Since my border has a border image, I set it slightly smaller to the parent so the border will be visible). This will be our **Scroll Rect** control but let's add its content child next.
5. Add an **Image** as a child to the **Scroll Rect** GameObject; this is for the content that you want to be scrollable. Make its Rect dimensions larger than the parent (say 1024 x 448). I used the **Unity5 logo** image (provided in the downloadable assets) as the **Source Image** for the **Image** component. (The Unity Logo image is a 1024 x 448 image, far larger than the **Scroll Rect** dimensions of approximately 400 x 200).
6. Now returning to the **Scroll Rect** GameObject, we add a **Scroll Rect** component, setting its **Content** property to the child **Image** GameObject we created and also attaching the two **Scrollbars** to the **Scrollbar** properties of the **Scroll Rect** (just drag them from the project hierarchy to the relevant properties of the **Scroll Rect** component).
7. Finally we add a UI **Mask** component and an UI **Image** component to the **Scroll Rect** GameObject so we can only see the part of the image underneath, that is within the boundaries of the **Scroll Rect**.

[We have to add an **Image** for the **Mask** component to work as it works with the **Graphics Raycaster** to only render the masked area.]

The **Scrollbars** are completely optional of course as we can manipulate the scrollable area either with the **Scrollbars** or just by touching and dragging within the **Scroll Rect** area.

This kind of pattern could be used for any scrollable type of UI, from inventory items to Mini-maps, it's very flexible.

Navigation

We close his chapter with a quick walk-through control navigation, or the ability to change focus from one interactable control to another using the keyboard.

> At the time of writing, tabbing between controls is not supported. Selectable's are only navigated between each other using direction keys (up, down, left, and right); there is no Control order to tab through. You could of course write your own system (for which there is an example in *Chapter 6, Working with the UI Source*).

As we have seen in many of the inspector screenshots earlier in this chapter, most controls come with built-in **Navigation** behavior properties including a button called **Visualize** to view the navigation in the editor, as shown here:

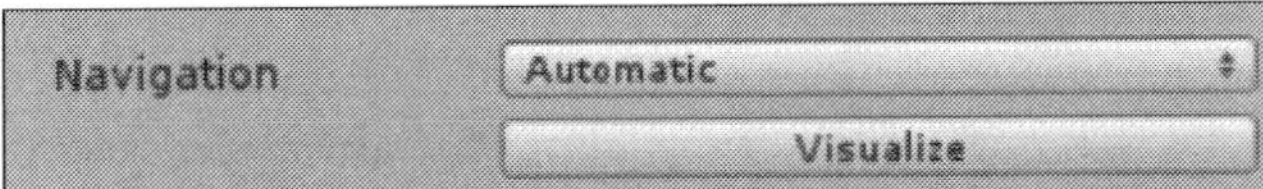

> Note: **Navigation** features are limited to those **UI** controls that implement the **Selectable** component, be it the built-in controls such as buttons, sliders, toggles, and so on, or those controls you build yourself.

By default (automatic), Unity will navigate from control to control by its nearest neighbor in the direction the user navigates (up/down/left/right); if we align controls vertically and horizontally, this would produce the following navigation pattern:

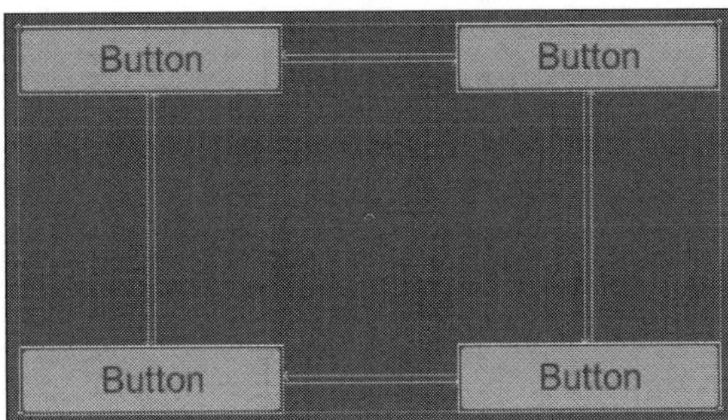

With each movement moving to the next control in that direction, if we rearrange the controls in a cross style pattern, then this nearest neighbor pattern becomes a little more obvious:

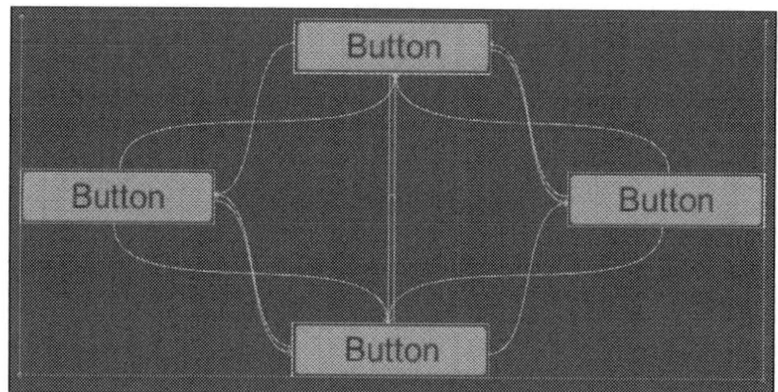

As you can see in the preceding screenshot, Unity does a good job of ensuring navigation flows unilaterally between each control; if you want a little more control, however, there are a few other options using the **Navigation** selection:

- **Automatic**: (shown above)
- **Horizontal**: This limits the navigation to only left and right as shown here:

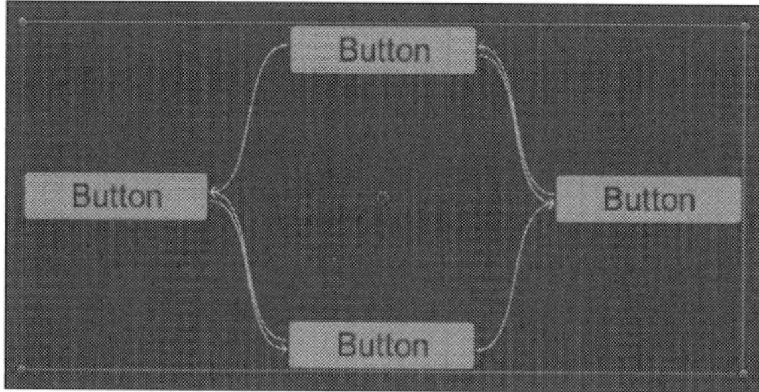

- **Vertical**: This limits the navigation to an up/down movement as shown here:

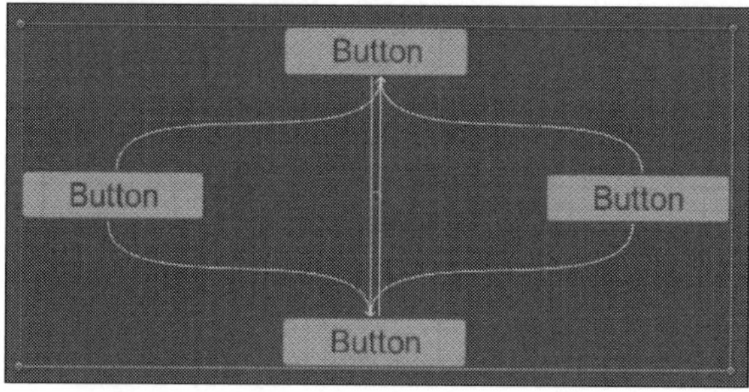

- **Explicit**: If none of the automatic options really take your fancy and your control setup is a little bit more bizzare, for situations such as this there is the **Explicit** option. This basically allows you to specifically select which control will be navigated to, based on the direction selected by the layer. If you look at the inspector, you can see this is very easy to configure:

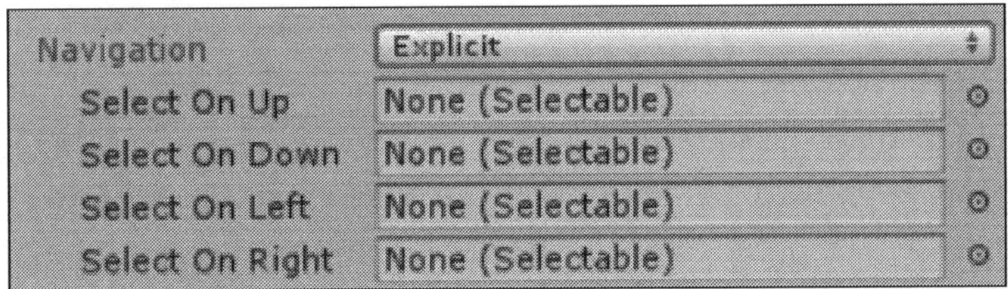

- Just point each direction at the **Selectable UI** control that you want, which is completely optional, you don't have to configure a direction if you don't want to.
- **None**: Nothing, absolutely nothing, do nothing ever, nothing works. You get the picture, navigation is disabled.

A word on shaders

A last word on our wonderful world of UI components is that you will note that each and every one has a **Material** property. Through this, you can apply a shader directly to each component by adding a custom material with a shader attached. Granted shaders are a bit out of scope for this book, so feel free to play to your heart's content.

Summary

Well, that was fun and we have still only just scratched the surface of what is possible with the new UI system. We've looked at all the *out-of-the-box* controls and some potential uses along with the default selectable navigation system.

Hopefully, you can start to glean the ultimate flexibility of the new **UI** system and its component based makeup. It's now even easier to strip down what is available and start expanding on or just writing your own controls.

Since the new UI is open source, you will also have access to all the code that goes into the new UI system, making this expandable journey even easier.

In this chapter, we covered the following topics:

- More framework stuff
- All the base controls
- How controls have been manufactured and laid out
- The possibilities of making your own controls
- Navigation

In the next chapter, we'll delve deeper into the layout features and the awesome anchoring system before returning back to the very beginning. We will also take a look at the different Canvas modes available and some truly interesting possibilities with the new UI, including placing dynamic UI directly into your 3D world, crafting away.

4
Anchors Away

In the next two chapters, we start to work a lot more closely with our UI. Sure, we can throw a bunch of controls at the screen and arrange them here and there, but what happens when the screen resizes, the perspective changes, or it's run by someone with an 80 inch screen; what happens to our UI then?

With game development, we usually take this into account with our game world, just shrink and/or resize it to fit the device. The same cannot be said however for our UI. Text can become unreadable, and buttons may become too small or too big or even become unusable. There truly isn't one size that fits all, or is there?

Through the new Anchoring system in Unity UI, we can finally build a dynamic and responsive design that will look like the way we want it to, no matter the resolution it is displayed in. This is then complemented very well with a scaling component that slots straight onto our Canvases.

The following is the list of topics that will be covered in this chapter:

- Positioning
- Anchors
- Scaling UI with the Canvas Scaler
- Building a responsive health bar
- Attempting to sail our ship through dangerous waters

Dropping Anchor

I wonder whether I'll be able to keep up with the nautical theme for this entire chapter.

As we venture into this strange land, we can begin to look at what Unity gives us out of the box and where to find all these Anchor settings before we delve into what they really mean.

If you recall, back in *Chapter 2, Building Layouts*, we introduced the new **Rect Transform** component that replaces the traditional transform component for UI elements, which looks like this:

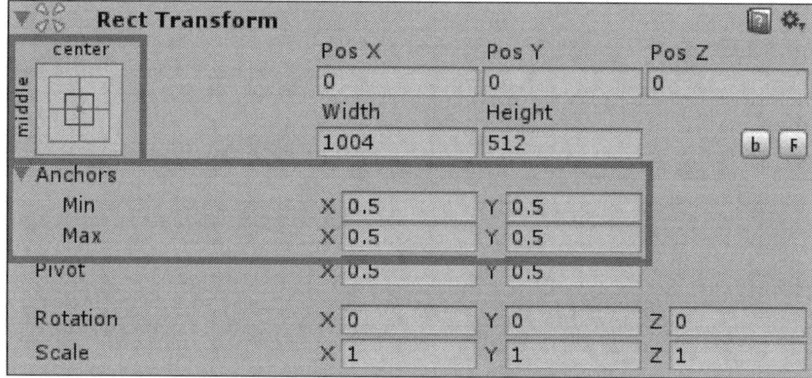

Highlighted in this screenshot are the new Anchor properties that will take a **Rect Transform** and bind it to a certain area of a parent **Rect Transform**. I say parent because an **Anchor** can be set against the borders of any parent UI GameObject, not just a Canvas..

Clicking on the top-left graphic also reveals the **Anchor Presets** (or **Common Configurations** as Unity likes to refer to them), as you can see here:

These Presets provide a quick and easy way to apply the most common patterns to bind your UI within the Canvas. However, you are not limited in any way because you can also manipulate the Anchors whichever way you want to create your desired effect or the UI layout.

When we look at the scene view, we also see the editor handles for the **Anchor** that depict where in the **Canvas** space the **Anchor** points are bound to (these being the top-left, top-right, bottom-left, and bottom-right corners).

The Anchor handles

So what does it all mean? What do these darn Anchor things actually do? We'll cover these with an example in its use and by the end, hopefully, you'll get the picture.

Put a nail in it, and trim the sails

Starting with fixing the UI to a specific point, we begin with the foundation to understand how **Anchors** work:

1. Create a new scene and add a **Slider** control to it using **Menu** | **GameObject** | **UI** | **Slider**.
    - This will create a **Slider** control in our scene together with a **Canvas** and an **EventSystem**, nice and neat.
    - In its default setting, the Anchor is placed at the center of the **Canvas**.

It is relative to the **Canvas** because the **Canvas** is the parent of the **Slider** control. If you have the **Slider** as the child of another **Rect Transform** GameObject, then it would be relative to that parent and not the **Canvas**.

- This means that whatever the resolution, the **Slider** will always be drawn exactly with the same dimensions from the **Anchor** point to the pivot point of the UI GameObject (by default, at the center), no matter how the screen is resized, as you can see here:

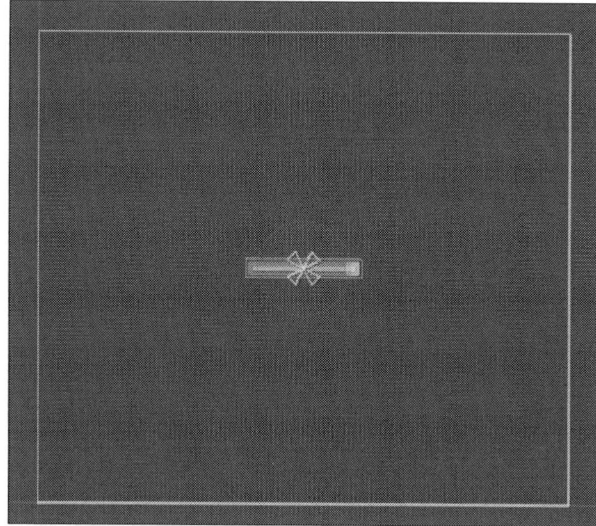

2. Next, click on the **Anchor Presets** graphics and select the **top** and **left** presets, as shown here:

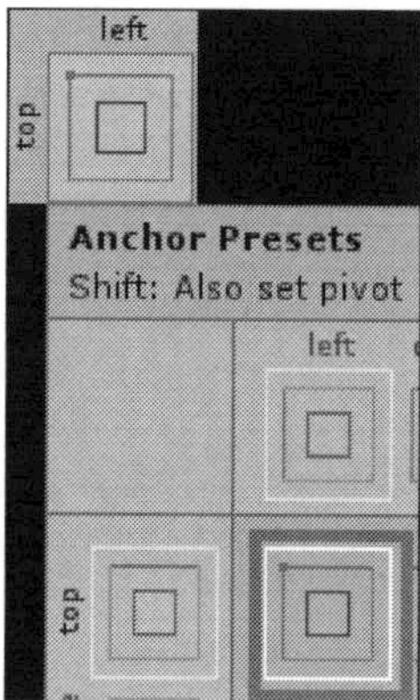

The top-left preset in the Common Configurations panel

This will reposition the Anchor for the **Slider** to the **top** and **left** corner of the **Canvas**.

[If you also hold down the *ALT* key when selecting **Anchor Preset**, it will additionally reposition the **Slider** control to the top-left corner of the **Canvas** as well.]

So what did this actually do for us? Couldn't we have just moved the **Rect Transform** of the **Slider** to the top-left corner?

Well, let's examine that. If we leave the **Anchor** at the center of the screen and just move the **Slider** to the top-left of the screen, then when the screen is resized down, the slider will retain the same distance from the center as it did before. This now results in the **Slider** being drawn off the screen, as you can see here:

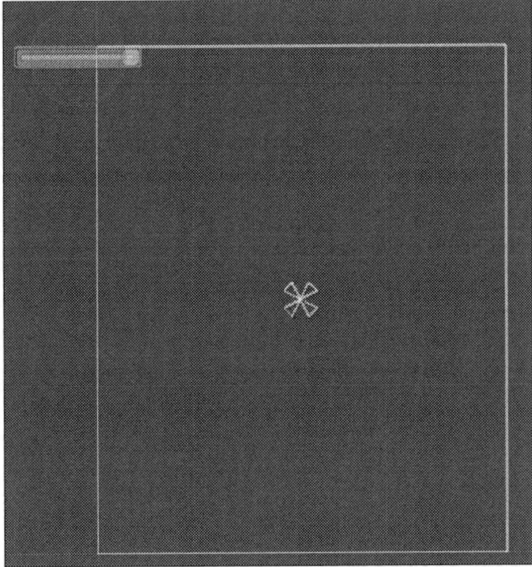

Screen width resized down - without being Anchored, the slider does not move

[It is worth pointing out that the **Anchor** holds the position of the UI directly to its **Pivot** point, not an edge or corner.]

However, by then moving the **Anchor** to the top-left corner of the screen, when we resize our screen, the **Slider** will remain where we put it simply because it is now Anchored to the top-left corner, as shown here:

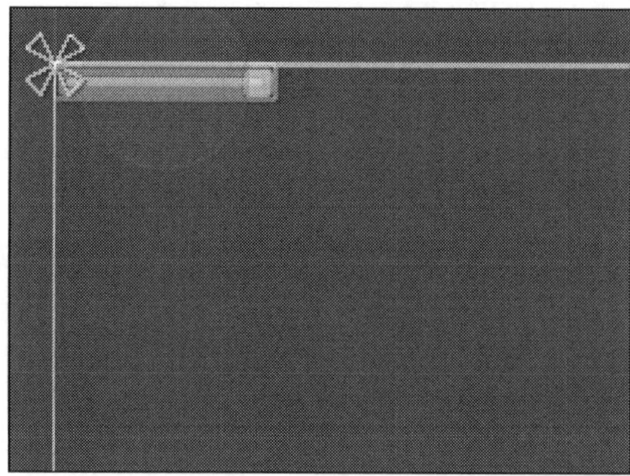

With the Slider Anchored to the top-left corner, it moves with the top-left when the screen is resized

Remember, if you hold down the *Alt* key when selecting a preset, it will also move the GameObject to the Anchor position as well, not just the **Anchor**.

This works for any position within a UI component's parent container, fixing the **Pivot** point of the UI GameObject to a set distance relative to its **Anchor**.

This helps us immensely when we create a screen the way we want it, position it where we like, and guarantee that all the elements within it will be positioned absolutely, for example:

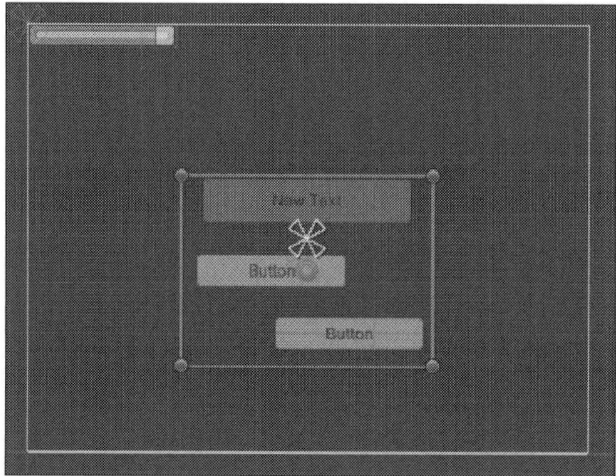

Here we have the following:

- An empty GameObject container with its **Anchor** set to the middle of the **Canvas**
- A **Panel** added to the top of the container, Anchored in the top-middle corner
- A **Text** control added as a child of the Panel, Anchored at the center of the Panel
- A **Button** Anchored in the top-left corner of the container, positioned at an offset
- A **Button** Anchored in the bottom-right corner of the container, positioned near the bottom-right corner

Now, no matter how the screen resizes, the position of all the elements within the Container will always remain the same, much the same way as if the entire container was an image.

Note though, if we resize the container, we can start to see the limitations of just using fixed **Anchor** points, as we can see here:

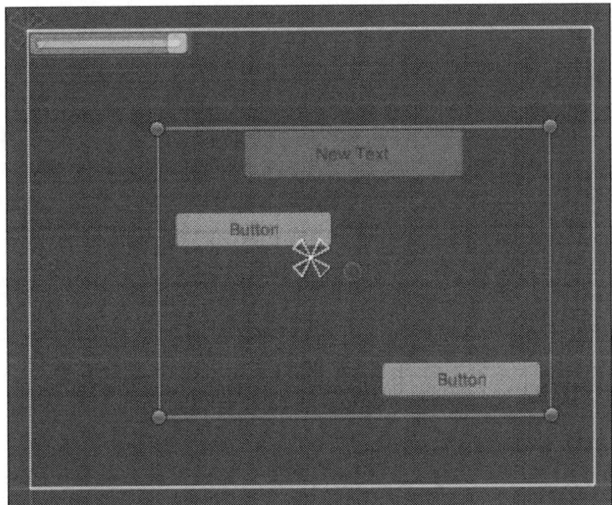

GameObjects remain locked with their Pivot point's relative to their Anchors

With the Container size increased, the buttons remain at their fixed point towards their respective corners, and the **Panel** is the same size fixed to the top.

So, what else can we do with this fancy Anchoring system? Can we make it so that resizing the Container does not lose our intended placement?

Stretch it, bend it

Now that we have mastered pinning our UI in place, how about some dynamic resizing? Time to set our course straight and true, *Warp factor 5, Mr. Sulu.* (Darn it! That's Star Trek, not very nautical is it?)

In a lot of UI designs, it is just not enough to have objects drawn in a particular position; we want them to always fill a particular portion of the screen, say 50 percent of the width. In these cases, just having it in a fixed place is no good if the screen resizes down below the width of the element we are trying to draw.

As an example, let's wipe out what we have done so far and build a health bar. The requirements set down by our really critical graphics designer are as follows:

- It should always be centered at the top of the screen.
- It should have a 20-pixel space between the top of the screen and the health bar.
- It should take up approximately 50 percent of the width of the screen on all devices. (But I'm targeting Android; that's impossible! Far too many resolutions to handle with any UI □)
- It should be 25 pixels high.
- It should fill from the left, with left being 0 and right being 100 health.

A simple request from our designer, but how do we achieve this in the new UI without a lot of complicated scripting? Easy, with our Anchors.

Let's start by adding a **Slider** to a new scene; in the example code, I called it **Resizing** UI.

We'll add a **Slider** and then configure its properties to give it a health bar look and feel (with my poor UX skills and lack of color coordination):

1. Add a new **Slider** to the Scene.
2. Expand the **Slider** control in the hierarchy and delete the **Handle Slide Area** (which will also delete its child **Handle** GameObject).
3. Select the **Slider** and click on the **Handle Rect** property; if it says Missing **Rect Transform**, then hit *delete* (to clear the property as we have no handle).

4. Set the **Target Graphic** of the **Slider** to the **Fill GameObject** by either using the **Object Selector** button to the right of the property or dragging the **Fill GameObject** from the hierarchy to the property. (This is just so when the user's mouse hovers over the control it will be highlighted; this is optional).
5. Set the Slider **Width** property to `200`.
6. Set the Slider **Height** property to `25`.
7. Select the **Background GameObject in the Hierarchy** and set the **Color** property of the Image to `Black` (the slider background).
8. (optional) Resize the **Rect Transform** of the **Background** GameObject to fill the area of the **Slider** GameObject).
9. Select the Slider again and set the **Max Value** property to `100`.
10. Check the box for **Whole Numbers** on the **Slider**.
11. Select the **Fill GameObject** in the project hierarchy and set the **Color** property of the image to `Green`. (Green is good for health, isn't it?)
12. (optional) Resize the **Rect Transform** of the **FillArea** GameObject to fill the area of the **Slider** GameObject).

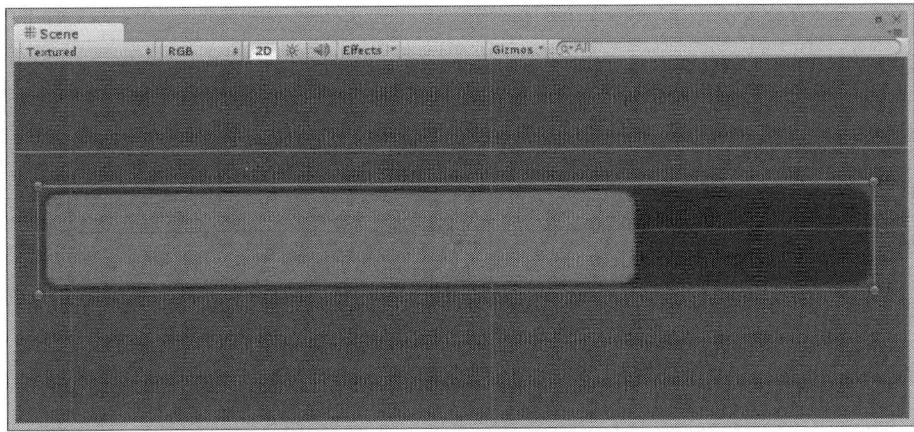

A screenshot showing the health bar Slider with its value at 80 (80%)

So we have our health bar; what about our other requirements? For these, we'll use our stretching Anchors. Select the **Slider** in the hierarchy and then click on the **Anchor Presets** button. Once it's open, select the **top** and **stretch** option, as shown in following screenshot:

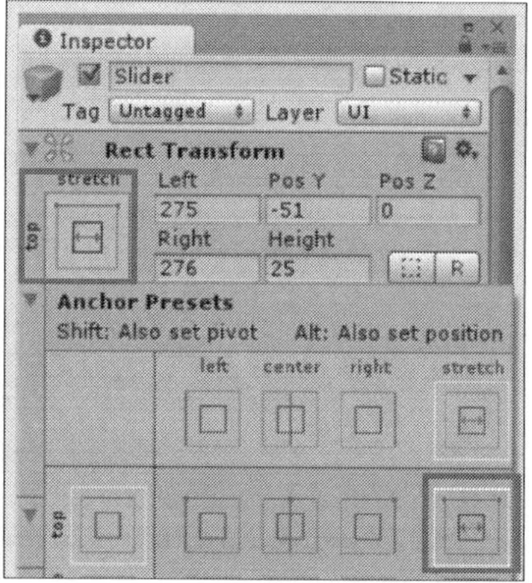

Now you have two options when selecting the preset: you can just click on it to alter the **Anchor** positions, or you can hold the *Alt* key and also move the GameObject, which will give you either of the following results:

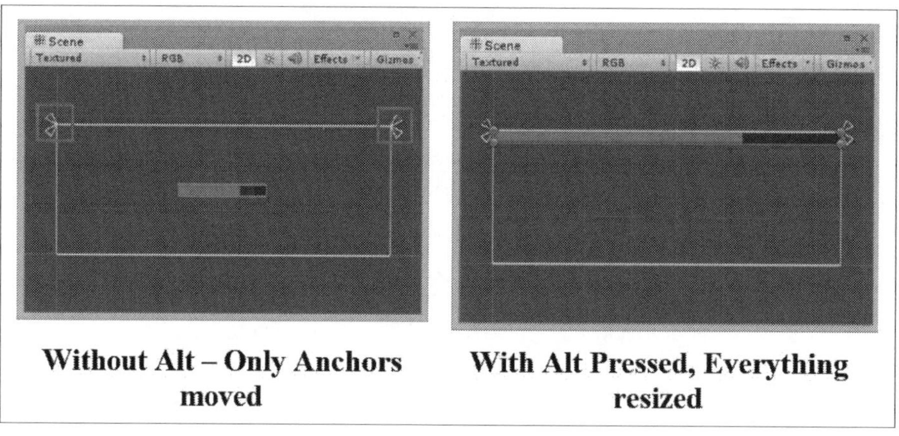

Without Alt – Only Anchors moved

With Alt Pressed, Everything resized

As you can see, in both instances, we still need to do some work to position our health bar how we want it to be; you just choose the path of least resistance for what you want to achieve.

To finish off, let's finalize the settings of **Rect Transform** for our **Slider** to position it how we want it to be. You will also notice that because we are now using Stretched Anchors, the **Rect Transform** position values have been updated to those shown in the following screenshot:

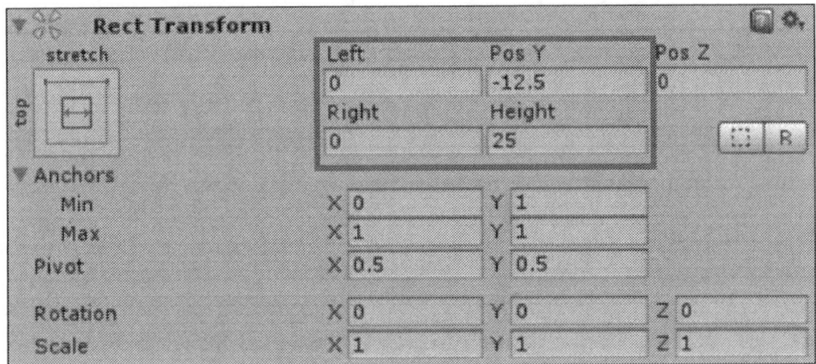

Position values after stretching the health bar

Because the **Slider** GameObject is now has stretched **Anchors** on the **X** axis, the **Pos X** and **Width** properties have been replaced with **Left** and **Right**. These now indicate how much padding is there between the GameObject's **Rect Transform** border and the left- and right-hand side areas of the screen.

If you set **Rect Transform Anchors** to the **stretch** mode on **Y** axis, the **Pos Y** and **Height** settings will be replaced with the top and bottom settings instead. If you set it to stretch the area completely, then all four settings will be updated.

If you now update the **Rect Transorm** values for the **Slider** with those shown in the following screenshot, we will achieve the laudy goals our designer required, well almost:

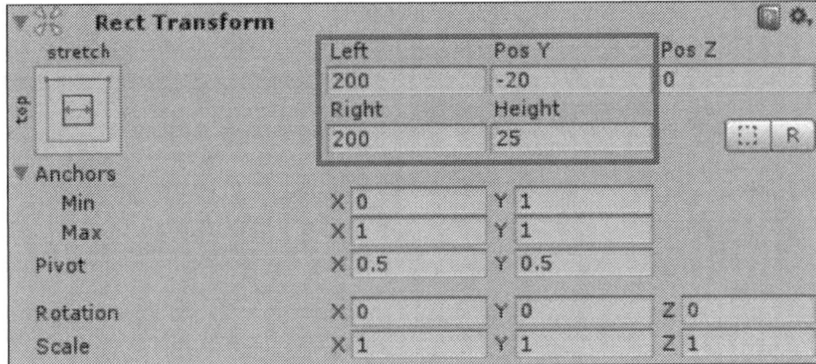

Updated position values

If you wish, you can now go back to the **Slider** and stretch the **Anchors** for the **Background** and **FillArea** GameObjects to make them fill the entire Slider.

The designer asked for 20-pixel distance between the top of the screen and the health bar, but at present, it's actually about 9 pixels from the top. (Why oh why? It's set to 20 in the preceding screenshot, isn't it!)

The reason is simple if you recall from earlier: the **Anchors** are positioned relative to the **Pivot** point of the **Rect Transform**, and our **Pivot** is still set to the default, in the center of our **Slider** ☺.

To correct this, include half the height of the Slider's GameObject in your **Pos Y** value of the Slider's **Rect Transform** (it's negative because we are counting from the top of the screen), edit the **Pivot** point to be at the top of the **Slider** by setting the value of **Pivot Y** to `1`, or use the **Rect Tool** in **Pivot** mode and drag the **Pivot** point (blue circle) to the top of the **Rect Transform** (which is what I did in this example).

Just be sure to check that the **Pos Y** value is correct after editing the **Pivot** point and that it hasn't moved the **Rect Transform**. If it has, then update it again to `-20`.

So we have met our goal; time to get paid, right? Actually, no because our designer simply failed to mention one little thing: it's meant to also run on a 4-inch Android device. This means our previous settings will not scale down enough and our health bar will not be drawn all because the left and right padding values are set to `200`. When the screen is scaled down, there won't be enough space left to draw the slider, whoops!

Note, you do not have to use just the **Anchor Presets**. If you wish you can also alter the **Anchors** manually by dragging each corner of the **Anchor** handle to the position you wish. In most cases the presets are enough but if you want more, you can just Do it Yourself!

Scaling and resolution

Time for a bit of tilt and sail.

If you recall, in *Chapter 2, Building Layouts*, we made reference to the **Canvas Scaler**, an automagical component that tells our **Canvas** how to draw the top-level **Canvas** to the screen. The **Canvas Scaler** is automatically added to a new **Canvas** when it is added to the scene, if you need to re-add it simply click **Add Component** | **Layout** | **Canvas Scaler** in the **Inspector** with the **Canvas** selected.

Working with the constant default

The default setting of the **Canvas Scaler** component for your top-level **Canvas** is **Constant Pixel Size** mode, as shown in the following screenshot:

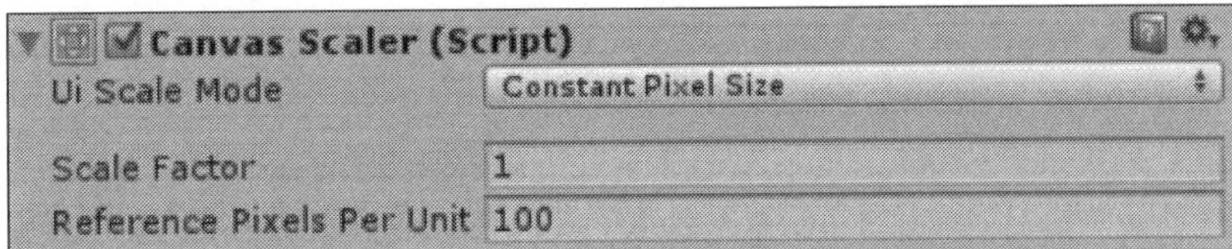

This just lets us set the default Sprite's **Scale Factor** and a **Reference Pixels Per Unit** value (for pixel-perfect drawing if the **Pixels Per Unit** setting is used in your sprites) for the **Canvas**, making it as steadfast as a ship run into the ground—this boat isn't moving.

> The **Pixels Per Unit** setting on a sprite sets how many in-game units a sprite takes up (how big it is in relation to your other sprites). This is then used by the **Reference Pixels Per Unit** value that decides how many pixels are in 1 game unit; `100` pixels in this case makes 1 game unit of width and height.
>
> For more information on this, check the Unity documentation at `http://docs.unity3d.com/Manual/class-TextureImporter.html`.

So what does this mean for our fancy health bar and other UI elements? Well, if we resize our gameplay screen, the result is fairly obvious.

If we compare what our **Canvas** looks like at the moment in various resolutions using the **Constant Pixel Size** mode, this is what we will see:

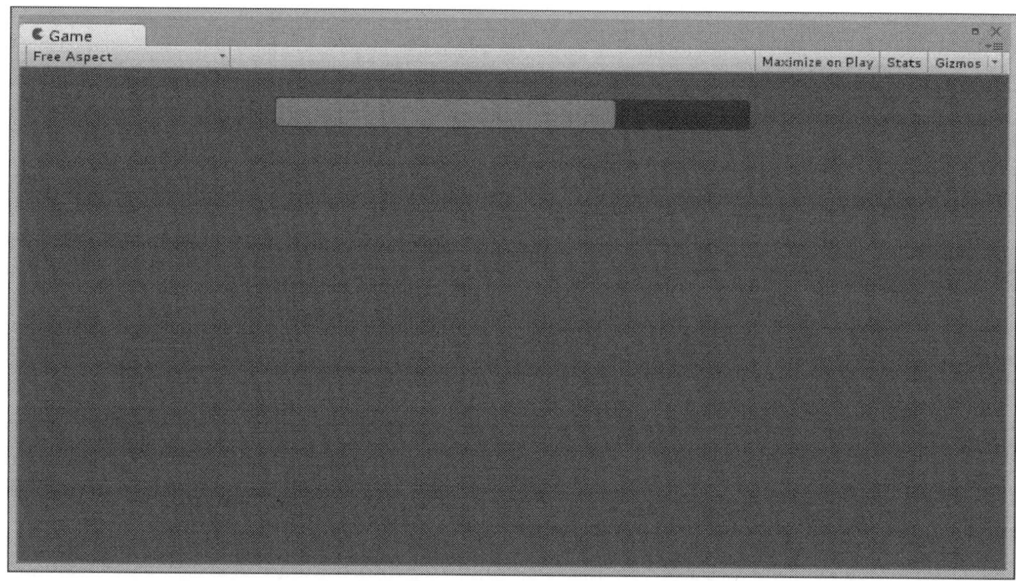

Slider as seen in the Free Aspect view using Constant Pixel Size

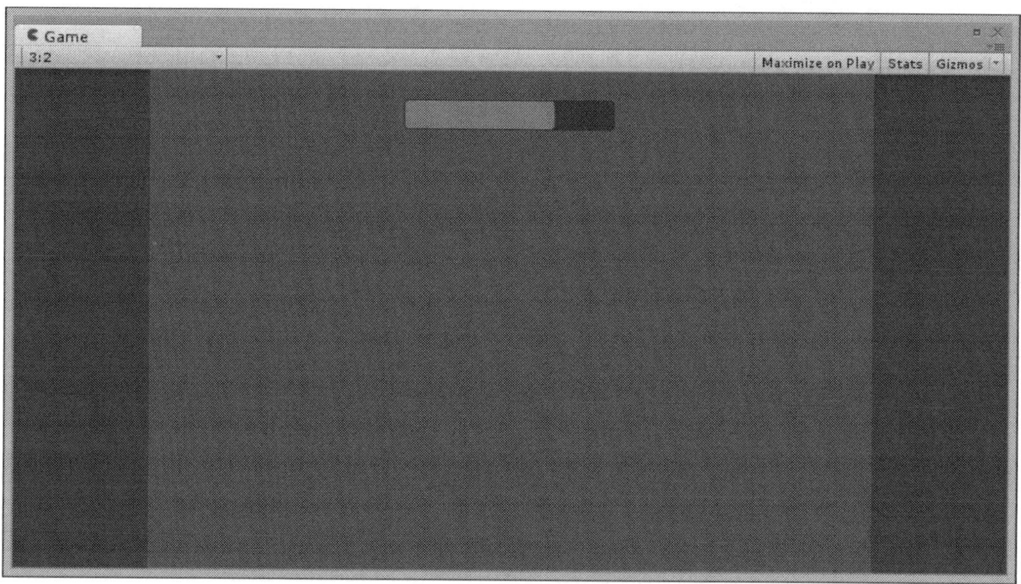

Slider as seen in the 3:2 aspect using Constant Pixel Size

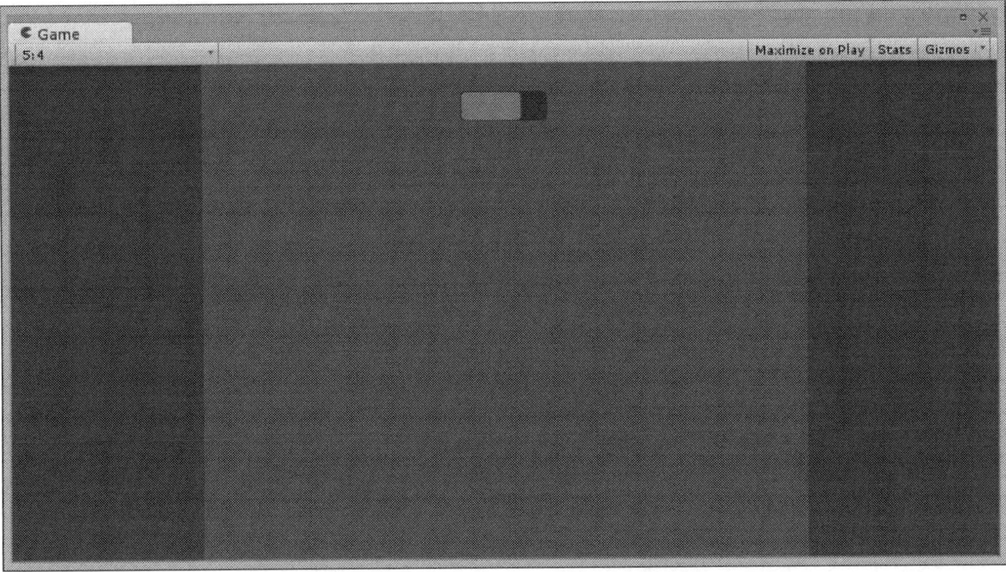

Slider as seen in a the 5:4 aspect using Constant Pixel Size

As you can see, using the **Constant Pixel Size** mode, every value we entered is adhered to regardless of the display resolution. So, the width of the **Slider** is dynamically updated because of its Anchors; however, the padding around the **Slider** remains constant.

As this is not desirable, let's look at how we can make our UI behave better when the screen is resized. This is important not just to work with smaller screens, but also when your game is displayed on huge 50 inch screens with desktops and consoles.

Scaling to my view

The next option we have in our arsenal with the **Canvas Scaler** is to use what is referred to as **Reference Resolution**. This simply means that the UI we are presenting will always have the same resolution on screen, no matter what its screen size is, setting our course straight and true.

In this mode the entire **Canvas** will make itself fit in the screen using our own preferred resolution scale. Looking at **Canvas Scaler** in **Scale With Screen Size** mode, we see the following:

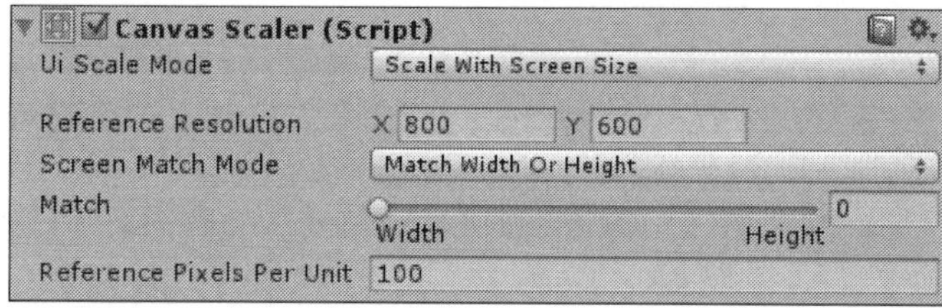

By setting up our preferred **Reference Resolution** to a virtual **Width** (**X**) and **Height** (**Y**), we can control how the canvas will be drawn. With the **Screen Match Mode**, we can also determine on which axis scaling should be controlled. Just the **Width**, the **Height** or a factor in-between using the **Match** slider; alternatively, we can just set it to only **Expand** or only **Shrink** if you so wish, all of which was explained in great detail in *Chapter 2, Building Layouts*.

So, using the **Scale With Screen Size** mode, we ensure what we originally configured in our UI will always look the same as shown in the following screenshots (using a **Match** width/height setting with a 0.5 **Match** value, balanced):

If we revisit our comparisons, they now look like this, using **Scale With Screen Size Canvas Scaler** (using a Match width/height setting with a 0.5 Match value, balanced):

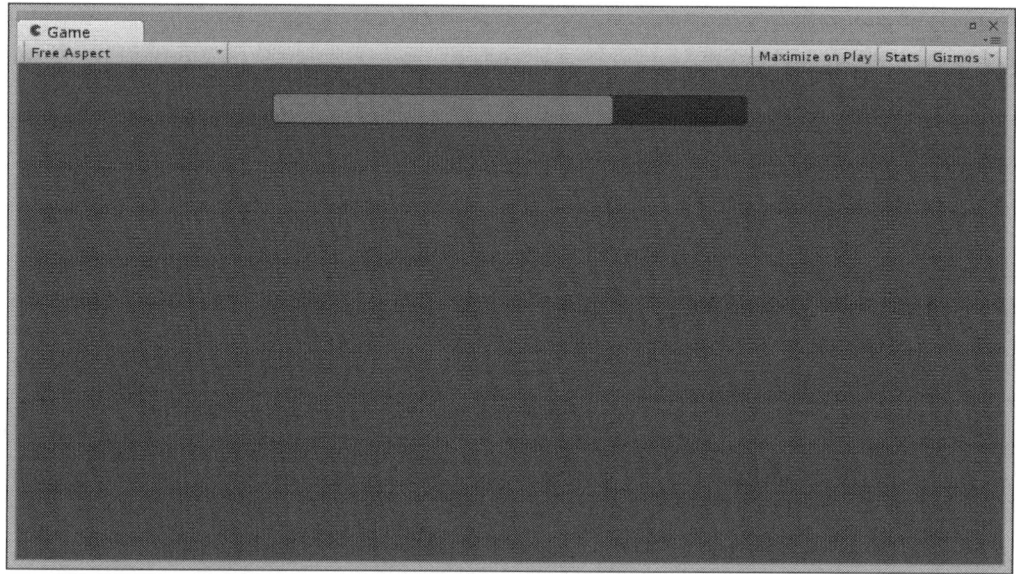

Slider as seen in the Free Aspect view using Scale With Screen Size

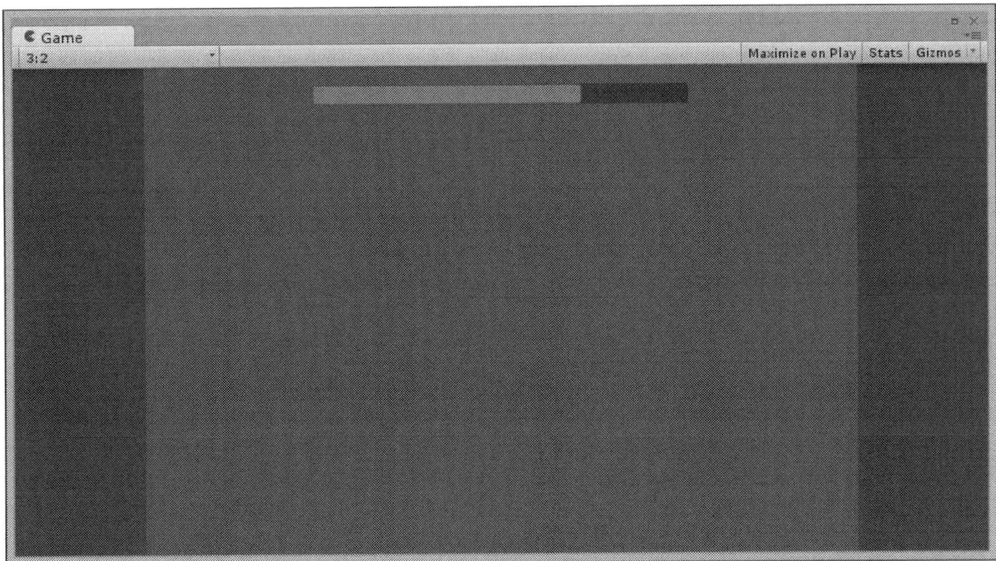

Slider as seen in the 3:2 aspect using Scale With Screen Size

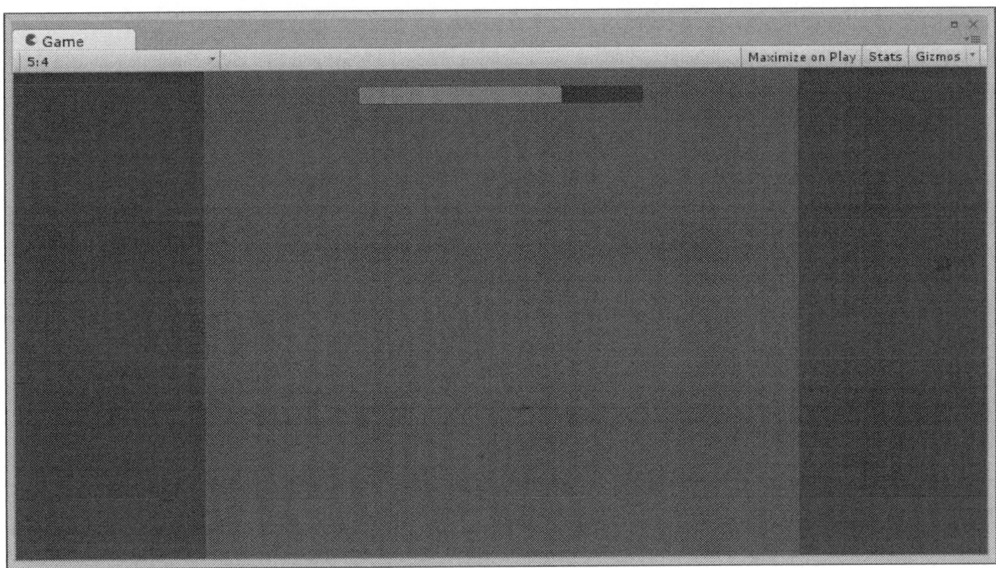

Slider as seen in the 5:4 aspect using Scale With Screen Size

This gives a much better result than not using any manual scaling at all, but as you can see, there is still some scaling going on: the bar is being shrunk to fit the desired area. In some cases this may not be the desired effect. We could increase the **Reference Resolution** but this would just make it a lot smaller on small screens and crisper on a large screen. It is a fine balance, but there is another option to consider.

Getting physical

When you want to get things exactly how you want them and when you want them, the final gate is to work with pixels. Shaders do it and meshes do this when you're working at the indices level.

By setting the **Canvas Scaler** mode to **Constant Physical Size**, you are in complete control of your destiny, as you can see here:

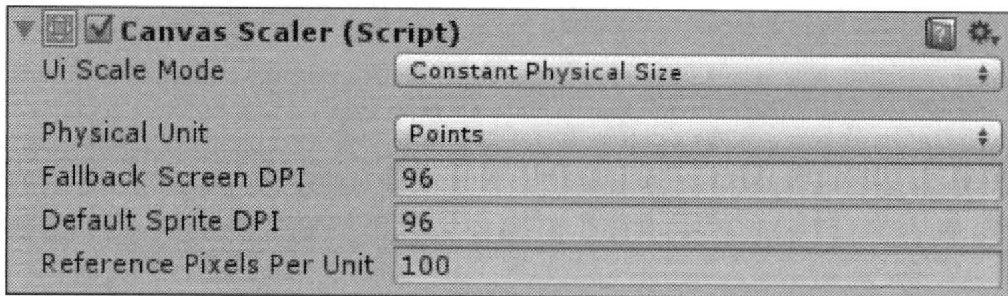

You are so much in control that you can even set your own measurements the way you want to, from Points (effectively, individual pixels) to real-world measurements in **Centimeters** and **Millimeters**. Then, you can set a default screen scale in **DPI** (or measurement per inch really), which decides what the full screen aspect would be.

On first reflection, however, changing our **Canvas Scaler** over to **Constant Physical Size** gives us some unintentional results, as you can see here (iceberg ahead):

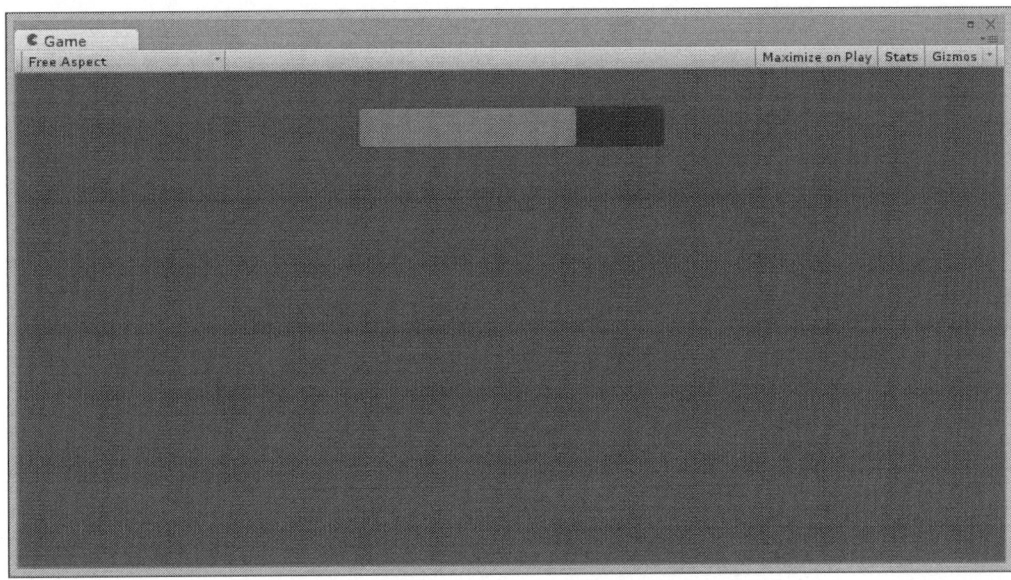

Slider as seen in the Free Aspect view using Constant Physical Size

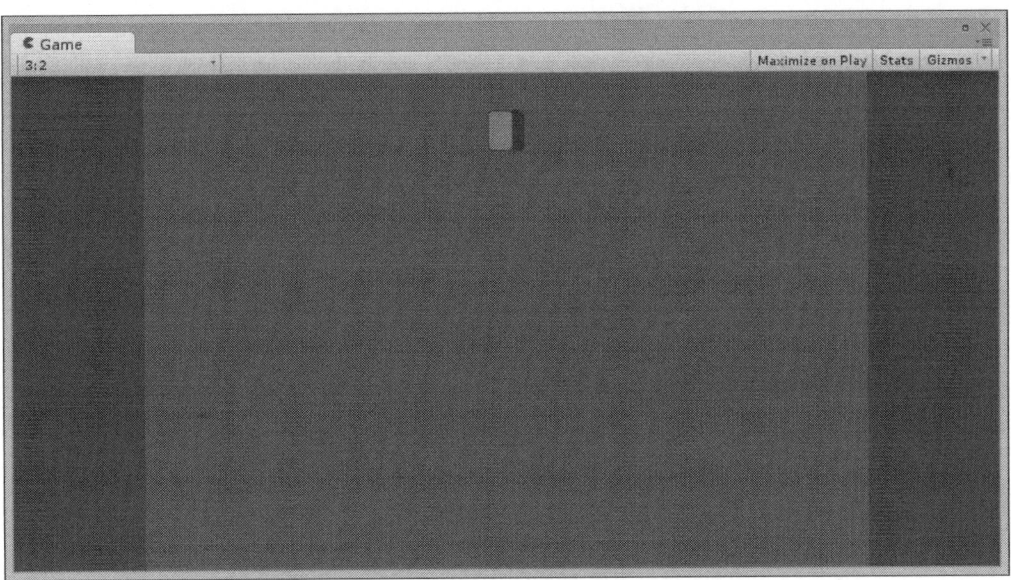

Slider as seen in the 3:2 aspect using Constant Physical Size

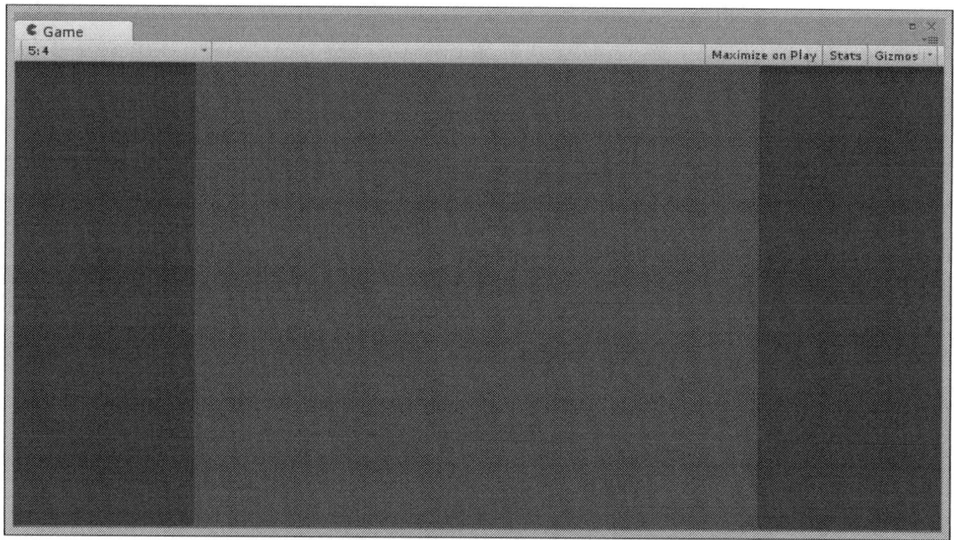

Slider as seen in the 5:4 aspect using Constant Physical Size

You will notice that in the 5:4 screen ratio, the slider has vanished completely. This is just because our **Slider** now has a negative width due to the padding and position values used on the slider's **Rect Transform**. If you check the scene view, you will see the following:

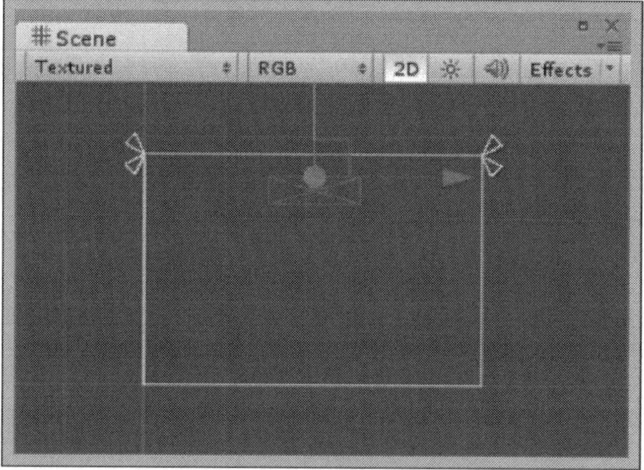

As you can see, the **Slider** is now drawn with a red cross; this shows that it is being rendered incorrectly. Effectively, its left and right edges have been folded over onto themselves (think of it like folding a piece of paper over itself), and because UI cannot be rendered backwards, it cannot be drawn.

The reason for this is quite simple. All our measurements for position and padding are now completely wrong; they simply haven't been scaled or factored into the new type of measurement we have selected using our **Canvas Scaler**.

> Granted, if you are starting a new Canvas and selected the Physically sized **Canvas Scaler** from the beginning, you won't have these issues simply because you started with the correct measurements.
>
> However, if you switch to using a different **Ui Scale Mode**, you will have to resize your elements again.

If we simply return and update the Rect Transform's **Left** and **Right** values to `100` (instead of the previous value of `200`), our **Slider** will again be positioned correctly and give the following results when scaled:

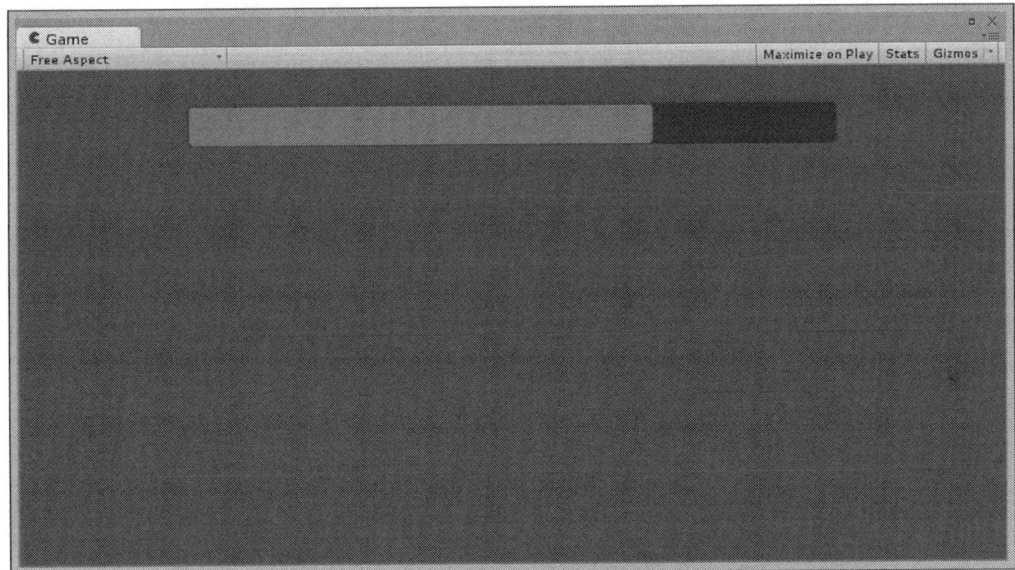

Slider as seen in the Free Aspect view using Constant Physical Size, that is now scaled correctly

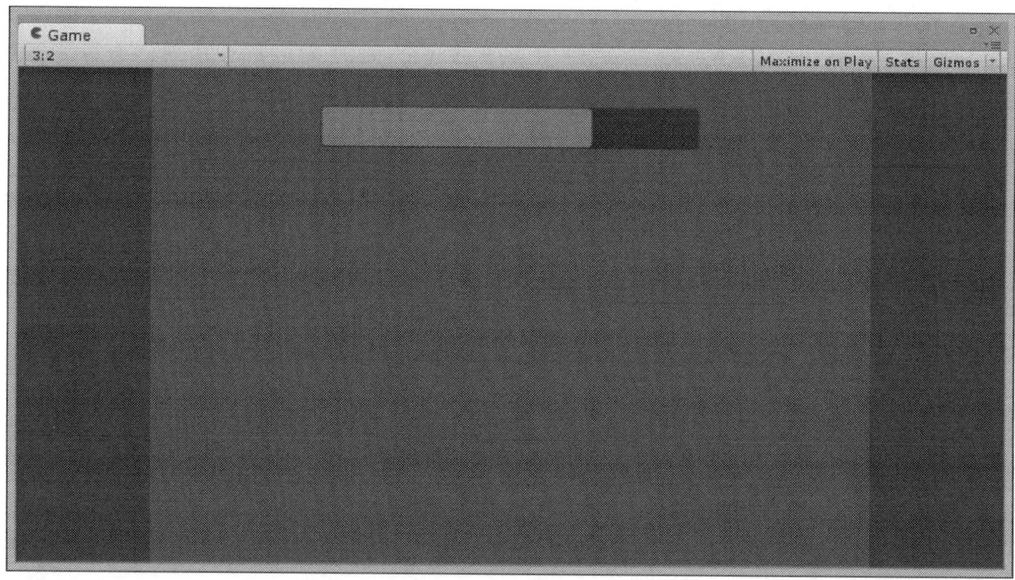

Slider as seen in the 3:2 aspect using Constant Physical Size, that is now scaled correctly

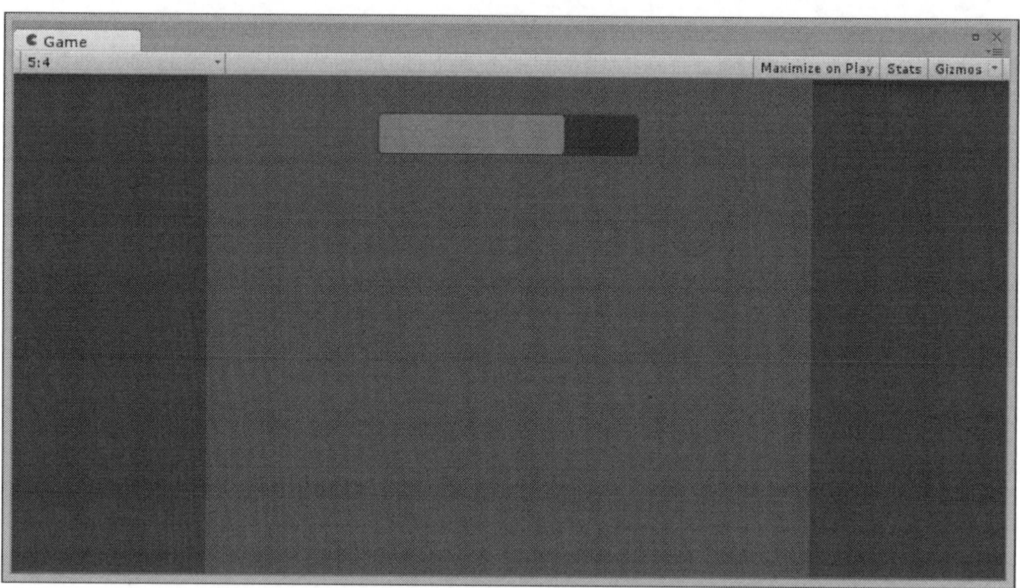

Slider as seen in the 5:4 aspect using Constant Physical Size that is now scaled correctly

Which to choose?

Each mode of the **Canvas Scaler** has its benefits and drawbacks, and you may even end up using more than one type of **Ui Scale Mode** on separate Canvases within a scene.

Planning a truly multiplatform UI is still hard, but at least Unity has now given you much better tools and layouts than the old legacy GUI system, plus the full source code should you wish to extend it in your own way.

Generally speaking, you will most likely use **Scale With Screen Size** mode of the **Canvas Scaler** for your topmost **Canvas** as it offers the best resizing options. However, the **Constant Physical Size** mode of **Canvas Scaler** is great for those pixel-perfect UIs where you want everything just so, which you will most likely use as a child Canvas of a top-level Canvas (remember, you can have any kind of depth for the Canvas you wish).

Of course, you can forgo all of this and leave the **Canvas Scaler** alone and build different UIs for each platform as before if you wish.

My best advice with all these options is to play with them and see what works for you as each UI situation is different. Remember, you are not limited in anyway, so if you want three parent Canvases, all with different scaling options, then go wild or create nested Canvases in your scene.

However, only use a new **Canvas** if you want to add the **Canvas Scaler** to it or a different **Raycast** system, else just use an empty GameObject and its **Rect Transform** to position, rotate, or scale your UI panel/window.

Summary

Working on a UI in any format and making it work for multiple platforms is hard, just ask any web developer who is building a responsive design for their website.

Coming up with a great UI design that works with your style of game is very tricky; thankfully though, the new Anchor system provided by Unity goes a great way to help you plan and layout your UI effectively. With the ever-increasing fragmentation of screen real estate on mobile devices (even Apple is at it now with multiple sizes of devices). It is more important than ever to get your UI working in a true multi-platform fashion across all devices rather than making specific ones for each resolution.

This evolution of a new layout system is certainly a breath of fresh air and welcome departure from the legacy, programmatic only, legacy GUI system.

Not sure whether I managed to keep up with the whole nautical theme, but I gave it a good try!

In this chapter, we covered the following topics:

- Positioning UI with Anchors
- Working with UI through multiple resolutions
- Handling UI scaling
- Working with the Canvas Scaler

In the next chapter, we will take things up a notch. So far, we have just looked at painting a single canvas and drawing it full screen; however, the Canvas component is capable of so much more. So let's turn up the heat and start having some real fun with our UI.

We'll also add a living, breathing 3D scene and dunk our UI in it, like a nice hot-brewed cup of tea with a lovely rich tea biscuit *Mr. Arthur Dent*. Now rest back on your towel and let us begin (bit of a Hitchhikers Guide to the Galaxy rift there).

5

Screen Space, World Space, and the Camera

So far, we have dealt with flat-style UIs; just take this and draw it there, scale, manage input, done. Granted, the new UI and layout controls make it a lot easier to get going (the placement and anchoring alone save you tons of time), but this is the future, so what else has the UI got for me?

As with any modern UI, your controls and drawing need to work with perspective within a 3D environment. Every game or title is looking to get deeper into the game world and get the player more involved, whether that's TV screens, more engaging menus, or third-person UX that is bound to game characters (such as Dead Space with its 3D inventory—`http://bit.ly/DeadSpaceUIExamples`).

In this chapter, we aim to break this perception boundary and plunge our UI into a 3D world.

The following is a list of topics that will be covered in this chapter:

- Overviews of the new Canvas modes
- Understanding the impact of cameras
- Simple and big UI examples

The Canvas and Cameras

So far, we have purely dealt with the basic **Screen Space – Overlay Canvas**, working through the controls and layout systems necessary to build our UI/UX.
This is all crucial to understand the new UI and what it takes to paint your canvas.

The journey doesn't stop there, however. Once you have your painting (a nice, easy way to depict a complete Canvas with the new Unity UI), you can go further. You can opt to apply some camera perspective to how your fullscreen UI will be drawn or take your painting and simply hang it where you want it in your game world.

As with everything, there are tips and tricks to make the most out of this new system.

Screen Space and World Space

Back in *Chapter 2, Building Layouts*, we walked over the canvas options for **Screen Space – Camera** and **World Space** Canvases:

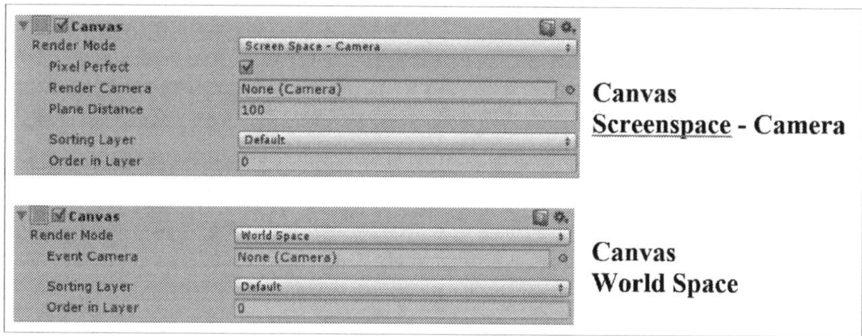

Each has its own capabilities above and beyond what the basic flat screen drawing canvas offers us:

- **Screen Space – Camera**: This takes the flat-drawn canvas and applies camera effects, such as perspective, field of view, depth sorting, and culling, and then applies this through the rendering cycle to the Canvas. This results in a **3D**-style-drawn **Canvas** UI rather than a flat system.

> Obviously, you could achieve the same effect by having your art assets created in a perspective view; however, this is time consuming and difficult to get right. It is far easier to have some high-fidelity flat images and then apply perspective while rendering (granted, there will likely be a lot of debate on the best *Quality* path for this).

- **World Space**: The other (and much more anticipated) view is to take your **Canvas** and embed it within **3D** worlds. This could be a TV screen, a computer console, interactive conversation elements, or even an inventory UI attached to the player. These scenarios were possible in the Legacy GUI; however, they were difficult to manage and get the perspective *just right*. Also, when text was used, scaling became a nightmare. All of this is so much easier now with **World Space** Canvases.

The Canvas, however, is only part of the picture. To make these elements work in a 3D way, they need to work with Cameras in the scene, not just be a flat 2D surface drawn on top of the screen, as with **Screen Space - Overlay** Canvases.

Cameras, when used with Canvases, fall into two categories:

- Rendering cameras
- Event cameras

Render cameras

In canvases, such as **Screen Space - Camera**, a second camera is used to render the UI.

> Actually, **Screen Space - Overlay** Canvases do this under the hood but you don't get to control the camera settings; it is just another sprite layer drawn in the scene.

The camera is used to provide the rendering settings for the UI. This is independent of any other cameras in the scene, such as the **Main Camera**.

As such, they can be placed elsewhere in the scene (doesn't have to be in the same place or direction as **Main Camera**) with their own settings, such as the following:

- **Clear flags**: These choose which part of the rendering path should be cleared (each frame)—this is set to *Don't clear* by default so that the UI is drawn on top of the scene.
- **Culling Mask**: This chooses what elements to draw in the view of the camera—by default, this is set to UI only (it's recommended to keep it this way).
- **Projection**: Setting a Perspective (3D) or Orthographic view (2D) - This should always be set to Perspective view, (which is the default) as an Orthographic will only give you the same as a **Screen Space - Overlay** view.

- **Perspective Field of View** (FOV): This controls the amount of perspective viewing angle in a camera's view, basically how bent the view appears.

You will likely tinker with this setting the most with **Screen Space - Overlay** Canvases as it plays with the perspective depth drawing of the UI, either causing rotation angles to appear elongated or take elements laid on top of each other (with different Z transform value depths) to be drawn out of the screen.

- **Viewport Rect**: This controls the size of the camera's viewport. Actually, playing with this is quite fun, but it will alter how the UI is presented and causes you a certain amount of rework. Set it and don't change it when building your UI.
- **Target Texture**: This is used to render this camera to a **RenderTexture**. You can use this if you wish, but it would be far easier to use a **World Space** Canvas. Only benefit is if you want the same UI painted all over the scene.

RenderTextures are a Unity Pro license-only feature.

- Other rendering settings (**Depth**, **Path**, **Occlusion Culling**, and **HDR**) can be set but do not provide any real value for UI systems. It's better to use the Canvas UI features.

Basically, you will want to use the **Screen Space - Camera Canvas** to liven up a flat UI or use it in conjunction with the Animation system to add an interactive 3D view to your UI.

Remember, the entire UI system can be animated just like any other Sprite using the Animation system. Play with it and you will have a lot of fun.

Event Cameras

The **Event Camera** is a lot simpler to explain. It is used by the UI system for **World Space** canvases to determine which camera should be used by the **EventSystem** for raycasting user input into the scene.

If you leave the **Event Camera** blank (null), it will use the **Main Camera** by default.

If you recall, in *Chapter 2, Building Layouts*, we determined where the mouse was and where the user clicked on or touched the screen by casting a ray (pointer) from the camera. It then passed through the scene in the direction the camera is facing until it hit either a UI element or passed straight through. This information was then passed back to the UI EventSystem for processing.

In most cases, you may want to just use the default (**Main Camera**). If, however, you are rendering your UI on a different camera, be sure to set it as the **Event Camera** or none of your input will work.

Getting some perspective

As we start to look deeper into the **Screen Space - Camera Canvas**, we will see a world of opportunity to enrich our boring, flat UI (although I quite like a flat UI for many things) and make it a little more engaging.

As we delve into this, we'll first look at some very simple examples before jumping into our main demo scene in 3D.

If you haven't started your project in **3D mode**, then it might be worth starting a new project for this chapter in **3D mode**.

It's not essential but will makes things a little easier.

As an example, we can work with the **Field of View** of our **Render Camera** to draw our UI out of the screen:

1. Create a `Canvas` and set the **Render Mode** to **Screen Space - Camera**.
2. Add a new `Camera` (**Layer** = `UI`, **Clear Flags** = `Don't Clear`, and **Field of View** = `1`) and name it **UICamera**.
3. Set the **Canvas Render Camera** to the new UICamera.
4. Add an **Image** with a **Button** on top of it (Button as a child of the Image).
5. Set each element transform's **Pos Z** value closer to the camera (Image 0, Button -10, and Text -20).
6. Now select the UICamera and switch to the **Game** view. Altering the **Field Of View** will now draw out each layer of the UI from the screen.

When we run the preceding example and try a few different Field of View (**FOV**) settings on the **Main Camera**, we get the following results:

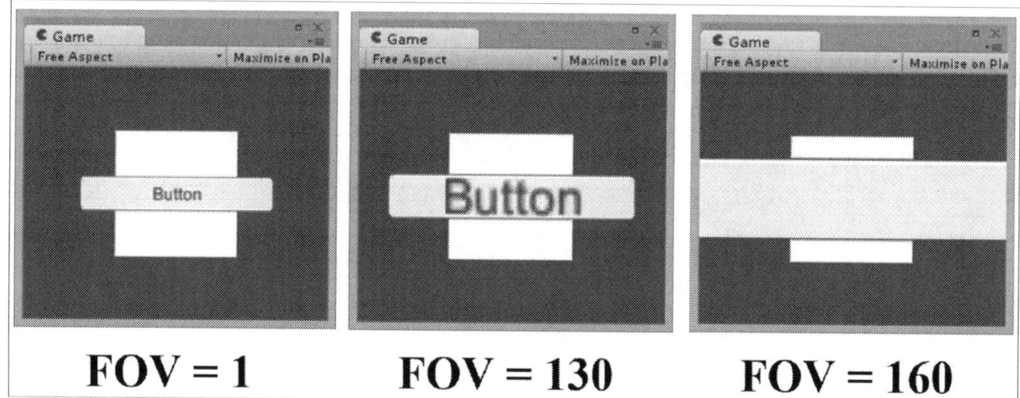

The **Text** on top of **Button** has now completely vanished at **FOV 160**, as it has passed the **Near Plane** of the **Camera** and isn't being drawn.

A bit hard to show in print, but the effect brings each element to the screen at a different rate until it passes out of view, based on its Z order depth. This would make a great animation to use this in reverse and slap each component down on the screen (maybe with a little shake on landing).

Another example of using the **Field of View** of **Render Camera** could be to use rotation to give perspective depth to the UI:

1. Reset the **Pos Z** values for all the elements in the previous example.
2. Set the Image's **Rotation Y** value to `10`.
3. Now select the **UICamera** and switch to the **Game** view again.

Altering the **Field Of View** will now draw out the side of the image closer to the screen, as shown in the following screenshot:

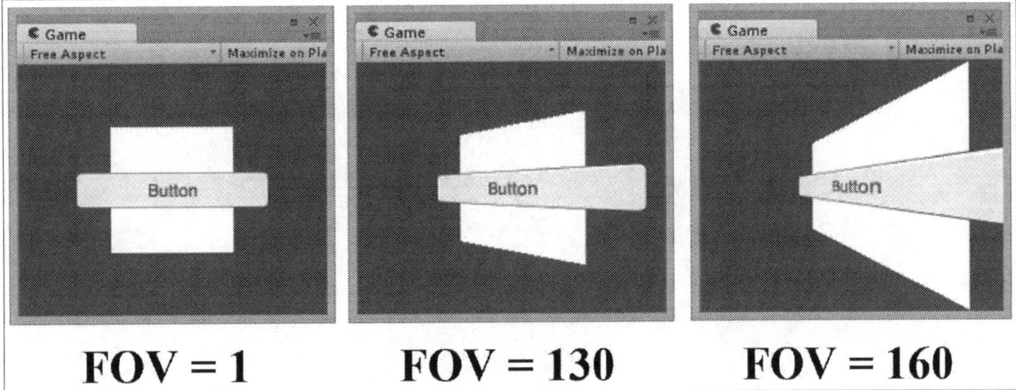

As you can see in the preceding screenshot, the effect is a little easier to see; altering the **FOV** extenuates the angle and alters the perspective depth that is drawn.

> An important point to note is the **Plane Distance** on the **Screen Space - Camera Canvas**. The value for this has to be within the **Near** and **Far Clipping Planes** settings for the **Render Camera**. Like any other 3D object, if it is too near the camera or too far away it simply won't be drawn.
>
> However, the setting is also invaluable to set how deep into the 3D scene the UI on the Canvas is when it is drawn. Have a play with it.

Setting up for the big game

Yeah true! The previous examples give a basic look to what the **Screen Space - Camera** gives us, but let's aim a little higher! So let's create something a little more interesting, like the following:

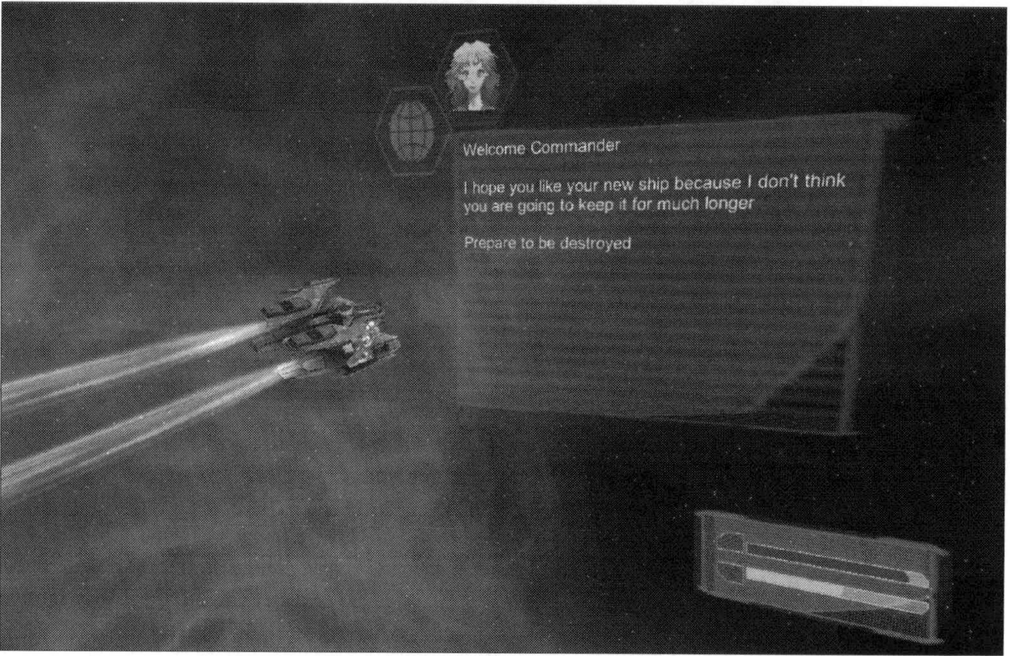

As building a fun 3D scene is a bit outside the scope of this title, full instructions on how to create the 3D backdrop and model are included in the appendix of this title. You can tackle this if you wish but it is not essential to learn the UI lessons in this chapter.

> You can also find the setup tutorial for the demo scene on my blog at `http://bit.ly/UnityUIEssentials3DDemoScene`.
>
> Or if you want, you can just import the demo scene using this handy asset package I created (aren't I just the nicest). Download it here: `http://bit.ly/UIEssentialsCh5DemoScene`.
>
> Then import it using **Assets** | **Import Package** | **Import Package** from the Unity editor menu.

If you are not using the demo scene, just create a new scene and add a 3D cube to the scene using **GameObject | 3D Object | Cube** from the Unity menu. Then, in the section that attaches the 3D UI to the ship, just attach the Canvas to the cube instead.

Some prerequisites

For the examples, we'll use some free assets from the Web. Be sure to grab them before we start building:

- Grab the free Doomstalker GUI assets from `http://bit.ly/DoomStalkerUI`
- Grab the `NobleAvatar V02.zip` file from `http://bit.ly/NobleAvatars` (great free asset to generate Avatar heads with some premade ones that we'll use)

These assets will help the UI look just a tad shinier.

Next up, some Sprite 2D work

As the new UI system predominately uses the new 2D sprite system, we'll need some assets to start building our UI. For this, import the `HUD_BaseA.psd` from the **Textures** folder of the **Doomstalker UI** pack you downloaded earlier and drop it into your project.

> Remember, if your project type is set to **3D**, it will import images as a **Texture** at first (unless you went 2D), so be sure to update the **Texture Type** to **Sprite (2D and UI)** for each image first.

With `HUD_BaseA.psd` selected in the `project` folder, set the **Sprite Mode** in the inspector to **Multiple** and then open the **Sprite Editor** (using the **Sprite Editor** button).

Looking at this spritesheet, since most of the artwork is transparent (which is brilliant for spacey effects), because of this however it can be a little hard to make out all the controls. So when viewing/editing this sheet, it's best to use the **Alpha** viewing mode by clicking on the button, as illustrated here:

This swaps the view from colored to the raw **Alpha mask**, as shown in the following screenshot:

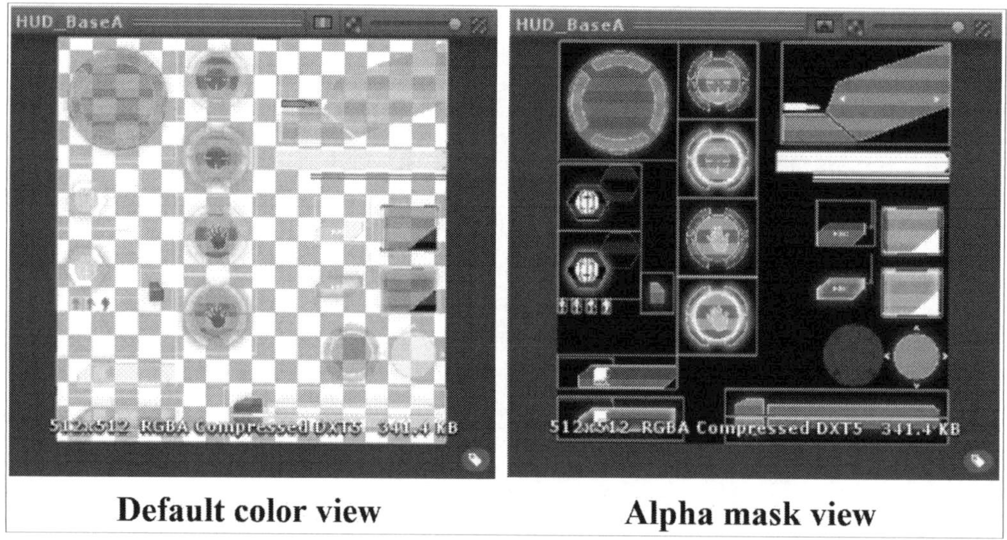

Default color view **Alpha mask view**

With the editor open, first use the **Automatic Slice** option. (By clicking on **Slice**, checking the **Type** is set to **Automatic**, and then clicking on the **Slice** button.) Next you will need to touch up the sprite regions, as follows:

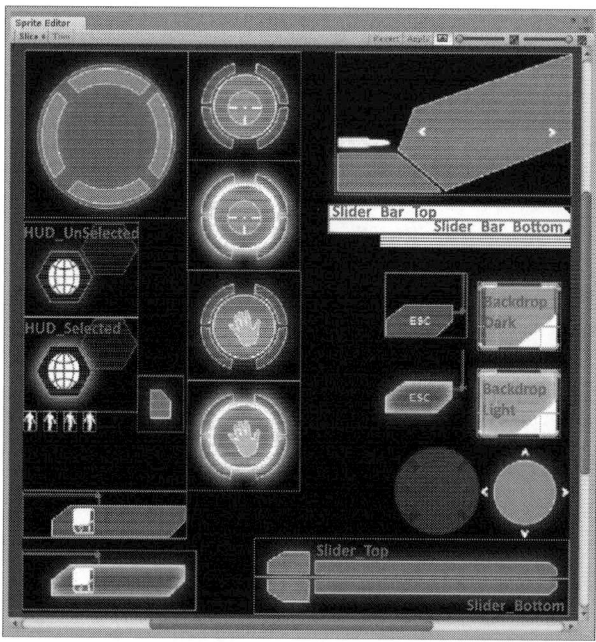

Of note, the Sprites (as shown in the previous sheet) that we are most interested in at this point are:

- **Slider_Top**: Position X 219, Y 35, W 293, H 35
- **Slider_Bottom**: Position X 219, Y 0, W 293, H 35
- **Slider_Bar_Top**: Position X 286, Y 360, W 226, H 13
- **Slider_Bar_Bottom**: Position X 286, Y 347, W 226, H 13
- **Backdrop_Light**: Position X 425, Y 163, W 78, H 62 - Border L 18, B 22, R 19, T 7
- **Backdrop_Dark**: Position X 425, Y 242, W 78, H 62 - Border L 18, B 22, R 19, T 7
- **HUD_Selected**: Position X 0, Y 184, W 108, H 85
- **HUD_UnSelected**: Position X 0, Y 271, W 108, H 85

Once you have these Sprites split and set up, we can continue building our **Screen Space - Camera** UI.

If you are unsure about how to use the Unity 2D **Sprite Editor**, then check out this short video tutorial on the Unity Learn portal: `http://bit.ly/Unity2DSpriteEditor`.

A Screen Space – Camera health bar

Now let's move on to building our UI. For this example, we will build a simple health chart for our fighter to track the shield and hull strength of our craft, as shown in the following screenshot:

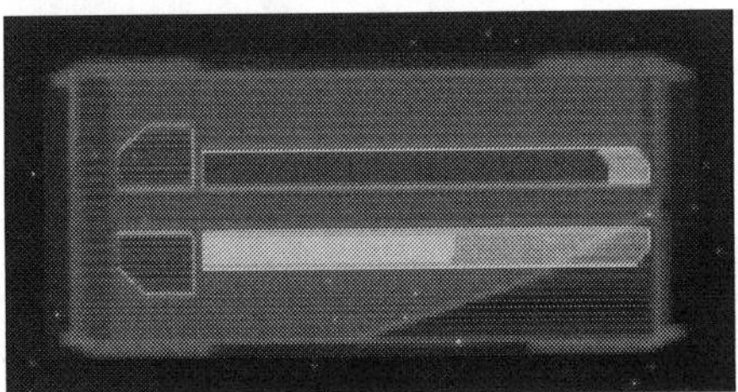

A top slider bar in blue for shields and a green bottom slider for health

Using our assets, let's throw this little gem together.

What's in a Canvas?

As a big tip, when you are working on just building UI elements and with positioning on a UI Canvas, it's best to switch to **2D** mode (using the 2D button at the top of the scene view). It just makes things a lot easier with the UI.

When you have finished working on the UI, feel free to flip back into 3D mode (tap the **2D** button again) to continue working with a 3D scene.

Granted, if you are creating a 2D game, you may never leave the 2D mode.

Firstly, add a new **Canvas** to the scene using **Create | UI | Canvas** from the project **Hierarchy** or **GameObject | UI | Canvas** from the menu and then rename it to `ScreenSpaceCameraCanvas`.

We'll just use the project **Hierarchy** from now on since you know where both the options are.

Now with the canvas in the scene, update its **Canvas Render** mode to **Screen Space - Camera** and you should see the following view:

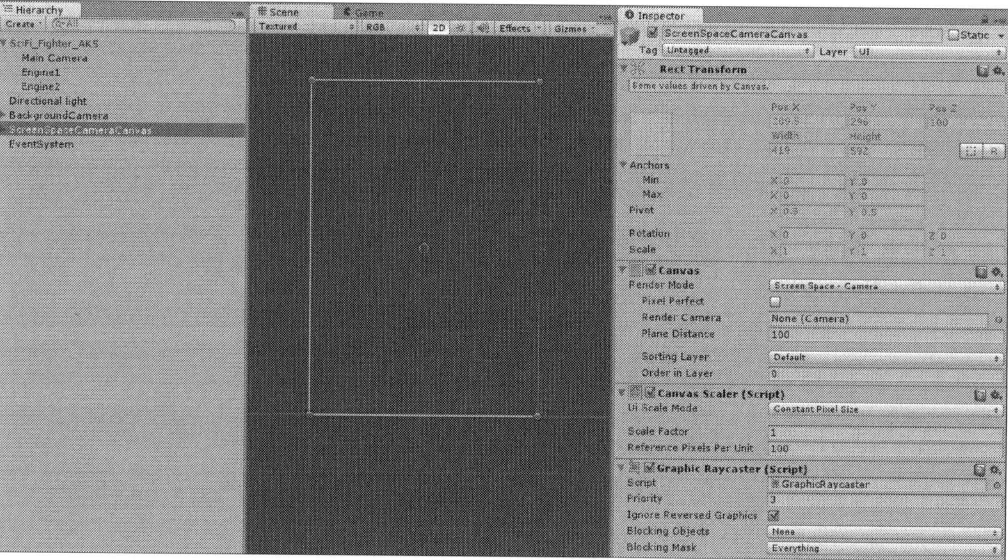

There are a few things to note:

- The bottom left-hand corner of the **Canvas** in the scene starts at the position of the topmost element in the project hierarchy, in this case, the fighter. Just an observation: the Canvas is not actually linked to it. It's still a **Screen Space - Camera** Canvas so its position doesn't really matter.
- The size of the **Canvas** will fluctuate based on the actual scene screen size. Resize the scene view and watch the width and height update. If you recall from the last chapter, this is something you need to watch out for, especially with multi-resolution support (supporting your game on different resolutions).
- The layer of the new **Canvas** is automatically set to **UI** by default. You can change this later if you wish. Remember this in your game if you are culling certain layers from **Camera** views (just as the Camera for this Canvas will only draw the UI layer, but we'll come to that in a minute).
- A new **Render Camera** option appears along with a **Plane Distance** option, which we'll look at next.
- There is nothing to see here. This canvas has been left intentionally blank (mainly because you haven't added anything to it yet, of course). If you recall, in previous chapters, when you added a UI element to a scene, it will have created a **Canvas** for you and then placed the new UI component on it. We have just created the Canvas itself, so it's brand new, yet to be unwrapped.
- An **EventSystem** was also added to the scene but you should have expected this by now!

Right! It's time to put our health bar UI into action.

We won't be playing with the **Canvas Scaler** in this chapter as we went through it in some depth in the previous one. **Canvas Scalers** only really becomes important when you are deploying your title and need to work with multiple resolutions. For this chapter, we are concentrating on creating the UI and working with the Canvas itself. (But don't let this stop you. Play with it as much as you like; it's your game as well, you know!).

Am I dead yet?

For the health bar, we'll reuse some of the tricks you learned in previous chapters but with some nicer graphics using our **Doomstalker** free UI bits.

So let's start by adding a panel to the **Canvas**. Right-click on the **Canvas** in the project hierarchy and select **UI** | **Panel**. Once done, rename this new GameObject `HealthUIPanel`.

> You could alternatively use the **Image** UI component as a start if you wish; they are pretty much identical. The only real difference, is that the **Panel** starts its life stretched to the full size of the **Canvas** and has a default background image, whereas the **Image** starts off smaller with no preset image. They are still exactly the same, but with different defaults.

Your **Scene** view will now look like what is shown in the following screenshot:

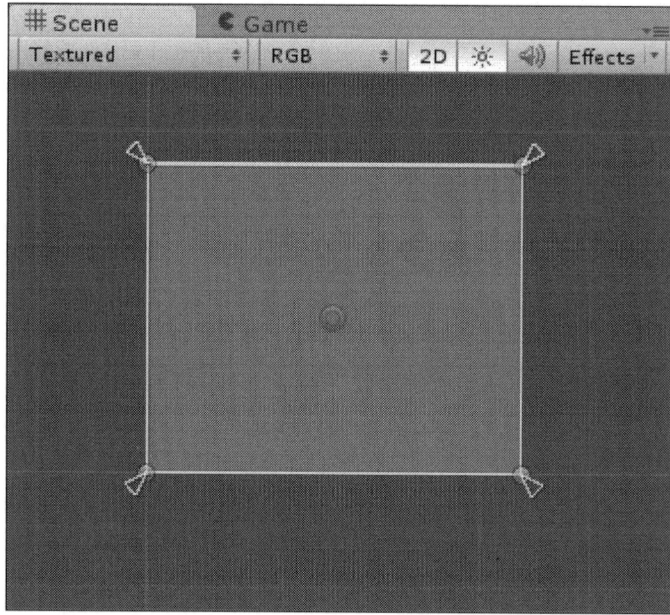

Not much to see here, so just resize the **Panel** down to the bottom right-hand corner using its Rect Handles (blue dots) and for good measure, pull the bottom right-hand corner back from the edge of the screen as well. While you are at it, change the **Source Image** of the panel to the `Backdrop_Light` sprite we created earlier from the `HUD_BaseA.psd` file. Since this is your UI, you decide on its final placement and size; the following screenshot is where I ended up:

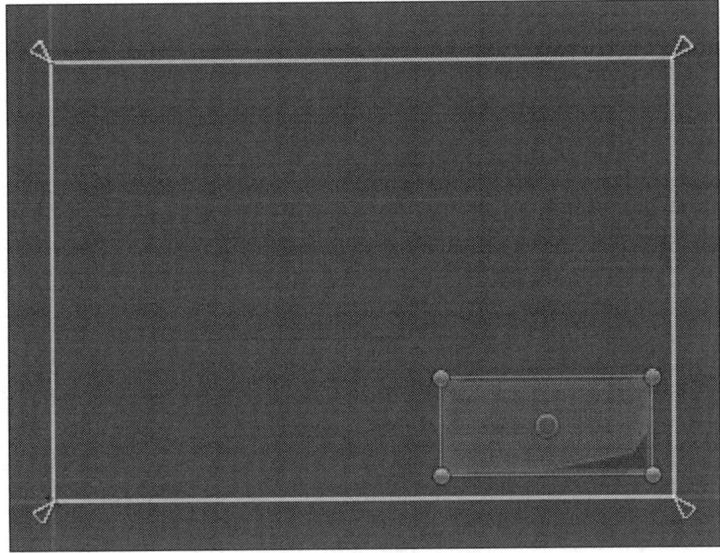

Because we started with the **Panel** UI control, the anchors are by default stretched to the size of the Canvas (its parent), and as such, will resize with the screen when it changes.

If you had started with an **Image**, the anchors would be set at the middle of the screen and would not resize.

Additionally, because we haven't applied a **Canvas Scaler**, the resizing will not be uniform with the screen as the spacing values would remain fixed.

Something to remember!

Since we are almost repeating what we did earlier in *Chapter 4, Anchors Away*, for the health bar, we will quickly whip through the steps for creating the Top blue health bar, which will be for our shields:

1. Right-click on the **HealthUIPanel** panel and select **UI | Slider**.
2. Expand the new slider in the project hierarchy and delete the **Handle Slide Area**.
3. Select the **Slider** and set the **Target Graphic** to the Slider's **Fill** GameObject (which is a child of the **Fill Area**).
4. Click on the **Handle Rect** property and hit *Delete* (or click on the circle icon to the right of the property and select **None**).
5. Click on the **Anchor Presets** of the **Slider** and hold *Alt* and click on the **Top Stretch** option (second from the top on the far right).
6. Bring in the left and right sides of the **Slider** (about 10 for Left and Right).
7. Select the **Background** GameObject (child of the slider) and set the **Source Image** to the `Slider_Top` sprite.
8. Resize the slider to give it a chunkier look (either by resizing the slider itself or altering the **Background** GameObject).
9. Select the **Fill** GameObject and set the **Source Image** to the `Slider_Bar_Top` sprite.
10. With the **Fill** GameObject selected, alter its **Rect Transform** handles to dock with its parent size (maximizing the **Fill** area's **Rect Transform**).
11. Still with the **Fill** GameObject selected, click on the **Color** property and set it to dark blue (H 244, S 255, V 255, A 255).
12. Select the **Fill Area** GameObject and resize it so that it covers the bar portion of the **Slider** Background image.

With this, you should end up with something like the following:

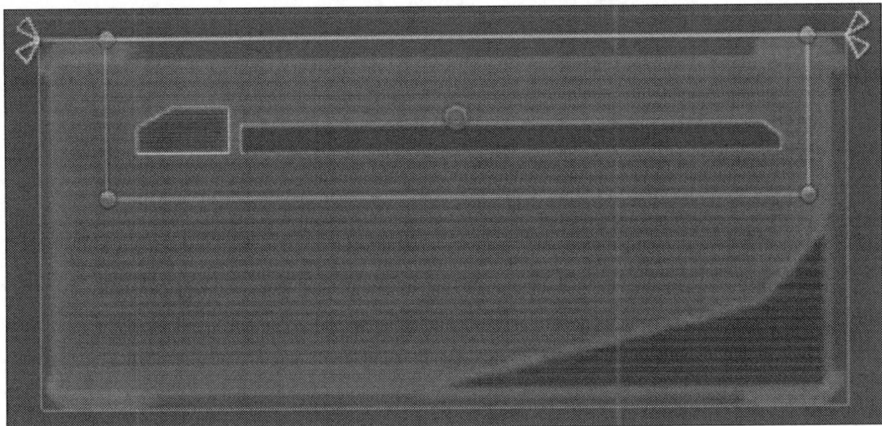

Obviously, feel free to play with the design and make it your own.

Now duplicate the Top slider, replace the **TOP** sprites with the **BOTTOM** versions and place them below the Top slider, remembering to position the **Fill** area over the new **Slider** area. (I'll leave it to you to decide whether you want to anchor the bottom slider to the bottom or top of the panel; each has its advantages.) Also, alter the color of the fill to green for ship/hull health; this is to give it a finished look, as follows:

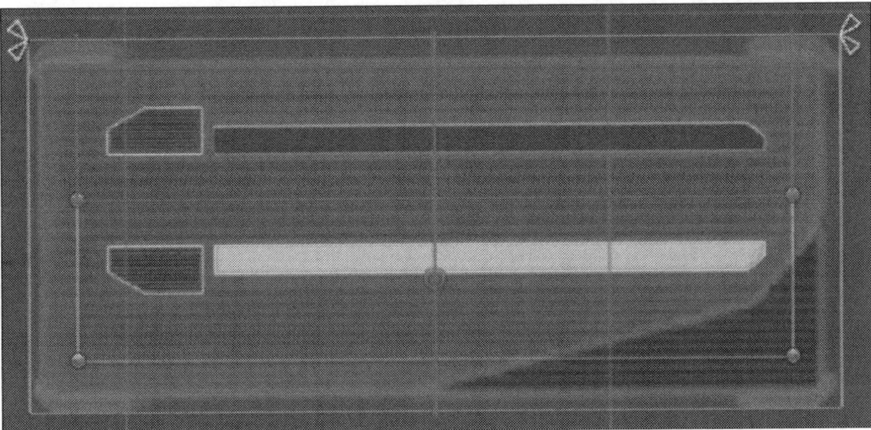

Now ain't that pretty? However, looking at the full picture and the game view, it still looks pretty much the same as a **Screen Space - Overlay** canvas. So let's do something about this.

In one test I sized both the **Background** and the **Fill Area** Rect Transform's to fill the entire of the **Slider** Rect Transform size. Just a thought, makes them bigger and easier to handle.

Reaching in

So we've got our fancy slider bars in play, but it still looks flat. To break this perception, we need to add some perspective and to do this we need a new **Camera**.

Without a separate camera, the **Screen Space - Camera** Canvas still operates exactly like a **Screen Space - Overlay** Canvas, as there is nothing to tell it how to draw differently. So let's add one.

Create a new **Camera** in the scene (**Create** | **Camera**) and name it `GUICamera`. The first thing you will notice (especially if you look at the game view) is that our scene has now vanished! Well, almost everything, the new **UI** we created is still shown. This is simply because both the new **Camera** you created and the **Main Camera** attached to the ship are both competing to draw to the same render depth, **Depth** `0`, as shown in the **Camera** properties. Because the new **GUICamera** is at the bottom of the project hierarchy, it is drawn last and wins.

Remember, in Unity 4.5, Unity Technologies changed how the rendering chain worked. Elements are now drawn according to the order they appear in the project **Hierarchy**, which by default is normally alphabetic.

Now, as this **Camera** is going to be specifically used for **UI** rendering, we can update its options to focus on just **UI** elements.

If you plan to use multiple **Screen Space - Camera** Canvases (which is possible), each with their own **Camera**, be sure to use separate **Layers** for each canvas unless you want them to draw each other! A fascinating bug that showed up while creating the demo scene, which saw my **World Canvas** UI flying along in the background of the scene. This was because it was drawing on the same layer as my **Main Camera**, which was very weird to see.

So, for GUICamera, update the following options:

1. Set the **Layer** property (the rendering layer) to **UI**.
2. Set the **Clear Flags** property to **Don't Clear** (since we want UI to be additive).
3. Change the **Field of View** property to `100` (just for a little extra depth).
4. Set the **Culling Mask** property to **UI** (select **Nothing** from the dropdown and then select **UI** to just select **UI**).

Now with the camera setup, just add it to the **Render Camera** property of the **Canvas** on the **ScreenSpaceCameraCanvas** GameObject and hey presto!

Wait, nothing happened! What's going on here? What kind of snake oil is this?

It's all gone a bit flat

So while setting up our **UI**, we attached a **Camera** with some funky settings to it but nothing changed! Why?

The answer to this riddle is very simple: if you set something flat, it's going to be drawn flat. It doesn't matter what funky perspective you apply to it; it's still flat.

So how to change this? (If you have read this chapter carefully, you should already know the solution! Hmm, let that settle for a bit.)

Earlier, I showed you a way to add perspective when drawing your UI, here we simply need to do the same thing. For this example, we'll just do something very simple; I will leave it to you to experiment further.

- Expand the **ScreenSpaceCameraCanvas** GameObject in the project **Hierarchy**.

> Note that all the **Rect Transform** properties are read-only.
>
> Both types of Screen Space Canvases (Overlay and Camera) take up the full screen. As such, their size, rotation, and scale are all determined by the device they are being run on, which includes the editor.

- Select the **HealthUIPanel** GameObject and set the **Rect Transform Rotation Y** value to `10`.

In the **Scene** view, you will see a minor change to the display of the **HealthUIPanel**. However, switch to **Game** view and you see the full effect of the rotation paired with the default **FOV** of the **GUICamera**, as shown here:

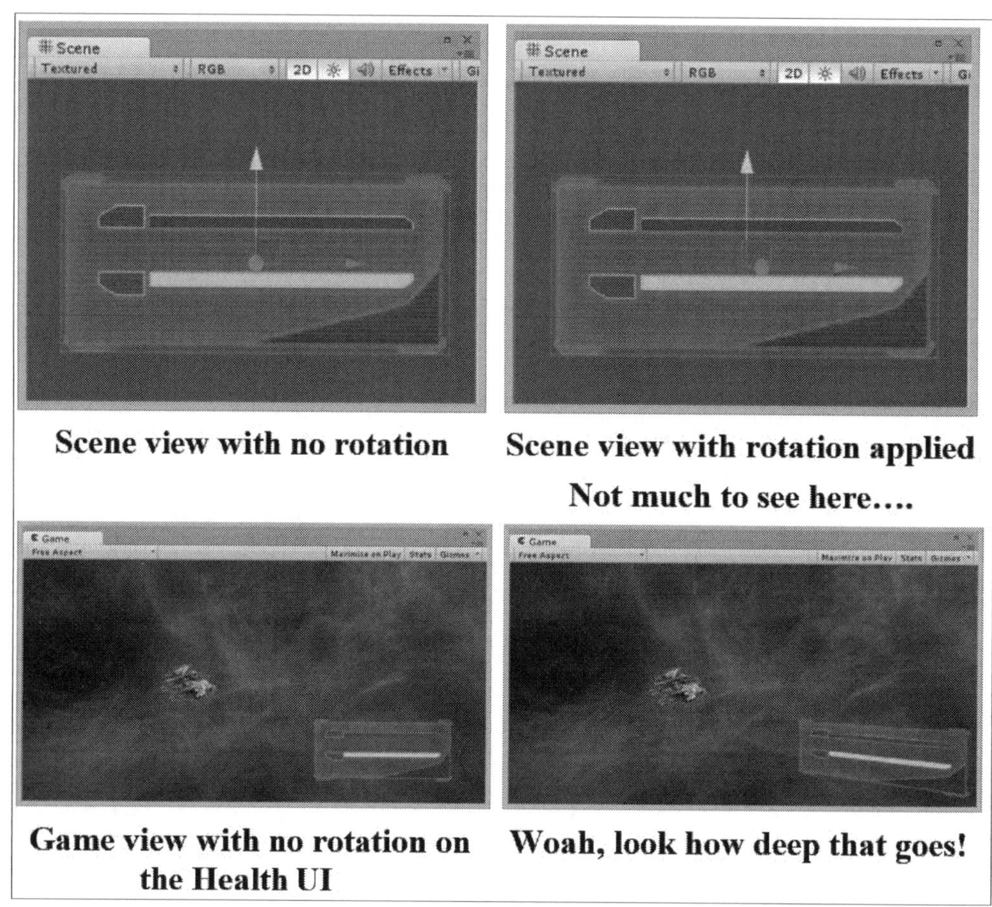

Scene view with no rotation

Scene view with rotation applied
Not much to see here....

Game view with no rotation on the Health UI

Woah, look how deep that goes!

As you can see, the **Screen Space - Camera** Canvas goes far to add some depth to an otherwise flat UI.

As detailed earlier, there are many options you can use with this, either tinkering with the camera, rotation, or depth of UI components.

Go wild and experiment!

Going deep

So far in both modes of the Screen Space Canvases, we dealt with a UI that was being drawn relative to the entire drawing space of the screen; each of the modes is intended to draw over or against the full screen.

However, in a lot of cases, this is not the desired effect. We want our UI to draw on surfaces, pop up message boxes within (not on) a scene, or even hover over the shoulder of a third-person character (as shown in the aforementioned inventory panel used in games such as Dead Space).

A lot of this is possible today, either using render textures (which require the pro version of Unity), twisting the legacy GUI through code (not very pretty), or using shaders in an intrinsic way (requiring an in-depth knowledge of shaders). All of these are usually outside the comfort zone for beginners or require a lot of time to set up and get right. This is where the new **World Space Canvas** comes in.

Hang your Canvas wherever you like

With the **World Space Canvas**, you literally get to take your UI canvas and place it where you want, positioned where you want, and rotated however you like, fully within a 3D environment. Unlike the Screen Space Canvases, they are not limited in any way. In fact, a **World Space Canvas** acts almost entirely the same as a **Render Texture** but without the limitation of requiring a Pro license—it is available to all.

A **Render Texture** is a special kind of texture that is generated at runtime using an independent camera. The view of the camera is output to a texture buffer instead of directly to the screen. This image can then be placed anywhere within a 3D scene to display the camera's output.

This is normally used for minimaps (where the map is rendered in view of a different camera) for rearview displays or circumstances where you want to show an additional view other than what the **Main Camera** is displaying. In one case, I saw a **Render Texture** being used in a **Portal** (`http://en.wikipedia.org/wiki/Portal_(video_game)`) clone, where one portal showed the view from another portal, in other words, the place where the port came out, which was obviously not what the player was looking at.

The big thing about Render Textures (as stated previously) is that it requires a Unity Pro license (for each platform) for it to be used, putting it just out of reach of users using the free license of Unity.

So once you have your **World Space Canvas** set up, the world is your oyster, enabling you to build such fanciful things as:

- A TV screen, showing a series of ads
- A floating information board
- Interactive text with in-game characters
- A computer terminal that the player can actually interact with

All of these can be fully animated through Unity's 2D animation system, which is pretty neat.

The showcase

Right, as a basic example of this, we are going to add a **World Space Canvas** into our scene and attach it to our ship so it follows it wherever it goes (or at least when a conversation needs to happen), as shown in the following screenshot:

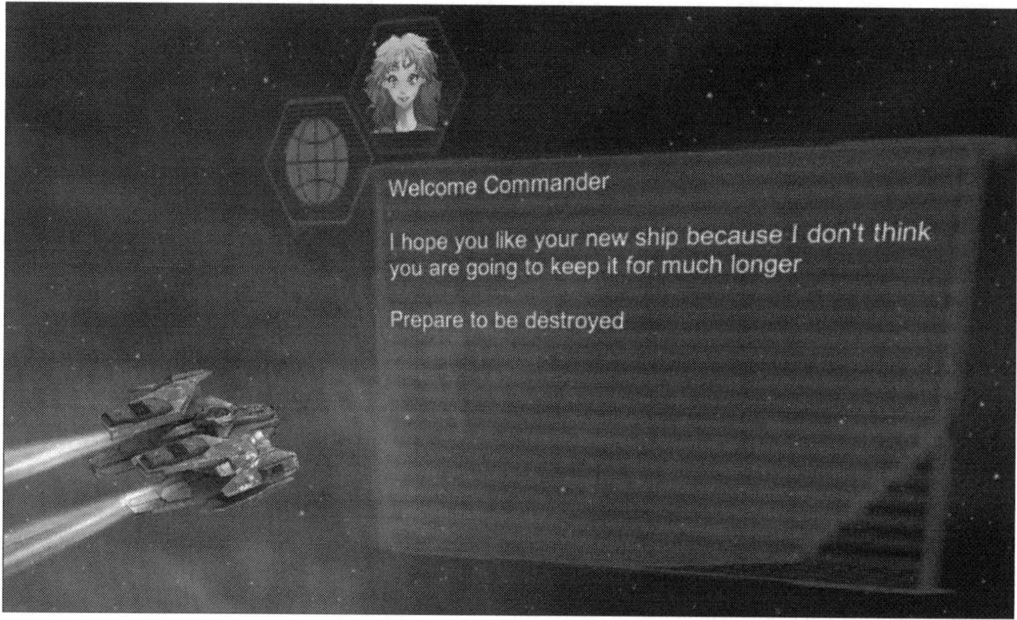

A World Space Canvas UI attached to the ship

The make-up of the UI is quite simple:

- One Panel in the top-left as an information image
- A child image for the Avatar placed relative to the empty slot in the top-left panel
- Another panel for the text background
- A Text control-sized for the panel area as a child of the text panel

However, in a break from tradition, I'm first going to show you the wrong way to build a **World Space** Canvas, so you can recognize issues it causes and then update to the better way.

> The reason I'm showing you the wrong way first is to show you why it's wrong; it's a learning exercise. It also points out why there are certain ways of doing things that may not appear obvious and what to expect when it doesn't go right; just bear with me.

Build your UI and place it in the scene

So, jumping in, let's add a new **World Space Canvas** to our scene:

1. Disable the **GUICamera** for now so we can focus on our new **World Space Canvas** (or just delete it; it's up to you).
2. Right-click on the **SciFi_Fighter_AK5** and select **UI** | **Canvas**.
3. A new canvas will appear in the scene offset and in a funny place; rename it to `WorldSpaceCanvas`.
4. Change the **Render Mode** of the **Canvas** to **World Space**.
5. Reset the **Transform** of the **WorldSpaceCanvas** GameObject (using the cog icon in the top right hand corner of the **Rect Transform** component in **Inspector** with the WorldSpaceCanvas selected, then select Reset).
6. Right-click on the WorldSpaceCanvas GameObject and select **UI** | **Panel** (this just adds a background image to our Canvas so we can see/position it).

If you now switch to the Game view, you will see your new canvas positioned relative to your fighter in the 3D scene (ain't no 2D on this bad boy), as shown here:

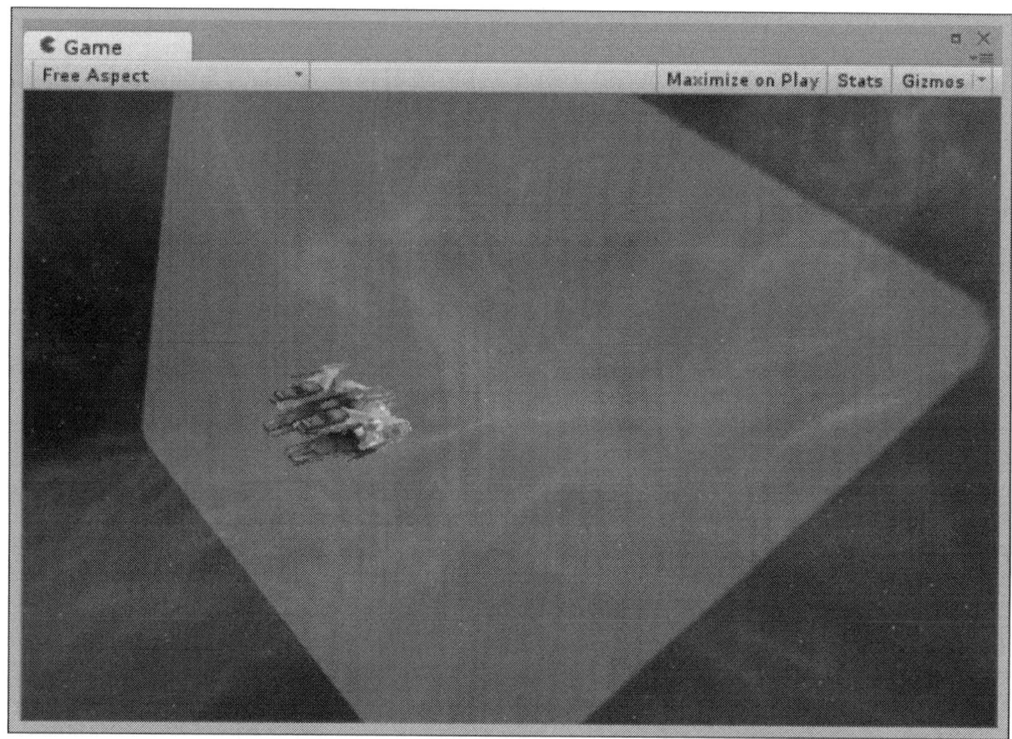

So we have our Canvas. If you return to the **Scene** view, you can see the first issue with first positioning your new Canvas in World Space in your 3D scene before adding UI elements, the Canvas is rotated and positioned at an odd angle in the other 3D scene. Granted, this isn't a big issue. As with any 3D development we are used to this, so we can do the following:

- Rotate the camera around until we are looking straight on at the **Canvas**
- Alternatively, switch on 2D view to flip to seeing the Canvas straight on (granted, it is still rotated when you use this method)

If you try to use the GameObject alignment options (**GameObject | Align with View or GameObject | Align with Selected in the menu**), then it will likely push our UI out of view. This is just my experience; yours may be different.

Regardless of which path you choose, let's set up our **Canvas** how we want it, so do the following:

1. Rotate and Position the **Canvas** so it's alongside the Fighter, as shown in the screenshot earlier in the *The Showcase* section.

I find it's easier to do this by undocking the **Game** view and placing it alongside the **Scene** view. This way, you can use the Rotation and Position handles to update the Canvas position/rotation and see the result while you edit it. Alternatively, you can use the preconfigured view modes for the editor (dropdown in the upper right-hand corner of the editor) and use the 2 by 3 or 4 Split options, which will arrange your editor view.

2. Rename the **Panel** that we added earlier to `TextArea` and resize it to the bottom right-hand corner of the **Canvas**.
3. Change the **Source Image** of the TextArea panel to the `Backdrop_Dark` sprite from the **HUD_BaseA** image.
4. Add another **Panel** to the **Canvas** and rename it `AvatarArea`.
5. Change the **Source Image** of the **AvatarArea** panel to the `HUD_UnSelected` sprite from the **HUD_BaseA** image.
6. Resize the **Panel** down to the top left-hand corner.
7. Tweak both the panels until you get something like the following in the **Scene/Game** view:

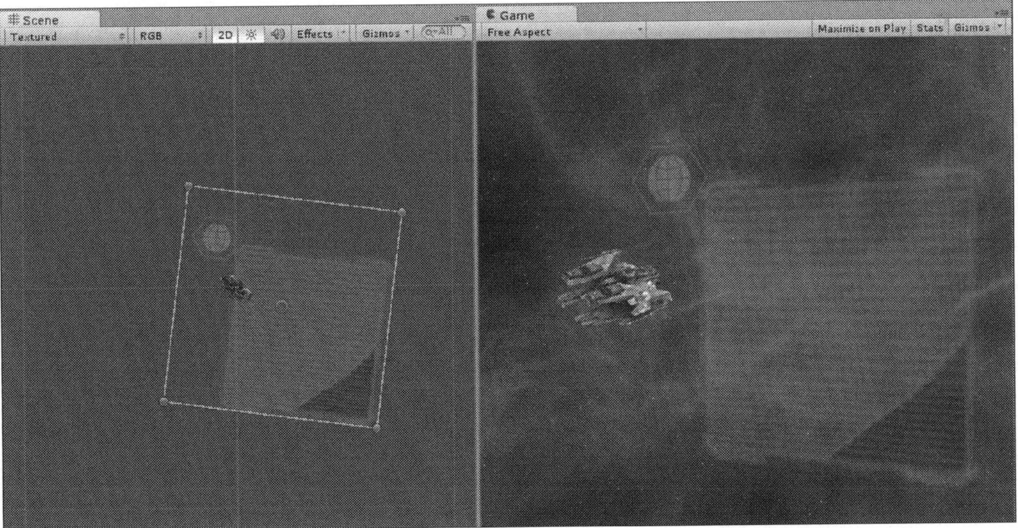

> Remember, this is a 3D object like anything else. So, when positioning it, position it in 3D space to get the view you want.

With these set up, let's add the **Text** and **Avatar** and we're done:

1. Import an Avatar head from the **NobleAvatar** pack mentioned earlier (make sure you set its **TextureType** to `Sprite` after importing).
2. Right-click on the **AvatarArea** panel and select **UI** | **Image** and change its **Source Image** to the imported **Avatar**.
3. Resize and position the **Avatar** over the empty hexagon on the **AvatarArea**.
4. Right-click on the **TextArea** and add select **UI** | **Text** to add a **Text Component**.
5. Resize the **Text Rect Transform** to fit comfortably within the **TextArea**.
6. Set the **Text Color** to `White`.

Now, if we examine our creation, you will find it looks pretty awful:

- The images look grainy
- The text is massive
- If you set the **Font size** of the text down, it looks horrible

So just what is going on here? Why does this look so bad?

Troubles with scale

The simple answer to the previous question, is scale. If you check the size of the **Rect Transform** of your **WorldSpaceCanvas** GameObject, you will see it is **100** pixels wide by **100** pixels high; in other words, it's tiny in your massive 3D scene.

If you take any image and resize it down to a minute size, it will look awful and cause all sorts of problems.

If you also recall, in a previous chapter, I noted that the text system hasn't changed in Unity 4.6. It has its flaws and doesn't scale well, which is why it looks its worst in the scene at the moment; the text needs to stay large (the larger, the better) to maintain any kind of quality.

So, the simple answer to this is to think bigger!

A better way

Now that we've ascertained just throwing the Canvas into 3D space isn't enough, what can we do?

We simply need a bigger Canvas, one drawn at a resolution that suits our art assets and works well with the text system as it currently is, then lean on the rendering path used by the **Canvas** system and scale it down to the size we need.

This way, the **Canvas** is rendered at the resolution we want, and then once rendered, is scaled down to a texture for drawing in our scene.

To do this, do the following:

- Either start fresh or simply set the appropriate width and height values for the canvas to the resolution we want (say 700 x 400 for example, but it could be any resolution you want)
- Resize and move the **Canvas** components (its children) to fit the new resolution (basically, make them bigger)
- Once you are happy, just scale down the Canvas, either using the scale tool in the scene view or by manually altering the scale values on the **WorldSpaceCanvas** GameObject in the inspector (I'd recommend using the Scale Tool)

Once you have done this, the quality will go up considerably because the **Canvas** is working at a much better resolution.

In practice, the way I would recommend creating **World Space** Canvases would be the same as working with Render Textures, for example:

1. Create your **Canvas** and switch to 2D mode.
2. Set the **Render Mode** of the **Canvas** to **World Space**.
3. Set the **Width** and **Height** to a good resolution for the type of element you are trying to create. If you are using text, the bigger the better (just don't go silly; use what you feel works best with the font you are using, and try not to oversize). I set mine to a **Width** of `700` and a **Height** of `400`.
4. Add **UI** elements to your **Canvas** and configure/arrange it how you want.
5. Once complete, place and scale it down to where you want it in your scene.
6. Done.

You can of course just create it in the overlay mode and then change the **Render Mode** afterwards; it's up to you. However, you will then not get a feel of the resolution of your **Canvas** that works best for what you are creating.

You will notice I didn't delve into **Anchors** for the **World Space** Canvas. They aren't as important with World Space UI due to them being rendered in 3D; however, I would recommend that you use them where possible to ensure you keep in the habit of using them.

A final word on Event Cameras

Now, as the previous **UI** didn't have any interactive elements on it, we didn't bother setting up an Event Camera for the **World Space** Canvas. You only need to apply an Event Camera if you want to alter the rendering of a **World Space** Canvas and thus need to specify a different camera to do the raycasting for the UI input.

The Unity examples (`http://bit.ly/UnityOfficialUIExamples`) already do a good job of demonstrating this, and in most cases for **World Space** UI, you will not need to define a separate **Event Camera**.

Remember, if you don't specify an **Event Camera**, it will use the **Main Camera** by default.

If you don't have any buttons, sliders, or other interactive elements, there isn't much point setting one.

So, either the **UI** will be in the main view and use the **Main Camera**, or you will need to draw it in a particular part of the screen (say an Inventory UI). In this case, you will use a separate camera (like what was done with the **Screen Space - Camera** examples earlier), which will be used as the **Event Camera** and help you to provide direct (simplify) input and render the **World Space** UI.

Summary

This chapter has been the most fun and I could have really run away with it, showing a lot more examples using these two canvas modes, but where's the fun if I do it all for you? Go create! Think up weird and wacky ideas that are not just flat or information; throw stuff in your game world like never before and go wild.

The Unity 5 preview presentation on UI (`http://bit.ly/U5Preview` at about the 1-minute mark) showed some other excellent examples of using these Canvas modes, including using a **World Space Canvas** attached to a block that pops up a conversation window aligned to the object in the game (not the player as I've shown here). The UI system it shows is actually from 4.6 that has been ported to U5, so everything you see is possible today.

Unity really listened to customer feedback when creating all these options with the new **UI** system, and these modes really deliver on the dream of a full 3D-embedded **UI** without the hacks.

In this chapter, we covered the following topics:

- UI and 3D
- Added a **Screen Space - Camera** Canvas and played with perspective
- Added a **World Space** Canvas and played with 3D placement
- Tips and tricks to use both the Canvas modes; no more flat stuff

In the next chapter, we will bring the title to a close and start to delve deep into the coding side, building **UI** through code, and delve into the open source code (and get it running) and what secrets it uncovers.

The fact that Unity has published the new UI system source using an open source license is beyond amazing and gives you, the developer, the power to create whatever you want using actual real-world examples of Unity code as the base. If you are feeling really adventurous, submit your ideas to Unity and see whether they make it back into the core product itself!

At this point I'd really urge to use what you have learned this far and rip into the Official Unity UI examples.

With everything I have shown you, you should be able to understand how all the parts of the demo fit together. It also has some good examples of interactive UI screens (such as a keyboard) and a working example of a Drag and Drop system (although you will need to look at the code section in *Chapter 6, Working with the UI Source*, to understand the scripts attached to the Drag and Drop demo).

The Official Unity UI demo sample can be found here `http://bit.ly/UnityOfficialUIExamples` and has several scenes, each showing a different UI pattern.

I will also be following up on my blog with more samples and UI layouts, so keep an eye out!

6

Working with the UI Source

So far we have done most things through the editor, which is fine. Adding Canvases, scaling them, throwing oodles of new UI at the screen, and even driving around in space getting veiled threats from passing spacefarers. All in a day's job!

Behind all this UI wonderfulness, there is a powerful new mechanism that keeps the UI in line and also offers an abundance of extra functionality that you make use of.

So let's delve into the underbelly of the new UI system and uncover its secrets.

The following is a list of topics that will be covered in this chapter:

- The **Event System** and what it does
- Events and delegates
- Examples to learn by
- What is open source and how to take advantage of it

Note: This is a more advanced chapter than the previous chapters in this book, there is a lot here and it will come in useful for your game development journey but it isn't essential if you just want to use the editor-only features of the new UI system. I leave it in your hands.

Unravelling the Event System

The **EventSystem** is a powerful yet simple manager providing such capabilities as:

- Cataloging all the input systems available
- Monitoring the current input state
- Maintaining the currently selected GameObject
- Updating all the various input systems
- Marshalling Raycast testing between input and screen objects (and not just UI GameObjects!)

We'll discuss what these mean in detail, shortly.

It's worth noting, there can only ever be a single **EventSystem** manager in any scene, no matter how many you try to add. At the core of the **EventSystem** is a static instance that ensures there can be only one.

The **EventSystem** uses all the Event logic described in the following sections of this chapter and manages the state of the UI and even processes the events for selected objects (as described previously).

The Event System loop

Like most managers and Unity itself, the **EventSystem** runs on a loop that looks like the following:

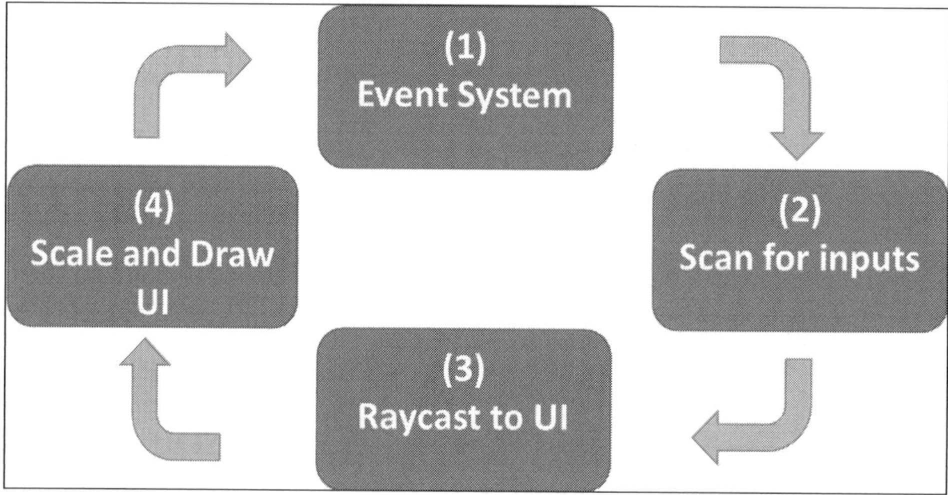

1. **The Event System itself**: At the start of the loop, the **Event System** verifies it has the details of all the active input systems present in your scene and then kicks off the next stage to test those inputs.
2. **Scanner on the scent**: Once the manager knows what types of input are available (such as mouse, keyboard, touch, and so on), it tells each input system in turn to gather their current state.
3. **Casting out the net**: When each input system has its state, they call back to the **Event System** to begin raycasting into the scene using the available raycast systems (Physics raycasters, Graphic raycasters, and so on) to determine if any GameObjects were interacted with by the user's input.

   This then causes the relevant events to be fired informing the relevant GameObjects. (Remember, this affects any GameObject, not just UI. If you only want input to affect UI you have to ensure the **Canvas** blocks raycasts into the scene using a **CanvasGroup**.)
4. **The final frontier**: Once the **Event System** has finished processing, rendering takes place and the **Canvas** draws itself into the scene. This is quite efficient and ensures any user interactions have been dealt with before the drawing takes place (such as a Button highlighting from the user's mouse hovering over it).
5. **Back to The EventSystem itself: And the dance begins again**: Obviously, when you finish the dance you start all over again, once Unity has finished whatever else it needs to do. You know all the other 3D/2D rendering and such.

Controlling state

In its other roles (because it is the only one), the **EventSystem** ensures what the current state of play is in whatever it does, whether that's:

- Which input system is being tested
- What is currently selected (important for the UI navigation system), including what the first (the default object) and previously selected objects were

These are key states that need to be tracked at all times through the game loop, understanding what is being processed at this point in time.

Raycast Marshalling

The **EventSystem** is also the go-to manager for raycast testing. As ever, all roads lead back to the **EventSystem**.

When an input module needs to verify if something needs to be notified by a specific input interaction, it asks the **EventSystem** if anything is in the vicinity of the current coordinates for the input action (mouse pointer or touch). The **EventSystem** then takes this position and then loops through all the raycast modules you have registered on your Canvas to see if anything was hit. The currently supported raycast modules are:

- **Physics Raycaster**: Tests 3D objects within the scene
- **Physics 2D Raycaster**: Tests 2D objects within the scene
- **Graphics Raycaster**: Test UI objects within the scene
- **Another Raycaster**: Build your own raycast test component!

These tests simply return a set of raycast results (if anything was interacted with by each progressive raycast test) for the input manager to handle.

> If you are unfamiliar with Raycasting, check out the Unity documentation at `http://unity3d.com/learn/tutorials/modules/beginner/physics/raycasting`.
>
> Basically, Raycasting is a simple test that takes one coordinate (say the position of a mouse) and a second coordinate (usually dynamically created through the scene using the camera) and tests to see if anything lies between those two points; if anything is hit, this results in a Raycast hit with relevant data about what it was.

Working with events

Behind the new UI system is the introduction of a new **UnityEvent** logic that is intended to standardize and delegate managed interactions between GameObjects in a scene; primarily, it focuses the input interactions with the new UI but it doesn't have to stop there.

At the core of the new UI system there is a new type of delegate manager called the **UnityEvent**. This manager allows you to create, add, and remove multiple delegate functions to it and execute them all at once.

The **UnityEvent** is an extension of the base delegate pattern that is found in most programming languages, obviously now tuned to work better from within Unity's own engine and language interpreter.

For more detail about delegates, see:

- `http://bit.ly/CSharpDelegates`—MS Reference
- `http://bit.ly/CSharpDelegateTutorial`—MS Delegate tutorial
- `http://bit.ly/PowerOfDelegates`—Power of delegates

Starting simple, we'll create a script that will output to the console to show the event has occurred. Create a new `c#` script called `SimpleEvent.cs` and replace its contents with the following:

For standards stake, you should add scripts into a folder called `Scripts` and scenes into a folder called `Scenes`. It's up to you; this isn't mandatory or anything.

```
using UnityEngine;
using UnityEngine.Events;

public class SimpleEvent : MonoBehaviour {
  //My UnityEvent Manager
  public UnityEvent myUnityEvent = new UnityEvent();

  void Start () {
    //Subscribe my delegate to my UnityEvent Manager
    myUnityEvent.AddListener(MyAwesomeDelegate);
    //Execute all registered delegates
    myUnityEvent.Invoke();
  }

  //My Delegate function
  private void MyAwesomeDelegate()
  {
    Debug.Log("My Awesome UnityEvent lives");
  }
}
```

Now, create a new scene and add an empty GameObject into the scene, then rename it to `SimpleEventObject` (as this GameObject is just there to attach the script to, it doesn't matter what it is actually called). Then either drag the script to the new `SimpleEventObject` GameObject or click on **Add Component** in the inspector (with the new **SimpleEventObject** GameObject selected) and find the **SimpleEvent** script to add to it.

Once you have added the script to the **SimpleEventObject**, then you see the following view in the Inspector:

Inspector showing the UnityEvent property drawer

You should recognize the property drawer shown as it's the same one that's used by the built-in UI components that can be interacted with, such as the Button, Slider, and so on. It works the same way too because they also use **UnityEvents**.

Note that it doesn't have to be a UI object you attach the script to; it doesn't even need to have an **EventSystem** in the scene for **UnityEvents** to function!

With the **SimpleEvent** script attached to the **SimpleEventObject** GameObject, when you run your project now, the script will:

1. Call the `Start` method when the scene runs.
2. Register the `MyAwesomeDelegate` function as a delegate of the new **UnityEvent.**
3. `Invoke` (run) the `UnityEvent`, which causes all delegates to fire.
4. Run the `MyAwesomeDelegate` method and output to the debug console.

This is all nice and neat but pretty much the same as what you can do with regular delegates. However, as with the other **UnityEvent** implementations, we can also configure the **UnityEvent** in the inspector thanks to its very useful **Property drawer**.

To show this, let's add an additional method to the previous script (a public one this time) as follows:

```
public void RunMeFromTheInspector()
{
  Debug.Log("Look, I was configured in the inspector");
}
```

Then in the inspector, do the following:

1. Select the **SimpleEventObject**.
2. Click on the **+** symbol of the **UnityEvent** property drawer to register a new **Event**.
3. Leave the **Runtime Only** option alone, since we don't need it running in the editor.

The option **Editor And Runtime** is effectively the same as using the `[ExecuteInEditMode]` code attribute you can use in code. Just runs it continually while the editor is open as well as when the game is running.

Refer to `http://docs.unity3d.com/ScriptReference/ExecuteInEditMode.html` for more information.

4. Select the **SimpleEventObject** using the object selector in the field below the **Runtime Only** option (or drag the GameObject from the scene on to the field). This selects the object the **Event** is to fire against.
5. Finally, use the drop-down box to the right of the **Runtime Only** option to select the action to fire on the selected GameObject. In this case, select the **SimpleEvent | RunMeFromTheInspector()** option to run our new delegate function we created earlier.

This should result in the following view in the **Inspector** with the **SimpleEventObject** selected in the hierarchy:

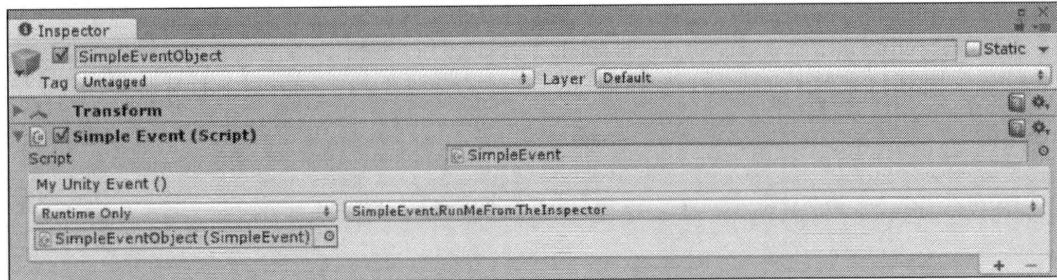

When the project is run this time, it will give us the same effect as with the code declaration. However, it is now being performed using the editor configuration, a world of choice at your fingertips. (You should see two output events, one from code and one from the editor configured option.)

Well, that is all well and good being able to click on something and start an action, but what about if we also want to send some data?

Using a parameter

We can expand on the previous example by using a set of parameters as part of the `UnityEvent` call. First you need to declare a new class type using the parameter pattern you wish to use. This needs to derive from (or be based upon) the `UnityEvent` class using the data type of the information you want to pass. For example, let's create a new `C#` script called `MyParameterizedEventClass` that will derive from `UnityEvent` using a string parameter as follows:

```
using System;
using UnityEngine.Events;

[Serializable]
public class MyParameterizedEventClass : UnityEvent<string>{}
```

If you don't add the `[Serializable]` attribute tag to the class type, the `UnityEvent` will not be available in the editor inspector! (Which you may want to enforce.)

Also, don't forget to add the following `using` statement to the script file (for the `Serializable` attribute), else you will get errors:

```
using System;
```

With our new type, we can now create and use the event as before but now with an optional parameter. So create a new `C#` script called `SimpleParameterizedEvent`, and replace its contents with the following code:

```
using System;
using UnityEngine;
using UnityEngine.Events;

public class SimpleParameterizedEvent : MonoBehaviour {
  //My parameterized UnityEvent Manager
  public  MyParameterizedEventClass myParameterizedEvent =
new MyParameterizedEventClass();
```

```
    void Start ()
    {
    //Subscribe my delegate to my parameterized UnityEvent Manager
      myParameterizedEvent.AddListener(MyOtherDelegate);

    // Execute all registered delegates with the string parameter
      myParameterizedEvent.Invoke("Hello World");
    }

    //My parameterized Delegate function
    private void MyOtherDelegate(string arg0)
    {
      Debug.Log("Some Message - " + arg0);
    }

    public void RunMeFromTheInspector(string arg0)
    {
      Debug.Log("What are you telling me? : " + arg0);
    }
  }
```

If we then add this to our scene as before on a new empty GameObject called **SimpleParameterizedEventObject** and also configure it in the editor as before using the static version of the `RunMeFromTheInspector(string)` method as shown in the following screenshot, we get the same as before but we are now passing it some additional information in the call using the new value field:

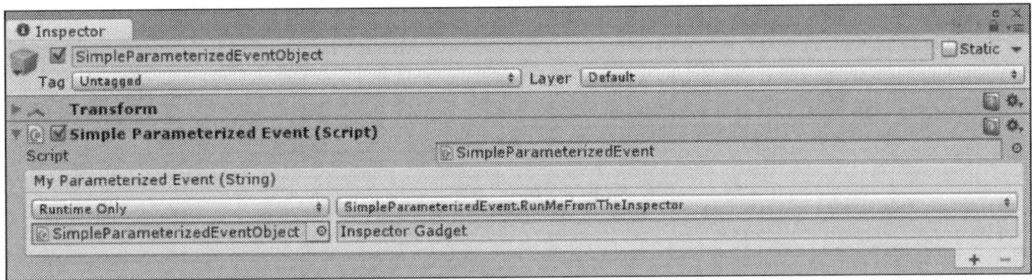

So when we run the project with the previous configuration, we get one message from the code saying **Some Message - Hello World** and one message from the editor configuration saying "**What are you telling me? : Inspector Gadget**".

It's a little more complicated but also gives you a little more freedom.

A word about parameter types

It is worth noting that at present, Unity only supports the `C#` base types (`bool`, `string`, `int`, and `float`) and Unity types (GameObject, and so on) as parameter types with UnityEvents.

See this video at the 10:30 timestamp for more details on the supported data types `http://bit.ly/UnityEventSupportedTypes`.

You can have up to four parameters in a single method with the current version of the `UnityEvent` class at present but you can extend that, if you wish, in the source code (see the *Getting access to the source* section later in this chapter)

Built-in event interfaces

For the UI system, Unity has built a horde of event types and interfaces to support these events, ready to use, straight out of the box. Each of these is implicitly implemented in the Input handlers to ensure all the events occur at the right time depending on user input.

The events that are currently available in Unity 4.6 broken down in to their respective groups are as follows: (which could change over time):

The Pointer Events:

- `IPointerEnterHandler`: This occurs when a cursor (for example a mouse cursor) enters the **Rect Transform** area of a UI object
- `IPointerExitHandler`: This occurs when a cursor leaves the **Rect Transform** area of a UI object
- `IPointerDownHandler`: This occurs when input presses on a selectable UI control (for example, a button)
- `IPointerUpHandler`: This occurs when input is released on a selectable UI control
- `IPointerClickHandler`: This occurs when input clicks (presses and releases) on a selectable UI control

The **Drag Handlers** events:

- `IInitializePotentialDragHandler`: This is the first point at which a drag could be taking place
- `IBeginDragHandler`: This means a confirmed drag action has begun
- `IDragHandler`: This means a UI component is being dragged (pointer down and cursor movement)
- `IEndDragHandler`: This means a dragged UI component has been released (pointer released when dragging)
- `IDropHandler`: This is the same as end drag but without drag data

The **Miscellaneous** handler events:

- `IScrollHandler`: This occurs whenever scrolling is detected from an input device; for example a mouse scroll wheel
- `IUpdateSelectedHandler`: This occurs when the selected UI control is updated/changed
- `ISelectHandler`: This occurs when a UI control is selected/focused upon
- `IDeselectHandler`: This occurs when a UI control is unselected/loses focus
- `IMoveHandler`: This occurs whenever a controller moves (uses `Input.GetAxis`)
- `ISubmitHandler`: This occurs whenever a **Submit** button is pressed (default, the *Enter* key)
- `ICancelHandler`: This occurs whenever a **Submit** button is pressed (default, the *Esc* key)

By using these interfaces in your scripts, you can automatically bind to these events when they occur. Now that we know what's available, how do we use them?

Executing events

To use the built-in events (so your script reacts when the event occurs) is quite simple. As an example, we'll put together a simple script that shows a tooltip when you hover over a UI element.

First create a new `C#` script called `Tooltip` and replace its contents with the following:

```
using UnityEngine;
using UnityEngine.EventSystems;
using UnityEngine.UI;

public class Tooltip : MonoBehaviour
{
  private bool m_tooltipDisplayed = false;
  public RectTransform TooltipItem;
  private Vector3 m_tooltipOffset;
}
```

Next we'll add the two event interfaces we will use for the tooltip, `IPointerEnterHandler` (to detect when the mouse moves over a UI GameObject) and `IPointerExitHandler` (to detect when the mouse moves away from a UI GameObject). To do this, simply update the class definition to the following:

```
public class Tooltip : MonoBehaviour, IPointerEnterHandler,
IPointerExitHandler
```

When you create your own classes using the event handlers, the interface names are sometimes shown with red squiggles. To fix this just right-click the interface with the red squiggle and select **Resolve | using UnityEngine.EventSystems** menu item.

You can also just add the `using UnityEngine.EventSystems;` to the top of the script manually.

With the interfaces added, we need to add the handler methods for those interfaces, so add the following to your script:

```
public void OnPointerEnter(PointerEventData eventData)
{
  //Mark the tooltip as displayed
  m_tooltipDisplayed = true;
  //Move the tooltip item to the detected GO and offset it above
  TooltipItem.transform.position =
```

```
transform.position + m_tooltipOffset;
  //Activate the tooltip
  TooltipItem.gameObject.SetActive(m_tooltipDisplayed);
}

public void OnPointerExit(PointerEventData eventData)
{
  m_tooltipDisplayed = false;
  TooltipItem.gameObject.SetActive(m_tooltipDisplayed);
}
```

Alternatively, in Visual Studio or MonoDevelop, you can just right-click the interface name (for example, `IPointerEnterHandler`) and navigate to **Implement Interface | Implement Interface** to add all the necessary methods to your class automatically.

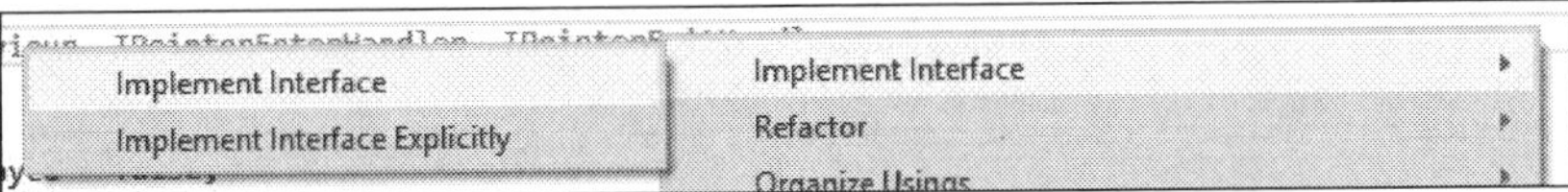

You just then need to add code to the generated method for what to do when the event occurs (as shown in the previous screenshot).

It is also worth noting that in different versions of MonoDevelop and Visual Studio, the public portion of the function may or may not be added. Either will work, and it's up to you whether you want to expose those functions outside of your script.

To finish, we just need to set up the properties for when the script starts by adding the following method to the `Tooltip` script:

```
void Start () {
  //Offset the tooltip above the target GameObject
  m_tooltipOffset =
new Vector3(0,TooltipItem.sizeDelta.y ,0);
  //Deactivate the tooltip so that it is only shown when you
//want it to
  TooltipItem.gameObject.SetActive(m_tooltipDisplayed);
}
```

Now that you have the script, in order to use it we need to:

1. Create a `UI` element called `HoverOverMe` on a **Canvas** and add the `Tooltip` script to it.
2. Create another `UI` element for the **tooltip**, say an image (add a `Text` component as a child if you wish). Make sure to position it off the UI Canvas so it does not block the UI on startup.
3. Select the **HoverOverMe** GameObject and set the **Tooltip Item** property of the **Tooltip** script to the UI element you created for the tooltip.

Done! Now when you run the project, the tooltip will pop up above the UI element you attached the script to when the mouse moves over it and when it moves away it will be hidden. In the example project, I created an **Image** and added the **ToolTip script** to it. I then added another **Image** called **ToolTip**, this time with a **Text** control as a child (setting the **Text Anchor** to **Fill**). Finally, I set the **Tooltip Item** property of the script on the initial **Image** to my new ToolTip Image/Text GameObject. This was the result:

Note, the Tooltip (shown in green) only appears when the mouse is over the GameObject (shown in white).

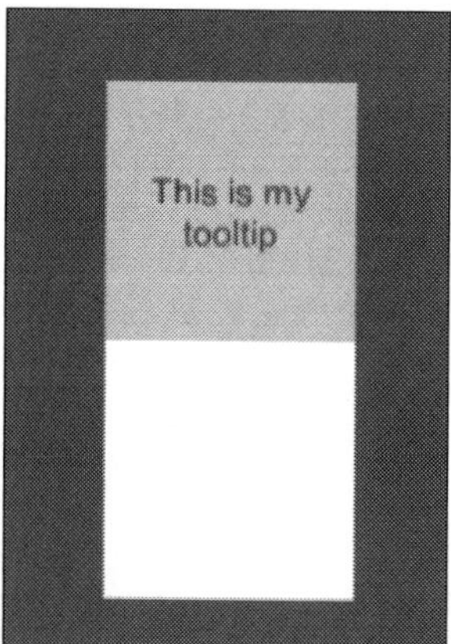

Note: This is a very basic implementation and only works for **Screen Space - Overlay** canvases. To use it with **Screen Space - Camera** or **World Space** canvases, you will have to translate the mouse position with the `ScreenPointToRay` function (check out the **UIWindowBase** example later for more details).

You could also have several objects using the same tooltip; or even make the tooltip dynamic and change its text/image based on the object it hovers over.

So how does this actually work then? Sure, we have this script but what does it all mean?

Since we added the `IPointerEnterHandler` and `IPointerExitHandler` interfaces, the following now happens:

> Note: If you only add the interfaces and not the implemented methods, your script will fail with a message like this:
>
> **Does not implement interface member** `UnityEngine.EventSystems.IPointerExitHandler.OnPointerExit(UnityEngine.EventSystems.PointerEventData)`'
>
> To fix this, add the methods you are missing manually, or by using the automatic method mentioned earlier.

- You have a script that implemented one of the previously mentioned events attached to a GameObject in a scene
- When an input handler (say the `StandaloneInputModule`) needs to fire an event it will search for relevant GameObjects that implement the interface for the event (this may be limited to those identified by raycast hits)
- If a GameObject is found to be implementing the relevant interface, it then executes the handler method for that interface and passes the necessary data for that event with it

Some events are managed by the Input handlers, others are managed by the Event system itself.

All this framework does, is to make it incredibly simple to add handling for these types of events to any script or component easily.

Building your own handlers or custom events

Now, you don't have to edit Unity's UI source code to build your own events; you can just write your own. It is a bit of a complicated setup but if you follow the standard, then it will be a lot easier to manage alongside Unity's UI framework (and if you find it immensely useful you could submit it to Unity later).

This is optional, of course, and you can still do your own thing if you are so inclined. However, a lot of thought went into the current event framework that Unity has built, so it's worth considering.

To build your own event, you will need to define the following:

- A custom event data structure (extending from `BaseEventData`).
- An interface for the custom event (extending from `IEventSystemHandler`).
- A static container class containing the Execute functions.
- (*Optional*) An Input module (extending from `BaseInputModule`) to process and execute your events. This could be done from anywhere, however.
- A class or GameObject that implements your interface (covered previously).

This sounds like a lot, but in reality it really is (just kidding)!

The main reason you would want to build your own events is to manage things going on in your game world that other objects need to know about, such as:

- An alarm system alerting all droids to swarm in
- Targeting data, to tell your starships to attack a certain point
- A conversation or event log system, where several parties needs to feed data in to be displayed

If we take the first example, let's walk through setting up our custom event handler. An alarm system is a great fit for this, especially with an **Input Manager** that monitors all cameras and sends all the droids if one detects something. (I really like this idea, as it could open up possibilities of hacking cameras to prevent the alarm being raised.)

A custom event Data Structure

When planning your custom event, the cornerstone is what data you consider to be important when this event fires. In the built-in interfaces, this can include information such as which GameObject is being affected, the mouse cursor position, and so on.

To start off, we'll create a new `C#` script to put all this code into one file, just so it's readable. To fully implement it, however, you would need an actual game to wrap around it. The main aim here is to set you on the path.

To keep this example simple, we will put all the **UnityEvent** code in a single code file called `AlarmSystem`. This is optional, of course, and you can create separate scripts for each section if you so wish.

Having the code all together like this will just make it easier to maintain all the crisscrossed event code.

So create a new `C#` script called `AlarmSystem` and replace its contents with the following (just the base using statements we need):

```
using UnityEngine;
using UnityEngine.EventSystems;
```

For our alarm, we only need the location of the alarm trigger point to send our drones in which would look like the following code, add this to our AlarmSystem script:

```
// Custom data we will send via the event system
public class AlarmEventData : BaseEventData
{
    public Vector3 AlarmTriggerData;

    public AlarmEventData(EventSystem eventSystem,
Vector3 alarmTriggerData): base(eventSystem)
    {
        AlarmTriggerData = alarmTriggerData;
    }
}
```

The important parts of this class definition are:

- The class derives from the `BaseEventData` class
- The class constructor passes the `EventSystem` for the event back to the base class constructor using the `base()` notation
- With our data in place we can now define our interface

I've used a `Vector3` here for the event data to identify the location of the alarm that has been triggered. If you were just doing a 2D game then this could be changed to a `Vector2`. Alternatively, you might want to add more data such as the direction of the camera with another Vector. The choice is up to you.

A custom event Interface

The interface for your event is by far the simplest part of the puzzle and looks like the following code. Just add this to the `AlarmSystem` script (after the `AlarmEventData` class section) we created earlier:

```
// The interface you implement
// in your MonoBehaviours to receive events
public interface IAlarmHandler : IEventSystemHandler
{
    void OnAlarmTrigger(AlarmEventData eventData);
}
```

Here we are simply defining:

- The name of the interface to be used on all classes implementing our alarm system (will this also include turrets?)

Standards suggest that all interfaces are prefixed with the uppercase letter I, so that they are easily distinguishable and easy to read.

- A simple method that will be used as the template in classes that implement the interface (there can be more than one if you support multiple actions)

Now that this is ready, it can be used on classes in the project; however, next we need to be able to handle the event.

A custom event static container

So that the Event System can call your custom event in the same way that it calls the rest of the events in its control, you need some boilerplate code so it can use it effectively, which looks like the following code. Add this after the `IAlarmHandler` interface in the `AlarmSystem` script:

```
// container class that holds the execution logic that is called
// by the event system to delegate the call to the interface
public static class MyAlarmTriggerEvents
{
    // call that does the mapping
    private static void Execute(IAlarmHandler handler,
BaseEventData eventData)
    {
```

```
        // The ValidateEventData makes sure the passed event
    // data is of the correct type
            handler.OnAlarmTrigger(
  ExecuteEvents.ValidateEventData<AlarmEventData>(eventData));
        }

        // helper to return the function that should be invoked
        public static
    ExecuteEvents.EventFunction<IAlarmHandler> AlarmEventHandler
        {
            get { return Execute; }
        }
}
```

There is not much to say at this point, when you execute the event you will pass the `AlarmEventHandler` that will in turn inform the Event System what the execute method is for the event.

Processing a custom event

Right with our `EventHandler` all written up, next we simply need to implement it within our sample game.

The last piece of the puzzle is the raising of the event, the point at which the event occurs and all objects implementing the interface are informed that the event has happened.

For this, we will need a separate `input module` script that we can attach to an Event System, so create a new C# script called `MyAlarmScannerModule` and replace its contents with the following:

```
using UnityEngine;
using UnityEngine.EventSystems;
//Custom input module that can send the events
public class MyAlarmScannerModule : BaseInputModule
{
    // list of objects to invoke on
    public GameObject[] TargetDroids;
    // Variable to store the location of a triggered alarm
      private Vector3 TriggeredCameraLocation;
    // Variable to denote if the alarm has been activated or not
      private bool alarmTriggered;

    // called each tick on active input module
```

```
        public override void Process()
        {
            // if we don't have targets return
            if (TargetDroids == null ||  TargetDroids.Length == 0)
                return;
            // If the alarm has already been triggered
    // then there's no point shouting
            if (alarmTriggered)
                return;

            //Placeholder to add some snazzy logic to locate triggered
    //alarms, just returns none for now.
            TriggeredCameraLocation = Vector3.zero;

            // for each droid invoke our custom event if the alarm
            // is triggered
            if (TriggeredCameraLocation != Vector3.zero)
            {
                alarmTriggered = true;
                var eventdata = new AlarmEventData(eventSystem,
                  TriggeredCameraLocation);
                foreach (var droid in TargetDroids)
                {
                    ExecuteEvents.Execute(droid, eventdata,
                      MyAlarmTriggerEvents.AlarmEventHandler);
                }
            }
        }
    }
```

The only important part of this script is the `Process` method, as this is called by the `BaseInputModule` class when it is this script's turn to run (called by the **EventSystem**). Within this script you need to go through whatever selection logic you need to use to identify those GameObjects that need notifying (in this case, the set of droids on our level looking for trouble), then for each droid we are calling Executing the event on that GameObject if it exists.

Granted, this is a very simplistic example, there are more complicated scenarios you can implement, most of which are implemented in the **Input Modules** in the UI source. Jump down to the *Getting access to the source* section and browse through the source if you dare!

You don't have to build an input system if you don't want to; this is just one example. If you wish you can simply call `ExecuteEvents.Execute` (provided you have a reference to the **Event System** from the scene) from anywhere in your code to fire an event, say for a Game Over event maybe!

The Roll a Ball Derby

If we take the previous system and put it into action in a simple example, we can start to see the possibilities of the new UnityEvent system.

> For this, I used Unity's own *Roll a Ball* example from their tutorial site, which you can follow along to create the base sample: `http://unity3d.com/learn/tutorials/projects/roll-a-ball`.
>
> To save time (and since Unity doesn't provide a finished version of the tutorial) I've created a Unity package you can import to speed along its creation, which you can download from `http://bit.ly/1AaDKF2` and then import into your project using **Assets | Import Package | Custom Package** in the menu. (It's also included in the code bundle for this project in the `Chapter 6` folder).

In the *Roll A Ball* example, we start off with a simple scene where our valiant hero ball is completely surrounded, as you can see in the following screenshot:

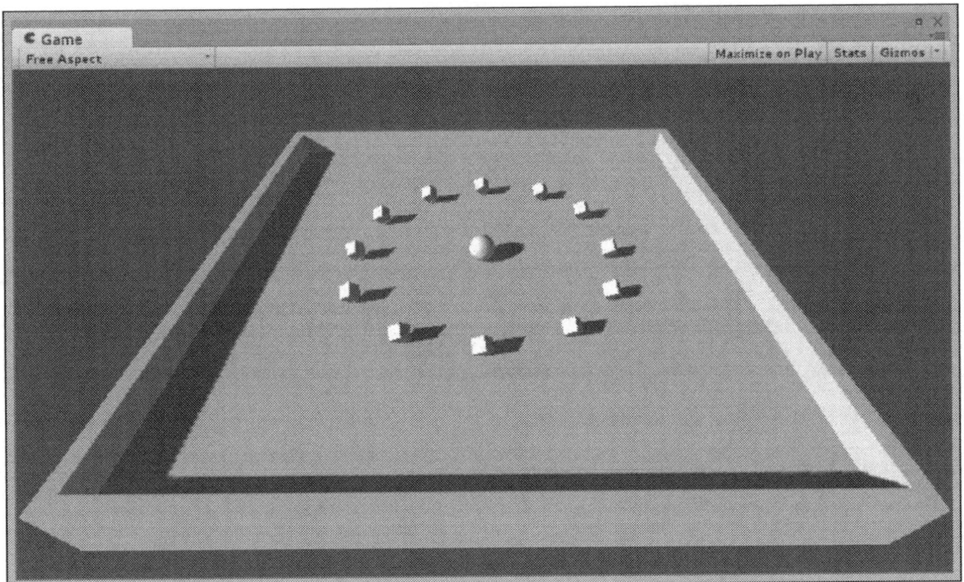

The completed Roll A Ball Unity tutorial (without the GUIText parts)

Make sure you have also added the **AlarmSystem** and **MyAlarmScannerModule** scripts from the previous section to complete this example.

In this example, we will add four alarm plates, which when triggered will cause all the enemy spinning blocks to charge in to attack the hero. (However, since the ball just collects the cubes, it really ends up more like Mario with a Coin hoover.)

To implement our fancy new custom event, we need a couple of things, namely:

- A script that implements our new event interface
- A script for the `Alarm` trigger that our Custom Input System will be watching out for
- Some logic in our Custom Input system to watch for triggered alarms (we just have boilerplate at the moment that does nothing)

All of this is very simple and basic.

This example has been greatly simplified in order to fit it within the scope of this title (else it could have been at least twice as big). I'll probably do a much larger example using these techniques on my blog at a later date (if I haven't yet when you're reading this). Keep an eye on the forums where it will be announced.

The Droid script

The script for our alert sentries, who are waiting for some kind of alarm to strike them into action is very easy to implement (especially if you have been following along). It is in effect no different to building a script that implements the built-in UI events.

First, create a new C# script called `DroidScript` (either in the **Project** script folder or in the **Roll a Ball** script folder) and either add the `IAlarmHandler` interface manually to implement that interface (using the handy trick I showed you earlier) or just replace its contents with the following:

```
using System.Collections;
using UnityEngine;
```

```
public class DroidScript : MonoBehaviour, IAlarmHandler {

  public void OnAlarmTrigger(AlarmEventData eventData)
  {
    //Intruder found, attack!!!
  }
}
```

So we have our event template, to this we'll add a simple `Coroutine` (after the `OnAlarmTrigger` function) that will make our cubes race to the alarm spot once it triggers, as shown in the following code (mainly to have something visible to see, I would have preferred turrets shooting at their foe but that would have been a lot more to script):

```
  //Coroutine that will move an object from its current
//position to another
IEnumerator MoveToPoint(Vector3 target)
  {
    float timer = 0f;
    var StartPosition = transform.position;
    while (target != transform.position)
    {
      transform.position =
Vector3.Lerp(StartPosition, target, timer);
      timer += Time.deltaTime;
      yield return new WaitForEndOfFrame();
    }
    yield return null;
  }
```

Next, we update the `OnAlarmTrigger` function for the interface, to call `Coroutine` when it's called:

```
  public void OnAlarmTrigger(AlarmEventData eventData)
  {
    //Intruder found, attack!!!
    StartCoroutine(MoveToPoint(eventData.AlarmTriggerData));
  }
```

To finish off, add the `DroidScript` script to the **Pickup Prefab** (select the **Pickup prefab**, click **Add** Component in the inspector, and select the script) and the rolling cubes of death will be ready.

If you add the script to the individual **Pickup** instances in the scene you will have to do it many times (and also you have remember to add it to any other pickups you add in the scene). If you add it to the **Pickup Prefab**, then all instances of that prefab will automatically be updated!

Now our cunning cubes will race to assault the intruder once the alarm fires, so now we need the actual alarm.

The Alarm plates

Again, we'll keep things simple. For the alarm trigger, we will just add some pressure plates to the floor that when the hero runs over them, they will mark themselves as triggered.

First add a new **Plane** (**Create** | **3D Object** | **Plane**) to the scene, reset its position (using the cog icon in the top-right hand corner of the **Transform** component in the **Inspector** window) and scale it down to a reasonable size (such as `0.15` on the **X**, **Y** and **Z Transform Scale** properties). Name the new **Plane** `Alarm` and also set its **Mesh Collider** to a Trigger by checking the **Is Trigger** property, as shown in the following screenshot (leave all the other options as per their defaults):

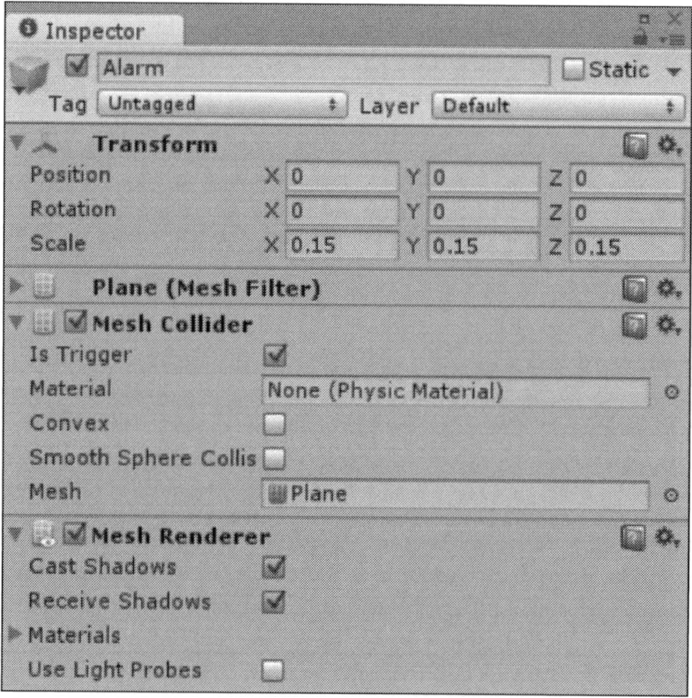

As we intend to have more than one alarm, make this new creation a **Prefab** by dragging the **Alarm** GameObject from the project **Hierarchy** to the **Prefabs** folder.

> The **Alarm** GameObject should now turn blue in the project hierarchy to denote it is now a prefab instance.

Now that we have our prefab, create an Empty GameObject in the scene, reset its position, and name it **Alarms** (this will be our **Alarms** grouping object). Then drag our current **Alarm** to the **Alarms** GameObject to make it a child, then reset its position.

Next position the **Alarm** in the scene at an appropriate point to trip the hero up (as shown in the following screenshot). I placed it to the side between the Hero sphere and the blocks (because I'm evil); additionally, (if you wish) raise it up a bit on the **Y** axis (say `0.1`) so that it is above the ground plane.

Now one **Alarm** is fun, but four are better, so duplicate the **Alarm** (by navigating to **Edit | Duplicate** in the menu or *Ctrl/Cmd D*) and move them to other positions in the scene. Here is a screenshot of what I ended up with (but the final placement is up to you!):

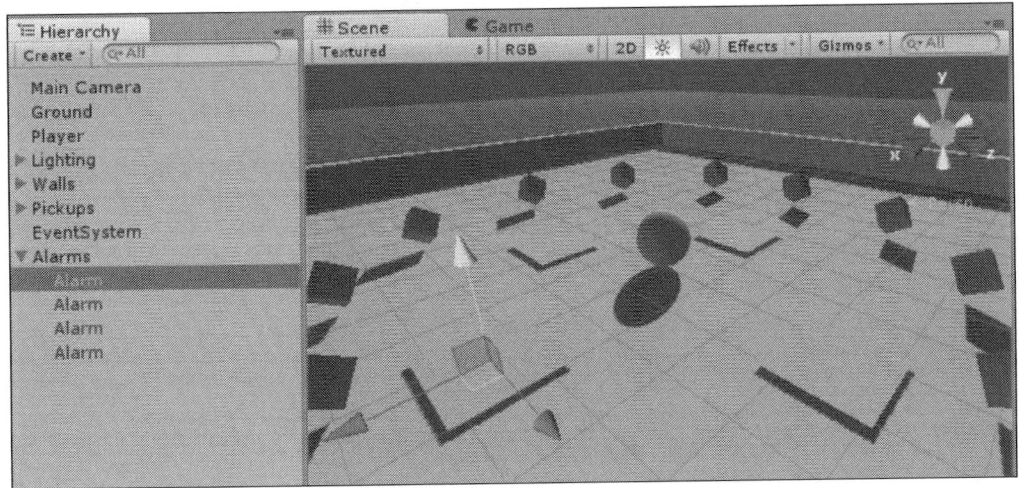

With our **Alarms** in place, all we need now is a simple script to change the state of the **Alarm** once the Hero triggers it. So create a new `C#` script called `AlarmScript` and replace its contents as follows:

```
using UnityEngine;

public class AlarmScript : MonoBehaviour {
  void OnTriggerEnter(Collider other)
  {
    gameObject.SetActive(false);
  }
}
```

Just a very basic script to deactivate the **Alarm** if the Hero's Sphere enters the alarm's plane collider, nothing fancy.

To finish off, add the **AlarmScript** script to the **Alarm Prefab** and we are set.

Who watches the watchers?

To close, we need to replace the boilerplate in our `MyAlarmScannerModule` input module that is managing the events to scan the alarms and send in the killer robots if any foolish Hero tries to plunder the gold.

To keep with the basic example thread, we will just add another public property to our custom input module that manages all the available alarms in the scene. We will then iterate over those alarms and look for any that have been made inactive by the clumsy Hero tripping over them.

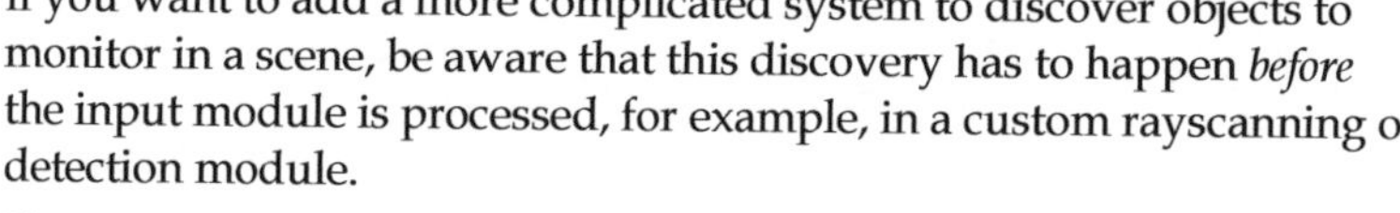

If you want to add a more complicated system to discover objects to monitor in a scene, be aware that this discovery has to happen *before* the input module is processed, for example, in a custom rayscanning or detection module.

If you try to build an array of objects (say using the `GetObjectsWIthTag` method) in the `Process` method, it will be unable to interrogate the list. It's not immediately obvious why this doesn't work, but if I was to hazard a guess, it's that the processing of the Input modules is either handled on another thread or is using some uber performant process. Simply put, it won't be able to see changes in your scene.

I'll see about adding a more complicated scenario in the follow-up example on my blog.

With that in mind, let's edit the `MyAlarmScannerModule` script and add a new public property for the `Alarms` as follows:

```
public GameObject[] Alarms;
```

Then replace the boiler plate line

```
TriggeredCameraLocation = Vector3.zero;
```

with the following:

```
TriggeredCameraLocation = Vector3.zero;
foreach (var alarm in Alarms)
{
    if (!alarm.activeSelf)
    {
        TriggeredCameraLocation = alarm.transform.position;
    }
}
```

This simply loops the alarms and if it finds one that is inactive, it sets the `TriggeredCameraLocation` to the position of the triggered alarm; this will then cause all the selected **Droids** to be activated.

With everything set, all that remains is to create an **EventSystem** in the scene (**Create** | **UI** | **EventSystem**), add the `MyAlarmScannerModule` script to the **EventSystem**, then add all the Pickups to the `Target Droids` array property and all the `Alarms` to the `Alarms array` property.

Note: We only add an **EventSystem** to the scene for the custom input module. We don't actually need a **Canvas** or any UI components!

If everything went well, when you run the scene and move the sphere using the arrow keys, when the Hero accidentally trips one of the alarms, they will be assaulted from all sides by the cubes.

> A handy tip when assigning multiples of anything from a scene to an array property in the inspector is to Lock the inspector and then drag them all at once.
>
> To lock the inspector simply click the **Lock** icon in the upper-right hand corner of the **Inspector** window. While locked, it will not change its view to any other objects selected in the scene. This allows you to multiple select all the **Pickups** or **Alarms** and drag them all at once to their respective properties in the **Inspector** window.
>
> For a visual explanation of this, check out the second image in the set of animated GIFs at `http://bit.ly/UnityAnimatedTips` (also check out the others while you are at it!).

Summing up the Event System

With great power comes great responsibility. This is so true with the new **EventSystem**; there is a lot going on under the covers and a lot of performance tweaks and enhancements that are unseen.

Granted, the previous example could have been achieved with delegates and a singleton manager coordinating everything, but it is a very basic example.

In truth, it could be a whole lot bigger with a scanner module that looks for collisions near the player that feeds into the alarm system, or independent radar style scanners for each alarm. Because the system is so modular, you can craft almost anything in a componentized fashion and it will be fast (provided you stick to the rules). Plus the interface design ensures it is fast and easy in a more object-orientated way to design your game and be sure it's not going to break in some freakish fashion.

I leave it to you to play further (or wait until I publish a new free, fully featured bonus tutorial on my blog).

Examples, examples, and even more examples

Now I could probably go on for several more books creating and walking you through many different code examples; however, this time I've created a public repository of all the scripts I have either come across, put together, or enhanced in my journey through the Unity UI, which can be found at `http://bit.ly/UnityUIExtensions`.

Keep an eye on the following thread in the Unity UI forums, where most of the scripts here came from, contributed from many stars of the forums:
`http://bit.ly/UnityUIScriptsForumPost`

At the time of writing, the following examples were found:

- **UI Window Base**: This example started its life on the Unity forums and was enhanced/updated and rewritten several times before I finally grabbed the best of all the changes into one final script. Its main goal is to add, drag, and drop support to any UI component. Additionally, this script now works with all types of Canvases, **Screen Space - Overlay**, **Screen Space - Camera**, and even **World Space** Canvases.
- **Curved Text**: This script still amazes me for both its simplicity and effectiveness. Add this to any **Text** component and watch your Text bend over a programmable curve, complete with intensity (careful, Intensity 1 is very strong, so you might want to use something more like 0.06!). This shows the power of being able to modify the vertex data of a UI graphics component.
- **Gradient**: This is another script from the same author as the Curved Text script, yet again, it's brilliant in its implementation. Simply put, add this to any component that provides vertex data and it will allow you to apply a color gradient to it. It's just fun to play with and breaks down how it works very clearly.
- **Tab Navigation**: This is a simple, yet welcome extension for anyone who needs to have forms in their title. Simply put, use *Tab* to go to the next field and *Shift* + *Tab* to go to the previous field.
- **RaycastMask**: This is an essential script especially if you have round or complex-shaped graphics. It ensures that raycast events only fire when the cursor is actually over your sprite not just the **Rect Transform**. This gives a more accurate and finer test if you need something more granular (such as individual image pixels) than just a box.
- More to come, keep an eye on the repository!

Getting access to the source

In a bold move, Unity released almost all the source code for the new **Unity UI** system as an open source project via `Bitbucket.org`. This isn't the first time they have made things public; back in October 2014, Unity released their Unit Test Tools and a bunch of examples on their new public account (check them all out at `https://Bitbucket.org/Unity-Technologies`).

Note: This section assumes you have either Visual Studio (2012+ express/community, pro, or ultimate), MonoDevelop, or Xamarin Studio installed to build and edit code. By default, you should already have MonoDevelop installed when you installed Unity.

You can browse the code all you like on the website, but to build/use it on your machine you will need a code editor and code build engine.

This is however, the first time they have released a core part of the Unity Engine for all to see (there have been a few other side projects but this is the biggest so far), to break it apart and even replace it in your own installs. Not only that, they are welcoming developers to review their code and suggest fixes/updates (within one week there were already 74 copies/forks of the new UI system); the world has become a very interesting place indeed.

Granted not everything is in there, the **Canvas** for example is a core engine component with specific rendering code so that isn't exposed, however, almost everything else is there to tinker with.

In this section, we'll walk over the repository itself (if you are not yet familiar with it), how you get access to the code, make changes, and even submit your suggestions.

Note: If you do find a bug and are unsure how to resolve it, then you should still use the Unity Bug Tracker built into Unity (**Help | Report a bug**) or pop along to the Unity UI forum located at `http://forum.unity3d.com/forums/unity-ui.60`.

The repository

As the code repository is completely open to the public, getting access to it is very simple. Just navigate to `https://Bitbucket.org/Unity-Technologies/ui` and you will see the following page:

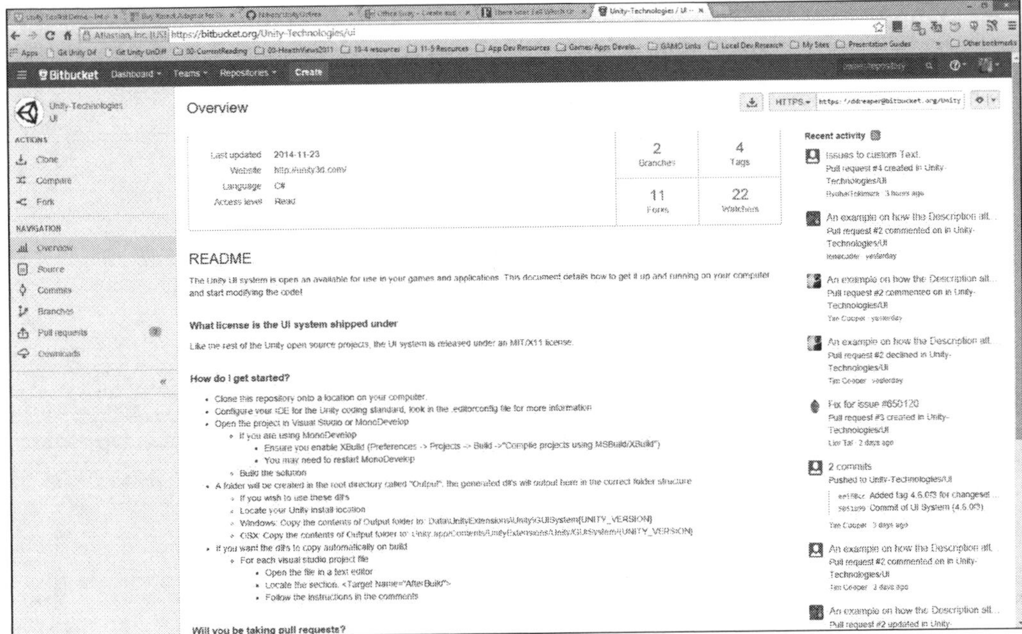

The Unity UI Bitbucket source page (at time of writing this)

From here you can browse the source using the **Source** link on the left or simply check out all the existing changes to the project through the **Commits** link. If you are feeling brave you can also see what other changes have already been proposed by other committed developers (or should be) using the **Pull Requests** link.

Additionally, you can see a feed to the right of all the recent activity.

The main part of the page is taken up with instructions for how to get involved and more importantly, how to run with the code in your local environment, but more on that later.

> Note: The source control system used by Unity is Mercurial (`http://mercurial.selenic.com/about`), a very similar distributed version control system (DVCS) to the other popular source control system, GIT. Keep this in mind if you have your own source control clients and want to connect to the UI project.

Getting forked

So you have decided you want to at least look through the code on your own machine and make changes for yourself; so, what next?

[Note: If you only want to download and examine the code you can skip this step and jump straight to the following *Downloading the code* section. You can change your mind at any time and return here if you suddenly have the urge to make changes.]

The first thing you do is to make your own source copy of the UI project; this process is called **Creating a Fork**. This clones the entire project into your own area on Bitbucket's own code servers, and every change you make within this new repository is your own and (more importantly) linked back to the original project.

[The link between your own copy of the project and the original is crucial if you later want to send changes back to the original (parent) project later.]

It is very simple to create your own fork:

1. First navigate to the Unity UI Bitbucket site (`https://Bitbucket.org/Unity-Technologies/ui`).
2. Log in to Bitbucket, if you haven't done so already.

[It's free to register and host your own projects on Bitbucket. So even after you have finished playing with the Unity UI code you can go and create your own public/private projects. If you also want to host your projects on Bitbucket it's free; just be sure to configure your Unity environment in the same way you do for GIT source control. Check out this post for more details: `http://bit.ly/UnitySourceControlSetup`.]

3. Click on the **Fork** action in the top-left hand corner of the Bitbucket page.
4. You will now see a form (as shown in the screenshot) for your copy of the project. Here you can select various options such as making it public or private (can the rest of the world see it), what permissions to assign, and whether you want a bug tracking system or **Wiki** attached to it.

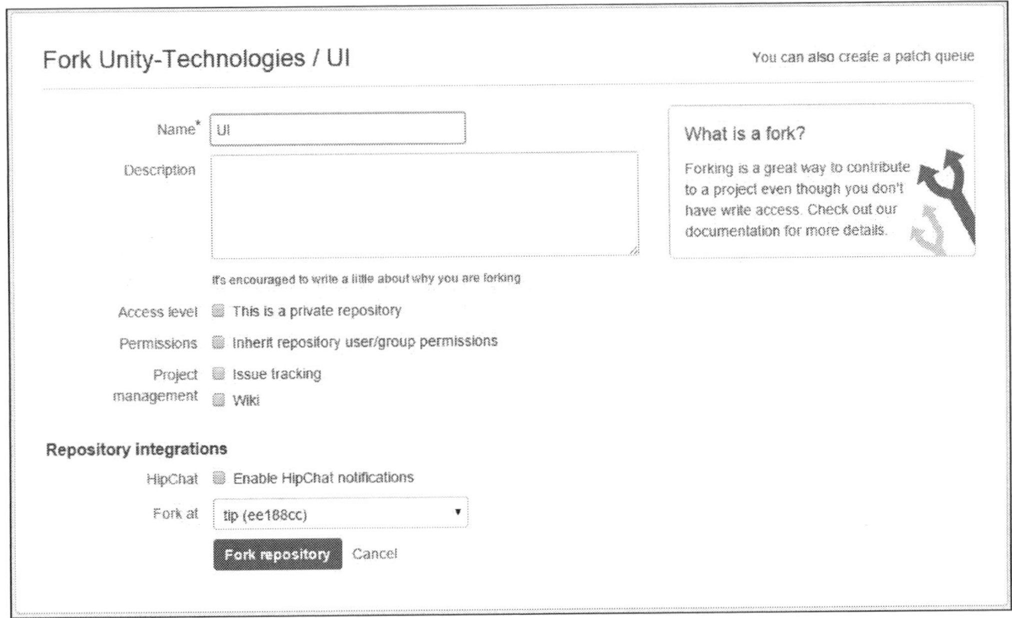

Bitbucket Fork request form

Once you have completed the form, the cogs at Bitbucket will churn for a while and then spit out your very own project. You will then be returned to the project's start page, however, this time it's your project, not Unity's.

When browsing any open source project via the source control website, be sure you are looking at the correct one. Don't get confused if you aren't seeing your changes when you accidentally look at the parent project.

With Bitbucket (as with most) it's easy enough to see whose project you are looking at; just check the top-left hand corner where the project information and owner are listed.

Expect a few double takes till you get used to it.

There are many other advanced options when creating a fork; however, most are only used within your own projects and not when working with someone else's project.

I actually had the fourth Fork of the Unity UI Bitbucket project but had to delete it for the purposes of the book—my claim to fame is gone. The first ever commit from the public was done by **Andreia Gaita**, which was accepted and merged. Well done Andreia!

Downloading the code

So you have access to Unity's UI project and possibly made your own Fork (copy) of the code (granted, completely optional). Now how do you get the code down to your machine.

> You can actually just download all the source code in a compressed file using the **Downloads** link on the left-hand side of the page. However, this isn't recommended as it will be disconnected from the main project (you won't receive updates) and any changes you make could be lost (if you don't back it up properly).
>
> It's an option but not one I'd recommend.

First off, you are going to need a source control client to pull the code from the server onto your computer and keep it linked. Here are a few possible options:

- **Atlassian SourceTree** (`http://www.sourcetreeapp.com/`): This is a nice graphical client that is available for most operating systems
- **Tortoise HG** (`http://tortoisehg.Bitbucket.org/`): This is my preferred client as it integrates tightly with Windows Explorer and offers several GUI management screens

> There are many other Mercurial clients for various operating systems that you can find on the Mercurial site at `http://mercurial.selenic.com/wiki/OtherTools`.

Bitbucket themselves (oddly enough since they make it) recommend SourceTree; you'll find links peppered around the website and they also offer integration with all projects hosted on Bitbucket. If you only use Bitbucket then it's not a bad option to choose.

> If, however, you work on several open source projects on many sites, I'd recommend the Tortoise source control clients. It's my preference; however, the choice is ultimately up to you of course.
>
> There's nothing particularly wrong with SourceTree and it will work with several DCVS systems.

Once you have your client installed, you need to get the **Pull URL** from the projects website as shown here:

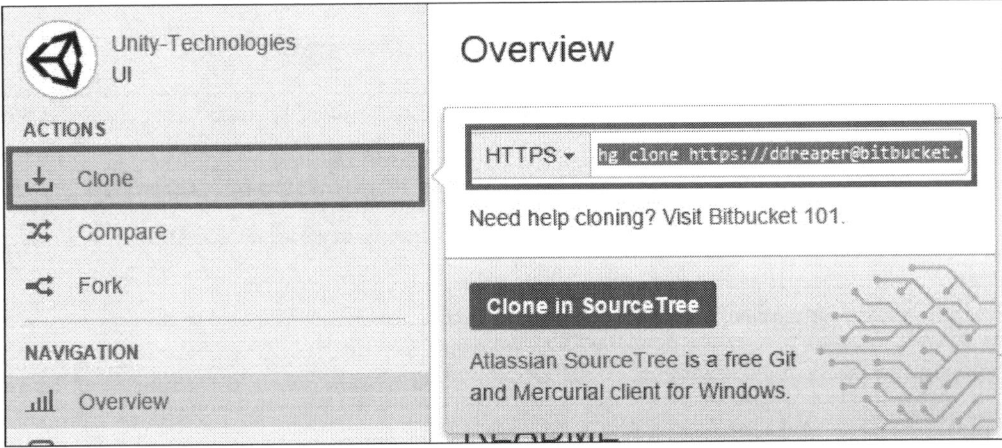

The Clone action on the Bitbucket site to get the code

If you have **SourceTree** installed, you can actually just click the **Clone in SourceTree** button as well. I did say the integration is peppered everywhere and aimed at beginner users.

Alternatively, you can also find this URL published on the front page of the project's website in the upper-right hand corner of the screen as shown here:

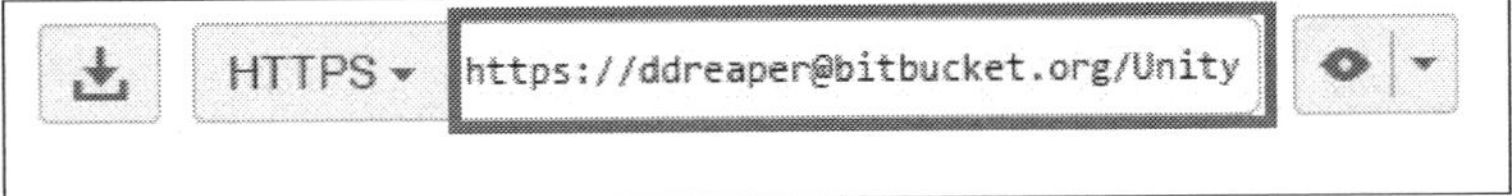

Once you have the URL, all that's left is to then clone the project to a folder on your local machine, assuming you are using **SourceTree** you will see something like the following once the operation is completed:

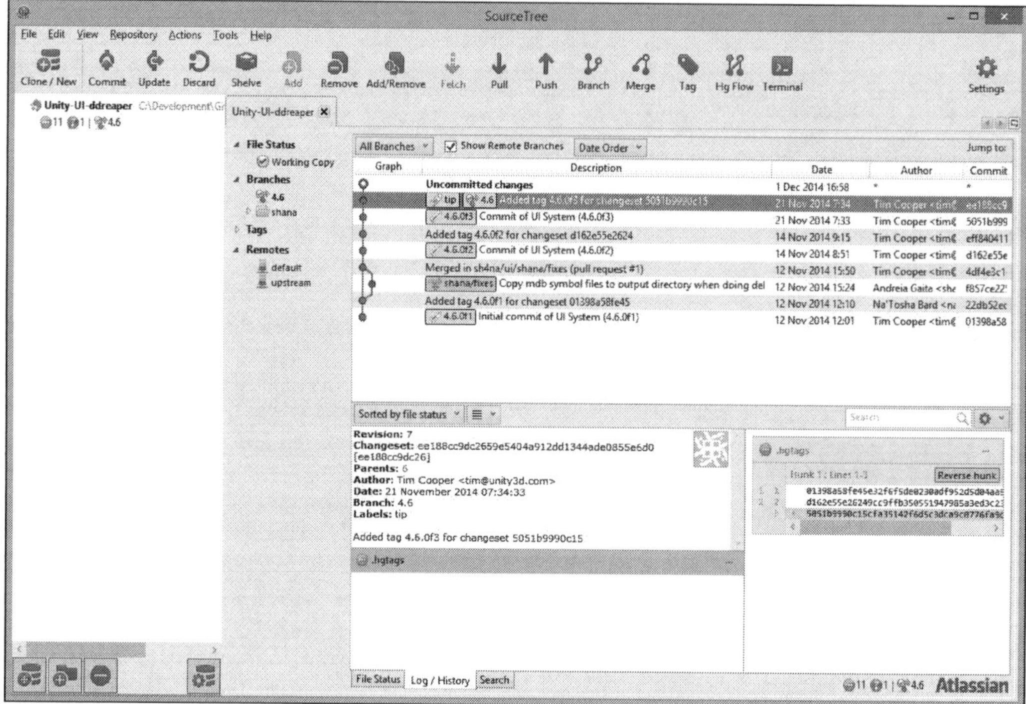

The UI project open in SourceTree

> With the Tortoise clients you need only:
>
> - Open **Windows Explorer**.
> - Navigate to where you want to download (clone) the code.
> - Right-click and navigate to **TortoiseHG | Clone**.
> - Give the destination folder a name (the source URL will be prepopulated from your clipboard, if it doesn't then just paste the URL into the source field and check your destination folder).
> - Click **Clone**.
>
> It's just my preference to use **Windows Explorer** really.

So you now have the code and can browse through it at your leisure and start making your plans to take over the world. Ahem, maybe that's just me!

As a *big* tip, if you are using **Visual Studio** to view the code, then I highly recommend downloading the **VisualHG** extension (**Tools | Extensions and Updates**) and then setting the source control manager for the project (**Tools | Options | Source Control**) to **VisualHG**. You will then see a graphically enhanced **Solution Explorer** and see the change state of each file. This gives you direct access to any modification/changes to source from within **Visual Studio**!

Keeping up to date

Over time with each new release Unity will be updating the source repository on BitBucket with changes and fixes, so you need to ensure you keep up to date.

When a new release is announced, be sure to pop over to your repository on the BitBucket website and use the **Sync** feature that will appear in the top-right hand corner of the page. This will automatically get any new changes and attempt to merge them into your own project. Then you will need to refresh your local code via your source control application so that you are now working with the latest source.

Be sure to check if any changes you are working on are affected by the Unity changes by updating any separate develop branches you have as well as by refreshing them. Each is a separate project in its own right.

If however, you have not created your own fork/copy, simply update/refresh your local Mercurial repository using your source control application to continue.

One great thing about the source being public is that you have more detailed information about what has changed in a file-by-file, line-by-line comparison between releases. The easiest way to see this is via the commit entries for the project.

What is in the solution?

Now you have the code on your machine, let's delve into what we have.

Open the folder where the Unity UI code has been copied to on your machine and open the `UISystem.sln` file by double clicking it and that will open your code editor of choice, such as **MonoDevelop**, as shown here:

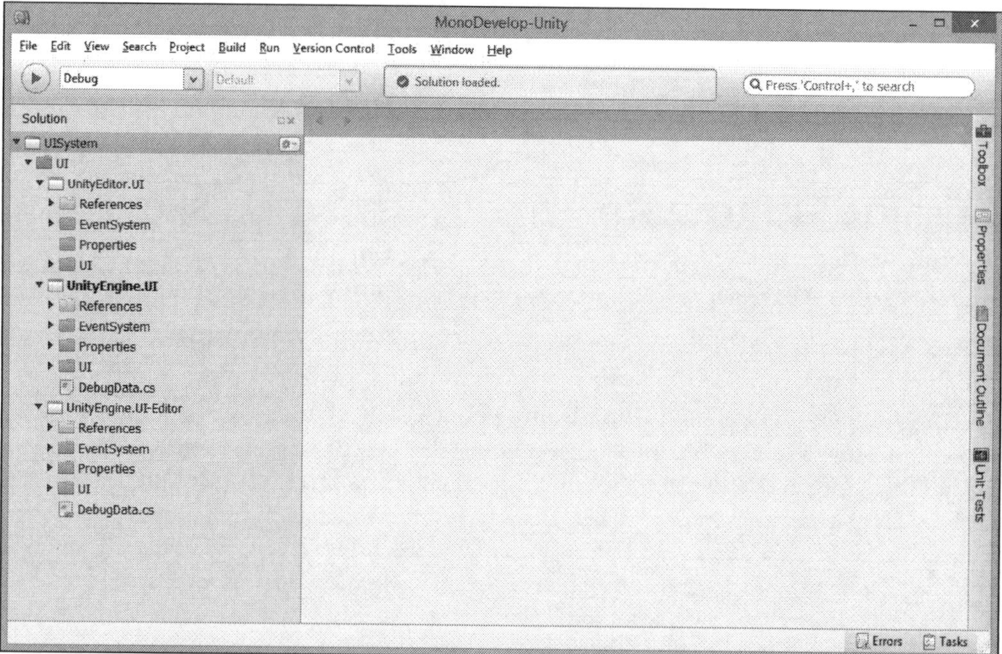

You will see three projects in the Unity UI solution:

- **UnityEditor.UI**: This contains all the Unity Property Drawers (`http://docs.unity3d.com/Manual/editor-PropertyDrawers.html`) and Custom Editor windows (`http://docs.unity3d.com/Manual/editor-CustomEditors.html`) for all the UI components. If you want to extend or add new Editor features, this is the place to add them.
- **UnityEngine.UI**: This contains the core UI classes and components, with everything from the Event System to **Images** and Toggles plus everything in between. If you are adding new controls or fixing existing controls this is the place to be.
- **UnityEngine.UI-Editor**: This is the editor version of the previous UI code.

The **UnityEngine.UI-Editor** project only contains linked files from the **UnityEngine.UI** project, meaning they are the same files. If you add more classes to the **UI** project you will also need to create a new `Linked` file in this project.

Navigating round the innards of the **UnityEngine.UI** project you will find the following folders:

Subject to change, it is an open source project after all.

- `EventSystem`: This contains core code and types to do with events, the **Event System**, and communication:
    - **EventData**: This contains structures and classes for event information.
    - **InputModules**: These contain the base input managers and delegate inputs from the Unity input event to the **Event System.**
    - **Raycasters**: This contains the base raycast modules that interrogate the scene based on the inputs. Note that it doesn't include the **GraphicsRayaster**, as this is located in the UI Core folder.
- `UI`: This is a structured folder for UI specific code. Code is located within the subfolders.
- `Animation`: This contains animation helper files.
- `Core`: At the moment, this contains everything else. So it includes all the components, types, modifiers, and utilities.

If you add a new type or class to the **UnityEngine.UI** project, be sure to also link that file in the **UnityEngine.UI-Editor** project, or it won't compile. The **UnityEngine.UI-Editor** project is essential for the inner workings of the editor and the main `UnityEngine.UI` project is what is deployed to the players.

There is certainly a lot of code to browse and get used to, so when you start I recommend you take your time walking through each component and understand how it has been implemented. (All the previous sections in this chapter were put together after spending a lot of time with the code.)

Adding your own version of UI to your project

So you got your code, what to do with it? The first step is to build the code, ready to copy it to your Unity installation.

> At the time of writing this, the only method of getting your own local code changes to the UI system into your Unity installation is to manually copy them. However, in the future this may be enhanced and made easier through the Module system in Unity (**Edit | Modules in Unity**) or some other method; they are aware this isn't simple yet and want to make it easier. So keep checking on Unity's site or the UI Bitbucket page for updates.

With your solution open from earlier, build the project and once it's complete we can start:

> I will be brief here as the full instructions are included with the project and on the Unity UI Bitbucket project page.

1. Open Windows Explorer on your computer (or the Finder on your Mac) and navigate to your `Unity installation` folder.
2. Open up the `Editor\Data\UnityExtensions\Unity\GUISystem` folder (or `Unity.app/Contents/UnityExtensions/Unity/GUISystem` on a Mac).

> By default, on a Mac, the filename extensions aren't turned on. So instead of **Unity.app** it will appear in the Finder (the Mac file manager) as just **Unity**. To be able to browse to the right folder, it's necessary to right-click on **Unity** (or **Unity.app**) and then select **Show Package Contents** from the pop-up menu. A new Finder window then appears that allows you to navigate from **Contents** onwards.
>
> This is a handy tip from one of my Mac owning reviewers, Simon Wheatley.

3. If you haven't done so already, back up the original folders within the GUISystem folder, which is the same as your installed version (for example, 4.6.0 for the initial release).

It seems on a Mac you may have trouble copying the folder in the same location, as the Finder (file manager) copy process appeared to virtually stop or hang. After several minutes, nothing had happened, so I cancelled the copy process. Copying the folder to a different location (such as a network drive) worked fine—and in an instant! Thanks again Simon Wheatley.

4. Now open the `Code` folder on your local computer in a new window and locate the new `Output` folder (if the project built successfully).
5. Double-check you built successfully and that the timestamp of the files/folders within the `Output` folder match!
6. Copy the contents of the `Output` folder (the `Unity Editor` folder, the `Standalone` folder, and `UnityEngine.UI.dll`) to the `version` folder in the `GUISystem` folder of your Unity installation.
7. Select **Yes** to overwrite any files.

Note: You must have administrative privileges to overwrite these files; if you haven't then uninstall Unity and install it to a folder on the computer you have write access to (you did know you can install Unity anywhere on your computer, didn't you?).

Now when you start up Unity (provided nothing went wrong!) you will be using your own copy of the Unity UI system with all your own fixes and changes (provided you made any).

If at any time you need to go back to the installed version, just copy your backup folder over the contexts of the `GUISystem` folder (you did make a backup didn't you?)

If you ever need to log an issue on the new Unity UI system, ensure you are using the version that comes installed with Unity. They will not be very forgiving if it's your own code that is breaking it!

Plus it is unlikely they will be able to replicate it if it is your code causing the problem.

Extra credit, push it back to Unity

So you have been going through the UI source and found a bug that you know how to fix or have some award-winning idea that you have implemented that you think is good enough to go into the main build, then thanks to the magic of a DCVS source control system, we have a way.

Note: The following pattern is meant only for submitting new features or fixed bugs. If you find something that is breaking or you don't know how to fix it, then use the standard Unity bug reporter (**Help | Report a bug**) to submit it. Don't submit a change with some notes saying it's broken because it will likely not be picked up by anyone.

Now to submit fixes or new features, you need to keep a few things in mind if you want it to be accepted (this is true for any open source project):

- **Keep it small**: Do this as large submissions will likely be ignored.
- **Keep it succinct**: Stay on target and fix one thing or add one feature at a time.
- **Document where possible**: This will help moderators who read the code understand it quicker and easier.
- **Plan ahead**: If you have a number of changes, either ensure they don't overlap/depend on each other or work with the moderators to ensure they are aware of what's coming. There is nothing worse than having a whole plan of work not accepted because it was too much or not what was wanted.

In the road to submission, we start from grass roots, which means you start planning for the change before you even start coding. The basic workflow is like this:

1. Create a new branch and keep the name simple and about your change.
2. Add your changes in one go or in a few commits/check-ins (too many commits in a request are bad).

Commits are when you are done making changes, then you use your source control tool to mark a checkpoint in your coding and then push/upload them to the server.

3. Commit your change to your branch.
4. Submit a Pull Request (PR) from your repository back to the main branch of the parent repository.
5. Monitor the request and answer queries.
6. If necessary update your development branch in your repository in answer to queries/requests.
7. Commit your fixes (no need to create a new PR, it will automatically be updated).
8. Once accepted, delete your development branch.
9. Refresh your repository from the parent.

Bitbucket has all this information to hand on their site, so check it regularly for updates.

If you have already made your changes to your own repository (some developers to have a playground where they test things), then do not fret. Simply create a new branch in your source code application from the last **Commit** point by Unity, then follow the previous steps and copy your change in.

It's quite normal to have a playground/sandbox area in your own repository; just be sure to start from a new branch in your local project before doing anything and above all else, keep the main development branch (the one from Unity) clean. *Do not commit directly to the unity main branch.*

Always use a new/clean branch of your own, or things will get muddled.

Happy coding!

A last note about submitting changes in the current process. Unity won't actually accept your change directly into their repository. The pattern currently being followed is that Unity will review your change and if it's deemed worthy they will copy your fixes/changes into their own code servers for consumption.

So they aren't using the source control in a normal fashion; they're just using it for people to highlight what they can easily fix/include. This may change over time as Unity get better working with Bitbucket.

Summary

This chapter has been really code heavy (as expected), with a lot of information to cover, however, the main aim was to get an understanding of the code and wiring underneath the hood of the new UI system.

At this point, you should be able to build your own events/event system handlers and if you have any flashy ideas, know how to submit them to Unity through their new open source offering.

With the code you can now delve into how Unity are building controls and the backend to support them so there is even more power in the hands of the everyday developer; there are grand times ahead!

In this chapter, we covered the following topics:

- Events and what they mean
- How to build your own events and handlers
- The Event System (and what has it ever done for us!)
- Learning through examples (and more to come!)
- Open source UI and how to read and contribute

As a closing note, I would love to hear from developers about the creations you make, so feel free to drop a note on the book form or contact me through my blog.

Also if you have more examples to add to the UI scripts extensions library I created with this book, then the same code management instructions (detailed above) apply. Just submit a PR (pull request) with your new script or a fix to an existing one and I'll add it in. Have you got a request for a new script/control? If so, just log an issue as a request; at the time of writing this I already have one and I haven't even shouted much about it yet!

The 3D Scene Sample

As part of *Chapter 5, Screen Space, World Space, and the Camera,* I set up a simple 3D demo scene with a few effects to make the UI really stand out and shine. However, as the focus of this book it has been moved to an appendix for you to follow if you so wish.

Additionally, the appendix is also available online at `http://bit.ly/UnityUIEssentials3DDemoScene`.

> If you want to skip the scene's creation or just use the completed version to follow through, then you can download the `.UnityPackage` asset for the demo scene from `http://bit.ly/UIEssentialsCh5DemoScene` and then just import it into your project as a **Custom Package** using **Assets | Import package | Custom Package...** in the Unity menu.

This chapter just works through a couple of 3D tips and tricks that you can use in any scene to help liven it up and work through some of the niggles of working in 3D scenes.

Setting up for the big game

To make any picture stand out, it needs a really good background, so in *Chapter 5, Screen Space, World Space, and the Camera,* I created this simple 3D space scene for us to paint our UI on:

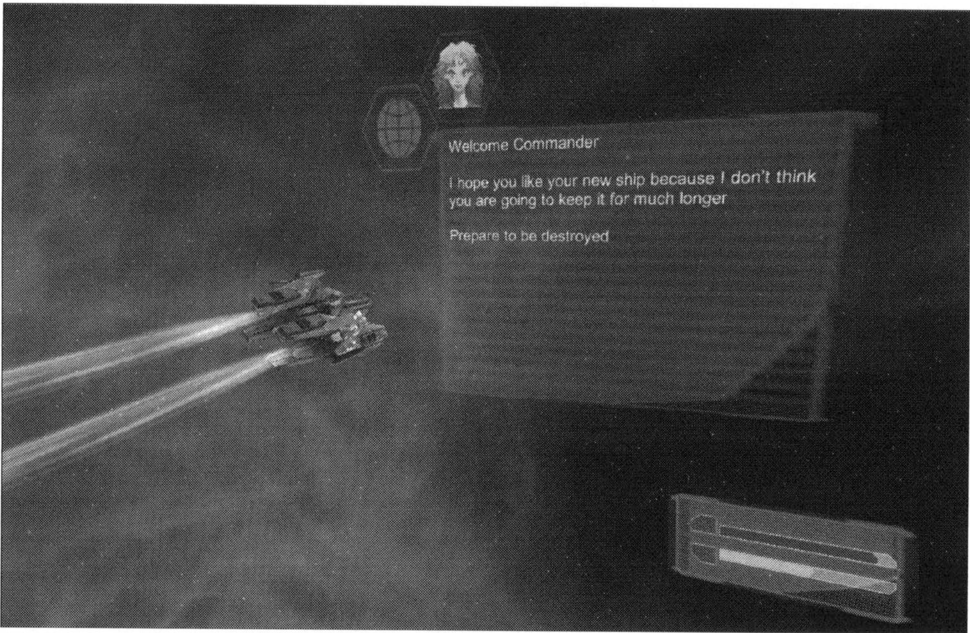

It's a cool mix of different Canvas UI elements displayed in a 3D scene, all with completely free assets!

First off, for our big example, let's grab a few things:

1. Start a new 3D project or just create a brand new scene for our playground.
2. Add the standard **Particle** project asset that comes with Unity (either when setting up the project or through **Assets** | **Import Package** | **Particles** in the menu).
3. Grab the **Skybox Volume 2 Nebula** asset package from the store (it's free and fantastic for demos – `http://bit.ly/NebulaSkybox`).
4. Grab the **Free SciFi Fighter** asset package from the store (it's pretty–`http://bit.ly/SciFiFighter`).

The free **SciFi Fighter** asset package when imported doesn't use its own folder (very annoying), so after you have imported it, create a new folder called `SciFi Fighter` and move its assets to this folder (the `Materials`, `Meshes`, and `Textures` folders and the `SciFi_Fighter_AK5` scene), just to keep the project structure tidy.

It is truly amazing what free stuff is available for game creators these days!

The initial 3D scene

I almost had a little too much fun creating this basic scene and even learned some new tricks along the way. It's not crucial for the UI setup, so you can skip it if you want to, but it'll only take 5 minutes or so to complete:

1. Start with a new scene (if you haven't done so already) and save it as `Example_UI`.
2. Drag the `SciFi_Fighter_AK5.fbx` mesh asset into the scene from the **Meshes** folder (either from the project root or the `SciFi Fighter` folder you created).
3. Change the **Rotation** of the **SciFi Fighter** to **X** `357`, **Y** `18`, **Z** `317`. This gives a nice outbound flight path for the fighter.
4. Drag the **Main Camera** (in the **Hierarchy**) as a child of the **SciFi Fighter** and reset its transform (using the cog icon in the top right-hand corner of the **Inspector** with the **Main Camera** selected, then select **Reset**). This ensures that the camera is always following the fighter and keeps it in view.
5. Set up the Main Camera's transform as follows:
    - **Position**: `X 38, Y 48, Z -47`
    - **Rotation**: `X 31, Y 340, Z 30`
6. Remove the **GUILayer**, **Flare layer**, and **Audio Listener** from the **Main Camera** by right-clicking on each component and selecting the **Remove Component** option. These just get in the way here because it's following the ship.
7. Set the **Clear Flags** property to **Depth Only** and the **Depth** to `0` on the **Main Camera** since this is just a tracking camera in front of a background (which we'll add in a bit).
8. Add a **Directional Light** using **Create | Light | Directional Light** to the scene to light the way.

Here's where you should be up to now, no UI yet, just the beginnings of a scene:

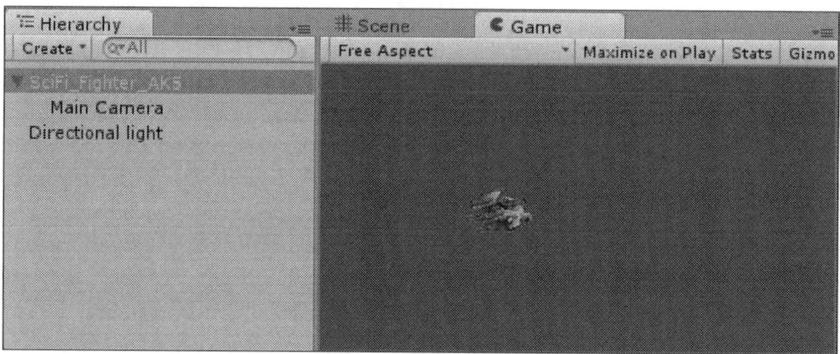

Next, let's smarten it up a bit with a background skybox and even a trail for the ship:

1. Add a new **Layer** to the project (through the **Layer** menu in the top-right corner of the **Inspector** for every GameObject) called **Background** (this just helps you identify background objects for the background camera). This should be in the **User Layer 8** field (but any position in the Layer array will do).

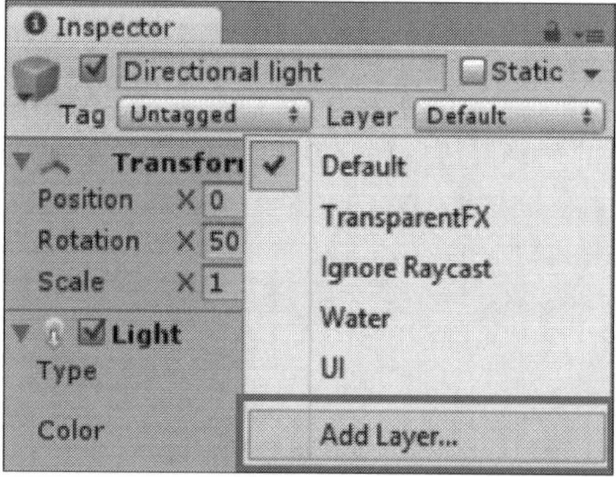

The Add Layer... option in the Inspector

2. Add a new **Camera** to the scene (using **Create** | **Camera**) and rename it to `BackgroundCamera`.
3. Set the **Depth** for the `BackgroundCamera` to `1`.
4. Set the **Layer** for the `BackgroundCamera` to the new **Background** layer using the Layer combobox shown earlier.

5. Configure the **Culling Mask** of the **BackgroundCamera** to just **Background** by selecting **Nothing** in the drop-down selection and then selecting **Background**. (For an added bonus, also remove the Background layer from the **Culling Mask** of the **Main Camera** so it does not render it.)

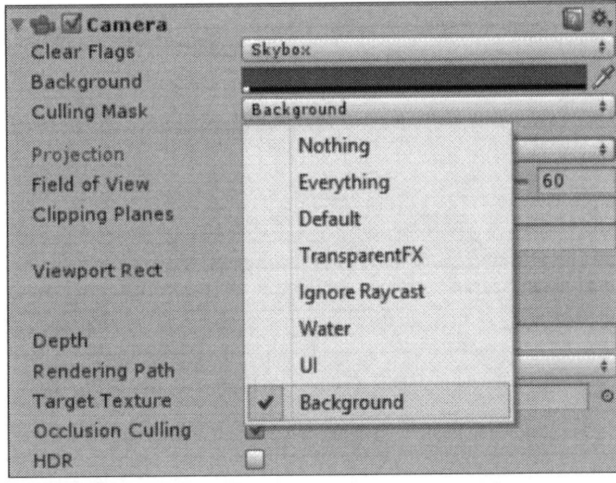

6. Add a **Skybox** component (**Add Component** | **Rendering** | **Skybox**) to the **BackgroundCamera** and set the **Custom Skybox** property to one of the skyboxes from the `SkyBox Volume 2` folder. You can do this by dragging the **DSG.mat** asset (the material, not the textures) to the **Custom SkyBox** property of the **Skybox Component**. I personally went for the `DeepSpaceGreen SkyBox` (in the folder of the same name under the `SkyBox Volume 2` folder).
7. Finally, add a new **Particle System** as a child of the **BackgroundCamera** (right-click on **BackgroundCamera** and select **Particle System**) with the following settings (any settings you won't alter are the defaults):
   - Transform
     - Position: X = **83,** Y = **28,** Z = **76**
     - Rotation: X = **10,** Y = **240,** Z = **1.8**
   - Particle System
     - Duration = **20**
     - Start Lifetime = **20**
     - Start Speed = **10**
     - Emission Rate = **5**

- Shape
  - Shape = **Box**
  - Box X = **50**
  - Box Y = **50**
  - Box Z = **5**
- Renderer Max Particle Size = **0.005**

The **Particle System** should now look like the following screenshot:

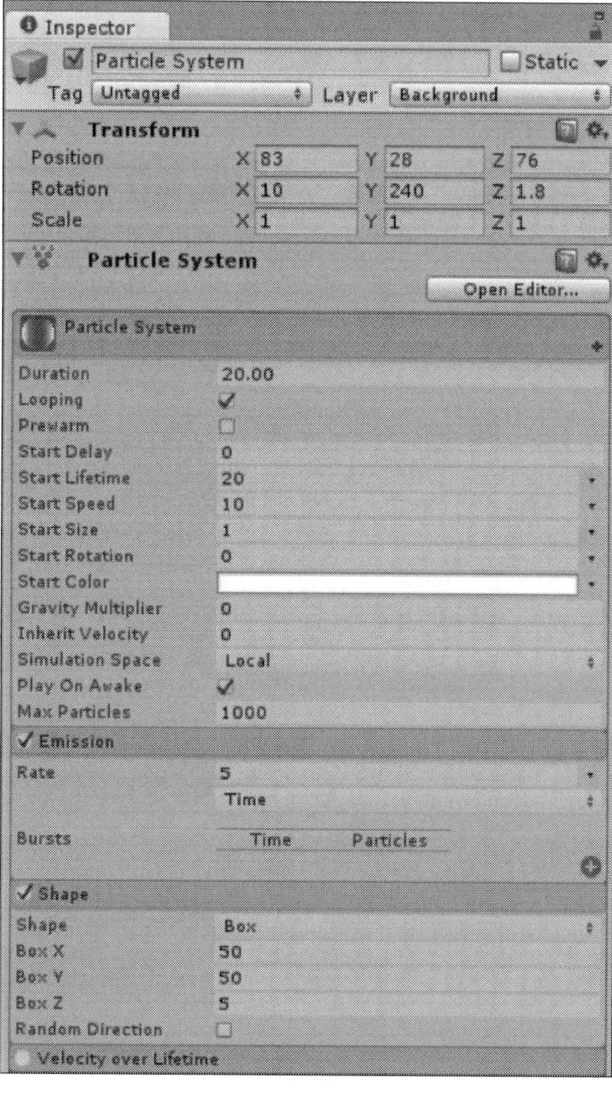

All this does is it simply adds some flavor to our scene so it's not boring.

I've found in situations where you want a background and a moving target that you want to follow, it is best to have the background and the target use separate cameras.

After all that, our demo scene now looks like the following:

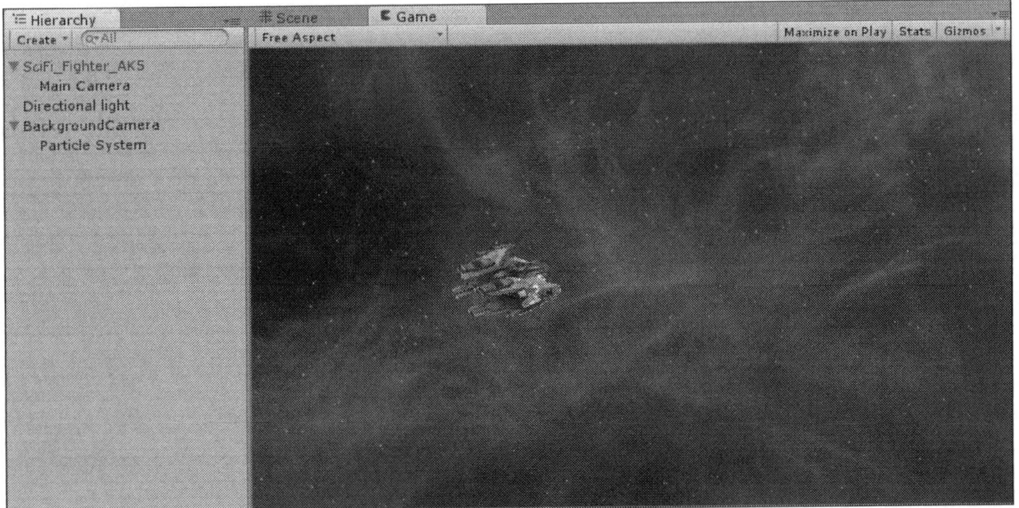

Lastly, let's kick our ship into action and make it at least look like it's moving:

1. Add a **Rigidbody** component (**Add Component** | **Physics** | **Rigidbody**) to the **SciFi_Fighter_AK5** and uncheck the **Use Gravity** property. (It's space; there is no gravity!)
2. Add two new Empty GameObjects as children to the **SciFi_Fighter_AK5** (right-click on the **fighter** and select **Create Empty**). Name them **Engine1** and **Engine2**.
3. For **Engine1**, set its **Transform Position** to **X** `-3.24`, **Y** `-0.04`, **Z** `-1.69` (**Rotation** values should all be `0` and **Scale** values should all be `1`).
4. For **Engine2**, set its **Transform Position** to **X** `3.49`, **Y** `-0.04`, **Z** `-1.69` (**Rotation** values should all be `0` and **Scale** values should all be `1`).

If, for some reason, this does not place the engine's GameObjects in the exhaust ports of the ship, just position them manually in relation to the SciFi Fighter.

5. Select **BOTH** the Engines in the project **Hierarchy**. Then, in the **Inspector** window, click on **Add Component** and select **Effects | Trail Renderer**.
6. Still with both the Engines selected, expand the **Materials** section of the **Trail Renderer** in the Inspector and set the **Size** to `2`.
7. Drag the **FlameE** material from the standard `Assets\Particles\Sources\Materials` folder onto **Element** `0` of **Trail Renderer Materials.**
8. Drag the **Smoke Trail** material from the standard `Assets\Particles\Sources\Materials` folder on to **Element** `1` of **Trail Renderer Materials.**
9. Set the **Time** to `2`, **Start Width** to `5`, and **End Width** to `0.5`.

The **Trail Renderer** is a great way of adding simple trails to GameObjects, whether it's a light cycle, a car, or, in this case, a spaceship. They float along behind the object as it moves round the scene.

The **Trail Renderer** in the **Inspector** window should now look like the following screenshot:

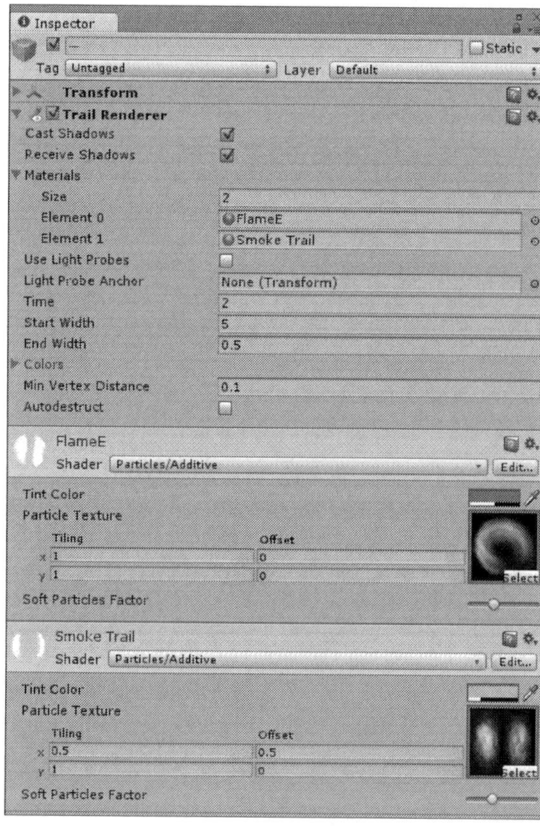

Almost there! One last thing remains. If you run the scene now, you won't see any change. There are no trails; the ship just sits there and does nothing. Simply put, it's doing nothing because we haven't told it to do anything. For the **Trail Renderer** to work, the ship has to move.

For the last touch, create a new C# script called `ShipMove` and replace its contents with the following:

```
using UnityEngine;

public class ShipMove : MonoBehaviour {
  void Start () {
  //Kick the ship in to action with a bit of force.
GetComponent<Rigidbody>().AddForce(Vector3.forward * 50,
 ForceMode.VelocityChange);
  }
}
```

Now, simply attach the script to the **SciFi_Fighter_AK5** GameObject and hit play and your fighter will be screaming through the stars on its way to oblivion.

Our sample scene is complete.

> The complete scene is also available as a Unity package and can be downloaded from `http://bit.ly/UIEssentialsCh5DemoScene`.

Now, return to *Chapter 5, Screen Space, World Space, and the Camera*, and start adding some UI to this amazing scene you have created.

Index

H

I

L

M

N

O

P

R

S

V

W

Thank you for buying

Unity 3D UI Essentials

About Packt Publishing

Packt, pronounced 'packed', published its first book, *Mastering phpMyAdmin for Effective MySQL Management*, in April 2004, and subsequently continued to specialize in publishing highly focused books on specific technologies and solutions.

Our books and publications share the experiences of your fellow IT professionals in adapting and customizing today's systems, applications, and frameworks. Our solution-based books give you the knowledge and power to customize the software and technologies you're using to get the job done. Packt books are more specific and less general than the IT books you have seen in the past. Our unique business model allows us to bring you more focused information, giving you more of what you need to know, and less of what you don't.

Packt is a modern yet unique publishing company that focuses on producing quality, cutting-edge books for communities of developers, administrators, and newbies alike. For more information, please visit our website at `www.packtpub.com`.

About Packt Open Source

In 2010, Packt launched two new brands, Packt Open Source and Packt Enterprise, in order to continue its focus on specialization. This book is part of the Packt Open Source brand, home to books published on software built around open source licenses, and offering information to anybody from advanced developers to budding web designers. The Open Source brand also runs Packt's Open Source Royalty Scheme, by which Packt gives a royalty to each open source project about whose software a book is sold.

Writing for Packt

We welcome all inquiries from people who are interested in authoring. Book proposals should be sent to `author@packtpub.com`. If your book idea is still at an early stage and you would like to discuss it first before writing a formal book proposal, then please contact us; one of our commissioning editors will get in touch with you.

We're not just looking for published authors; if you have strong technical skills but no writing experience, our experienced editors can help you develop a writing career, or simply get some additional reward for your expertise.

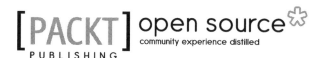

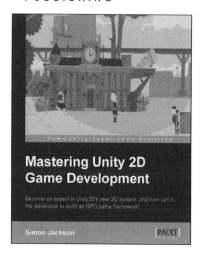

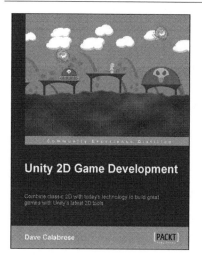

Unity Multiplayer Games

ISBN: 978-1-84969-232-8 Paperback: 242 pages

Build engaging, fully functional, multiplayer games with Unity engine

1. Create a variety of multiplayer games and apps in the Unity 4 game engine, still maintaining compatibility with Unity 3.
2. Employ the most popular networking middleware options for Unity games.
3. Packed with ideas, inspiration, and advice for your own game design and development.

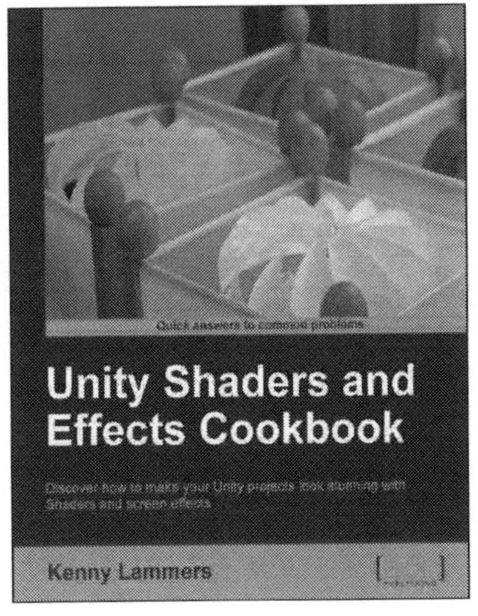

Unity Shaders and Effects Cookbook

ISBN: 978-1-84969-508-4 Paperback: 268 pages

Discover how to make your Unity projects look stunning with Shaders and screen effects

1. Learn the secrets of creating AAA quality Shaders without having to write long algorithms.
2. Add realism to your game with stunning screen effects.
3. Understand the structure of Surface Shaders through easy to understand step-by-step examples.

22925158R00158

Made in the USA
San Bernardino, CA
27 July 2015